The Nightmare Considered

The Nightmare Considered: Critical Essays on Nuclear War Literature

Edited by
Nancy Anisfield

Bowling Green State University Popular Press
Bowling Green, Ohio 43403

Acknowledgements

"Fatal Fiction: A Weapon to End All Wars" originally appeared in slightly different form in *The Bulletin of the Atomic Scientists*, November 1989; parts of it have been adapted from the author's *War Stars: The Superweapon and the American Imagination* (New York: Oxford University Press, 1988.)

"A Flash of Light: The Evolution of Anti-Nuclear Consciousness in an Alternative Literary Journal" appeared in *Samisdat* volume 56, number 1. Essay and excerpts reprinted by permission of *Samisdat*, Merritt Clifton, editor.

"The Days After Tomorrow: Novelists at Armageddon" was originally published as "Bangs and Whimpers: Novelists at Armageddon," *New York Times Book Review*, 13 March 1988. Reprinted by permission of authors.

"Psychic Numbing, Radical Futurelessness, and Sexual Violence in the Nuclear Film" originally appeared in shorter form in *The Journal of Popular Film and Television* 16, no. 3, pages 100-107, Fall 1988. Reprinted with permission of the Helen Dwight Reid Educational Foundation. Published by Heldref Publications, 4000 Albemarle St., N.W. Washington, D.C. 20016. Copyright © 1988.

"Post-Nuclear Holocaust Re-Minding" was originally read in shorter form at "The Fantastic Imagination in New Critical Theories," an interdisciplinary conference held at Texas A & M University, 1 March 1990.

"The End of Art: Poetry and Nuclear War," Copyright © 1990 Jan Barry. Essay and poem excerpts from *Peace is Our Profession* (Montclair, NJ: East River Anthology) reprinted by permission of Jan Barry.

Denise Levertov's "Watching *Dark Circle*," *Oblique Prayers*. Copyright © 1984 by Denise Levertov. Reprinted by permission of New Directions Publishing Corporation. World Rights.

"Haiku and Hiroshima: Hara Tamiki" appeared in *Modern Haiku* 9:11-17 (Winter-Spring 1988.) Reprinted by permission of the author.

"Nuclear Family/Nuclear War" appeared in *Papers on Language and Literature*, volume 26, number 1. Reprinted by permission of the journal.

"Thinking Woman's Children and the Bomb" is reprinted from *Explorations in Ethnic Studies*, journal of the National Association of Ethnic Studies.

An earlier version of "The Theme of Guilt in Vonnegut's Cataclysmic Novels" was presented at the annual meeting of the Popular Culture Association in 1987.

Contents

Introduction

Summer fields:
fragments of nightmare
flash before my eyes.

(by Hara Tamiki, trans. Richard Minear)

This is a difficult moment to present a study of nuclear war literature. As Soviet policies soften international relations, as the Berlin Wall is torn down, and as Eastern European countries reject communist rule, Cold War tensions are easing. The Persian Gulf war has refocused national attention on conventional warfare. A world-wide nuclear freeze movement has risen from the grassroots level, and in response, on March 6, 1990, *The Bulletin of the Atomic Scientists* reset its famous "Doomsday Clock" back four minutes, to ten minutes from nuclear midnight. Against this backdrop, arguing for the necessity of nuclear studies may seem both pessimistic and counter-productive. Yet the contradictions and debates inherent in such studies indicate the need still exists. Along with what appears to be an overriding desire to classify and categorize this literature, paradoxes abound, matched only by the oxymoronic euphemisms of nuclear rhetoric such as "peace keeper missiles" and "star wars defense." One paradox surfaces when, at the same time the nuclear threat seems to be diminishing, there is an outpouring of new post-holocaust novels. One debate centers on the relative merits of science fiction versus mimetic texts as the best conveyors of nuclear commentary. One contradiction lies in the argument that the eschatological capability of our nuclear arsenals provides a new literary subject, when in fact, there have been writings of apocalyptic doom for a long, long time. Hovering above these issues, however, is the general consensus that this literature is important and must be integrated into the classroom at as many levels as possible.

It is also important not to dismiss the critical studies of nuclear literature as merely esoteric resources for scholars only. Isolating the academic from the political is as naive as believing imaginative literature has no impact on history or societal change. Furthermore, as Daniel Zins suggests in his argument for nuclear criticism in the English department, "...what our students think about—or fail to think about—when they leave our classrooms and educational institutions forges an inevitable nexus between our activities and what we perceive as 'the real world' " (27).

1

The voices in this collection belong to teachers, editors, poets, novelists and political activists. They write about a wide range of fiction, film, poetry and drama. Their methods vary, some working with critical approaches such as deconstruction or feminist theory, some writing from the perspective of personal experience. What holds their studies together is their awareness of not only the political exigence of this material, but its literary richness.

I have divided these essays into two sections, hoping to direct students and teachers more easily to the type of study they seek. Part I, "Issues and Overviews," contains essays which discuss a variety of works through a survey or key critical argument. Part II, "Specific Texts," contains closer examinations of individual writers or works, many of which are part of the nuclear canon (if such a thing exists), or perhaps should be.

Acknowledging literature and film to be cultural reactions to contemporary ideas, anxieties, and desires, critics understand the very close ties between nuclear writings, nuclear policies, and nuclear awareness. Writers are confronted with the challenge of expressing the inexpressible, and readers are confronted with the difficulty of comprehending the potential horror and responding to it. Individually failing to respond, we create a small silence. This, in turn, may lead to a silence much greater. W.D. Auden wrote: "We are afraid/ Of pain but more afraid of silence; for no nightmare/ Of hostile objects could be as terrible as this void" (2). To this I add Terrence Des Pres' statement: "...the one clear thing is that we live by words" (12).

Works Cited

Auden, W.D. "If On Account of the Political Situation." *Writing in a Nuclear Age. New England Review & Bread Loaf Quarterly* V. 4 (Summer 1983): 1-2.

Des Pres, Terrence. "Self/Landscape/Grid." *Writing in a Nuclear Age. New England Review & Bread Loaf Quarterly* V. 4 (Summer 1983): 3-12.

Zins, Daniel L. "Exploding the Canon: Nuclear Criticism in the English Department." *Papers on Language and Literature.* 26:1 (Winter 1990): 12-39.

Part I:
Issues and Overviews

Fatal Fiction:
A Weapon to End All Wars

H. Bruce Franklin

The year is 1910. A young Missouri farmer carefully copies down ten lines of science fiction poetry from Tennyson's "Locksley Hall" and places them in his wallet. The lines depict ultimate aerial superweapons of the future, waging a terrible climactic war in the skies:

> ...there rain'd a ghastly dew
> From the nations' airy navies grappling in the central blue...

The horrors of this scientific warfare bring about universal peace and world government:

> ...the war-drum throbb'd no longer, and the battle-flags were furl'd
> In the Parliament of man, the Federation of the world.

Now it is July 1945. The Missourian, on his way to a historic conference, believes that he is about to gain control over the ultimate aerial superweapon. He pulls that now-faded slip of paper from his wallet, where he had been carrying it for thirty-five years, and recites the lines to a reporter (Smith 286).

If Harry Truman believed that the atomic bomb might bring an end to war, it was not because of a single poem. A typical American, Truman grew up in a culture bubbling with fantasies of ultimate weapons. Appearing first over a century ago as American science fiction, these fantasies helped to shape the nation's conceptions of nuclear weapons and responses to them, decades before those weapons materialized.

Such fantasies were kindled by the advent of modern technological warfare, which burst upon the industrialized world between 1861 and 1871, in the United States as the Civil War and in Europe as the Franco-German War. Dynamically interrelated with modern, industrialized war was a new literary genre that emerged in the 1870s: fiction envisioning future wars.

This essay originally appeared in slightly different form in *The Bulletin of the Atomic Scientists* November 1989; parts of it have been adapted from the author's *War Stars: The Superweapon and The American Imagination* (NY: Oxford University Press) 1988.

The typical European fantasy was militaristic propaganda designed to terrify its newly-emerging mass reading audience with a specter of their ill-prepared homeland invaded by some likely enemy, often armed with a deadly new weapon.[1] In America, however, authors churned out hundreds of novels and stories imagining future wars from a peculiarly American perspective. In these fantasies, the emergent faith in American technological genius wedded the older faith in America's messianic destiny, engendering ecstatic visions of made-in-America superweapons that would allow America to defeat all evil empires, wage war to end all wars, and make the world eternally safe for democracy. In the decades leading to World War One, this fiction was a main dish in the cultural diet of what is now called middle America.

Even before the discovery of radioactivity, American fiction was imagining weapons equal to nuclear weapons not only in explosive force but also in political and cultural power. A most revealing example is Frank Stockton's 1889 novel *The Great War Syndicate*. When war breaks out between England and the United States, twenty-three "great capitalists" form a "Syndicate, with the object of taking entire charge of the war" (12). The Great War Syndicate develops the "Motor Bomb," with the explosive force of an atomic bomb. Merely demonstrating this dreadful weapon brings victory. England is then allowed to join the "Syndicate of War" as a junior partner, and the world submits to the Syndicate's benevolent rule. In the novel's final words: "...all the nations of the world began to teach English in their schools, and the Spirit of Civilization raised her head with a confident smile."

The mercy shown toward the British did not apply when superweapons were used against non-whites, especially Asians. The fate of Hiroshima and Nagasaki was foreshadowed decades earlier in dozens of future-war novels and stories that raved about the Yellow Peril. For example, Jack London's 1910 short story "The Unparalleled Invasion" predicts that in 1975, when the world seems doomed to be overrun by hordes of Chinese, it is saved by a secret weapon developed by an American scientist. Fleets of airships shower China with "missiles" loaded with "every virulent form of infectious death," exterminating the entire Chinese population with "bacteria, and germs, and microbes, and bacilli, cultured in the laboratories of the West." This is, as London so aptly says, "ultra-modern war, twentieth-century war, the war of the scientist and the laboratory." Once the Yellow Peril is entirely expunged—"All survivors were put to death wherever found"—the world becomes a virtual utopia for the victorious forces of progress, led by America. London's story is a twentieth-century, American version of Tennyson's "ghastly dew" that rains from airships, thus ending war and bringing about a prosperous, unified world. It appeared in 1910, the very year that Harry Truman placed Tennyson's lines in his wallet. It was published in *McClure's*, a magazine that young Truman avidly devoured. As he wrote to his sweetheart Bess in 1913, "I suppose I'll have to renew my subscription to *McClure's* now so I won't miss a number."[2]

Truman's role in August 1945 was forecast by the first novel to imagine radioactivity used in a weapon of war: Roy Norton's 1907 *The Vanishing Fleets*, which was serialized in the *Associated Sunday Magazines*, a Sunday insert carried by most leading American newspapers (as the *Parade* of its day). Japan launches a sneak attack. But American scientists invent "the greatest engine of war that science has ever known" (223), giant "radioplanes" powered by radioactivity and capable of sweeping entire fleets of warships off the sea. The President, "his Americanism exceeded only by his humanitarianism" (237), decides that his solemn duty to humanity is to use this weapon in war—in order to end war. He explains why secrecy is imperative: " 'If our secret becomes known'," the Japanese might not continue the war, thus depriving us of the opportunity to actually *use* this " 'most deadly machine ever conceived...thereby ending wars for all time'." " 'Let us bear with fortitude whatever reproaches may be heaped upon us, for we are the instruments of God'," he declares (237). After American fliers win "the last great battle in history," the President announces: "The United States, having faith in the Anglo-Saxon race as...the most peaceful and conservative, has formed an...alliance with Great Britain" (341). Thus comes the end of war. American-Anglo hegemony and perpetual peace are guaranteed by the eternal American monopoly on the superweapon produced in secret by American ingenuity and merging air power with radioactivity.

The first truly nuclear weapon of war appeared in Godfrey Hollis' 1908 novel *The Man Who Ended War*. An American scientific mastermind invents a focused beam of "radio-active waves" which instantly disintegrates all metallic atoms into subatomic particles. When the major powers fail to comply with the scientist's ultimatum demanding immediate universal disarmament, he begins to annihilate their fleets with his radioactive beam. The nations disarm. "The man who stopped all war" then destroys his machine, his plans, and himself—so that no one will obtain the "secret" of the weapon and the world will therefore be permanently at peace.

This characteristically American fantasy presents a striking contrast to H.G. Wells' 1913-1914 novel *The World Set Free*, which imagines "atomic bombs" not as peacemakers but as the instruments of global armageddon. Whereas Wells recognized that the scientific knowledge required to produce atomic energy or weapons could never be kept private or monopolized, *The Man Who Ended War* promulgated the myth of the atomic "secret," an idea that critically influenced American politics and culture in 1940, through the Rosenberg case, and beyond.

The American mode of atomic fantasy evolved further in *The Man Who Rocked the Earth*, by Arthur Train and Robert Wood, which was serialized in 1914-1915 in the *Saturday Evening Post*, another magazine whose fiction was read eagerly by young Truman. The novel opens with the World War hideously stalemated, as millions are slaughtered by a multitude of novel weapons. Then appears an American scientific wizard who calls himself "PAX." PAX's ultimate weapon is a radioactive beam which can annihilate mountain ranges or armies. He fires this atomic weapon from an airship powered by "atomic energy" (100) generated by uranium forced into rapid disintegration. His atomic attacks produce scenes interchangeable with descriptions recorded by survivors of Hiroshima, including detailed accounts of death from radiation sickness (68, 134-35). Armed with atomic weapons, PAX declares that "either war or the human race must pass away forever" (142). Of course in the fantasy it is war that becomes extinct. Faced with the peacemaker's atomic arsenal, the nations destroy their weapons, abolish armies, and form a world government to guarantee perpetual peace.

Atomic energy and weapons remained a popular subject of fiction through 1940. Science, politics, and the mass media were not too far behind. By the end of 1939, World War Two had begun in Europe and physicists in Germany, Great Britain, the United States, the Soviet Union, Japan, and other nations were working on atomic energy. That year, scientists published almost a hundred articles on nuclear fission. By 1940, American newspapers and magazines—from *Popular Mechanics* to *Time* and *Newsweek*—were thrilling their readers with fantasies about the wonders to come from splitting the atom.[3] The public was told that the nuclear chain reaction essential for atomic energy, and possibly even atomic bombs, now depended mainly on developing practical means for producing significant quantities of the unstable isotope, uranium 235.

Simultaneously, a serialized science-fiction novel read by millions of Americans developed both the doctrine of U.S. global supremacy through nuclear weapons and a proposal for institutionalizing this hegemony almost identical to the Baruch Plan actually proposed after the war. The novel was *Lightning in the Night*, which ran in weekly installments during the pivotal months of August to November 1940 in *Liberty*, one of the three most popular magazines in America.[4]

The story begins five years in the future, after Germany and its allies have conquered Britain and France. Japan and the Soviet Union carry out a sneak attack on Hawaii. Formations of Soviet, Japanese, and Nazi bombers devastate American cities. Hordes of Reds, Japanese, Mexicans, and Germans invade on three fronts, inflicting on an unprepared United States the "macabre nightmare of modern warfare" (October 19 installment).

As the United States fights back, the Nazis arrange a meeting with the American president. Hitler begins by explaining the theory of atomic energy and summarizing the history of atomic research. The Nazi leader recalls that   " 'by the year 1939 the physicists of the Reich, of Denmark, and of America were frantically at work attempting to free and harness atomic energy' " (November 9).

" 'The secret of world mastery'," Hitler continues, of course would go to the nation that "'first could produce great quantities of pure U-235'," the uranium isotope sufficiently unstable to sustain an explosive chain reaction. The Reich, he announces, has discovered this " 'key to atomic energy'," and has begun production of pure U-235, with its " 'destructive power beyond present-day comprehension'," " 'the power to blow entire cities off the face of the earth'." " 'Within one month, that devastating power can be unleashed against your cities, your people'," Hitler boasts, so " 'further resistance becomes utterly foolhardly'." After this " 'month of grace' " he will unleash " ' literal and total annihilation'."

The President concedes that a nation without atomic weapons would be helpless against a nation with them. And so this November 9 installment (published just before the crucial presidential election of 1940) concludes with the United States apparently ready to surrender to the Nazis. Thus the millions of readers of *Liberty* confront a picture of their future if America were to lose a nuclear arms race with the Nazis.

But the final installment reveals that the United States had secretly been working on its own atomic weapons. Great cyclotrons and other marvelous equipment had been provided to the nation's "most ingenious and resourceful scientists." The President expounds America's vision of atomic energy, a vision like that of 1940 articles in *Harpers, Collier's,* and the *Saturday Evening Post*[5], a fantasy that would reappear after Hiroshima and Nagasaki under the slogan "Atoms for Peace":

We saw its potentialities as a weapon of war, but even more clearly as an unlimited source of heat, of light, of power for peaceful production and transportation—all this at an almost incredibly low cost....

...poverty would vanish from the earth. So would war itself; for the economic causes of war would no longer exist...that Utopia, if you like—was what we envisioned: a free world of free peoples living in peace and prosperity, facing a future of unlimited richness. (November 16)

Although the Nazis now have "the secret" of the ultimate weapon, they are too late. At this very moment, " '50,000 feet over the Atlantic, great United States stratospheric bombers'," specially modified for intercontinental flight and carrying atomic bombs, are " 'heading for every great city in Germany'."

The President next presents the American proposal for peace and atomic disarmament. This turns out to be a prototype of the only proposal for nuclear disarmament ever actually offered by the United States, the Baruch Plan of 1946: an organization dominated by American scientists would control both the world's supply of uranium and the licensing of nuclear energy facilities to other nations; the United States would maintain its monopoly on nuclear weaponry until some unspecified date in the future when it would be turned over to an international agency.

'We have no wish,' the President said, 'to assume for long the task of policing the world. When the world is restored and made free, a Council of Nations shall take over the task we inaugurate now.'

Germany surrenders. Japan and the Soviet Union capitulate a day later, after an American bomber drops one nuclear bomb on "the deserted Russian steppes." The American atomic bomb has brought the utopian Pax Americana to the planet.

The nation's motives for developing atomic weapons in the novel are precisely those of the Manhattan Project: to forestall Nazi use and to achieve a lasting peace. Like those who later were to make the decision to use atomic bombs, *Lightning in the Night* assumes that the first nation to deploy atomic weapons wins and ends the arms race. The fictional President, like his actual counterpart in 1945-46, fails to realize that the first atomic bomb might just accelerate the race for nuclear superweapons and open an epoch dominated by them.

In the fall of 1940 the U.S. government began to wrap atomic research in a shroud of secrecy. Even the secrecy itself was a secret. Newspapers, magazines, news services, and radio broadcasters were soon ordered not to mention atomic power, cyclotrons, betatrons, fission, uranium, deuterium, and thorium. Army Intelligence later even attempted to block access to back issues of magazines like the *Saturday Evening Post* containing popular articles on atomic energy in order "to wipe the whole subject from memory."[6]

Thus ended the free exchange of knowledge that had symbolized the community of science, to be replaced by one of the grotesque hallmarks of our era: the attempt to transform vital parts of human knowledge into secrets whose existence is to be classified by the state and kept inviolate by secret police. When the seventeenth-century Roman Catholic Church authorities forced Galileo to stop promulgating Copernicanism, at least they claimed they were prohibiting the dissemination of *false* belief. The U.S. government, however, was consciously outlawing scientific *truth* about the fundamental nature of the universe. As early as 1941, John J. O'Neill, president of the National Association of Science Writers, charged that this censorship on atomic research amounted to "a totalitarian revolution against the American people." Pointing to the devastating potential of an atomic bomb utilizing Uranium-235, O'Neill asked a fateful question: "Can we trust our politicians and war makers with a weapon like that?"[7]

So for the crucial years 1941-1945, public discussion of atomic weapons was banished from the nation that claimed to be leading the fight for democracy and freedom, while a handful of men secretly spent two billion dollars of public funds to develop these weapons. During these years, the only Americans exposed to public thoughts about atomic weapons were readers of science fiction. At first government censors ignored science fiction, which was considered a subliterary ghetto inhabited by kids and kooks. But then they became alarmed by every atomic bomb in science fiction. So even though there already had been widespread public discussion of the two main technical problems of atomic bombs—isolating sufficient quantities of fissionable material and achieving critical mass suddenly enough to set off an explosive chain reaction—government censorship clamped down on the imagination of fiction writers. When Philip Wylie submitted his novella *The Paradise Crater* to *Blue Book* in early 1945, an editor forwarded a copy to Army Intelligence, which had the author apprehended by a major who informed Wylie that he was personally prepared to kill him, if necessary, to keep the weapon secret (Moskowitz 292-93). Even science-fiction comic strips were censored. On April 14, the McClure Newspaper Syndicate ran strip one of "Atom Smasher," a new Superman series pitting America's favorite superhero against a cyclotron. The Office of Censorship promptly forced McClure to run a substitute series (in which Superman played a baseball game single-handed).[8]

The only citizens left to contemplate the consequences of atomic weapons were the readers of *Astounding Science-Fiction*, which stirred up a major security investigation when it published Cleve Cartmill's "Deadline" in the March 1944 issue.[9] The story suggested that the anti-fascist Allies would never use an atomic bomb because they realized that nuclear weapons could eventually threaten the existence of "the entire race," leaving nothing but "dust and rocks." This was not the view of the men who did decide to drop the bombs.

Today, few serious historians accept the original public position, still widely held, that the atomic bombs significantly shortened the war, eliminated the need to invade Japan, and thus saved hundreds of thousands of American lives. The historical debate instead focuses on the motives of the decision-makers, principally President Truman himself. Truman was aware of Japanese peace feelers. And he had been guaranteed that the Soviet Union would enter the war between August 8th and 15th, when a huge Soviet army would launch an all-out assault on the main surviving Japanese forces. Since he believed that this Soviet attack would end the war—"Fini Japs when that comes about," he secretly recorded[10]—did he have other motives?

The debate has tended to polarize between two positions. One suggests that Truman and his advisers intended the atomic bombs on Japan as what many believe they turned out to be—the opening shots in the Cold War against the Soviet Union. The other argues that the decision was made by default, through bureaucratic inertia and myopia, that there was just never any doubt that the bomb would be used.

But the President may have had another incentive as well. For Harry Truman and his key advisers evidently believed that destroying cities with atomic bombs might bring an end to war itself.

Thus President Truman reenacted the role of the President in *The Vanishing Fleets*, the novel that first imagined the United States wielding a weapon based on radioactivity, who decides that only by *using* this "most deadly machine ever conceived" can he end "wars for all time." Defending his role in the decision to use atomic weapons, Secretary of War Stimson explained that he was persuaded "that the bomb must be used" because "that was the only way to awaken the world to the necessity of abolishing war altogether. No technological demonstration...could take the place of the actual use with its horrible results."[11] Edward Teller argued that the bomb was so horrible that it might actually help "get rid of wars," so "[f]or this purpose actual combat-use might even be the best thing" (Szilard 209).

It was on his way to Potsdam that President Truman recited those lines from Tennyson prophesying that ghastly combat waged by airships would still "the war-drum" and bring about "the Federation of the world." Given details of the Alamogordo test, Truman recorded in his diary his thoughts about the atomic bomb: "It seems to be the most terrible thing ever discovered, but it can be made the most useful." When he learned of the devastation of Hiroshima, he proclaimed: "This is the greatest thing in history." Echoing the President in *The Vanishing Fleets*, who declared that America must " 'bear with fortitude whatever reproaches may be heaped upon us, for we are the instruments of God'," President Truman called the atomic bomb "an awful responsibility which has come to us," and told the nation: "We thank God that it has come to us, instead of to our enemies; and we pray that He may guide us to use it in His ways and for His purposes."[12] Did the President believe that he now possessed what Americans had long fantasized, the absolute weapon that could achieve perpetual peace under the global hegemony of the United States?

Within months of Hiroshima came the Baruch Plan, which some see as merely "an ultimatum" to the Soviets "to forswear nuclear weapons or be destroyed" (Herken 171). But the Baruch Plan—virtually identical to the atomic ultimatum issued by the President in the 1940 novel *Lightning in the Night*—may be understood more deeply as an expression of the treacherous mirage of the ultimate weapon endemic in American culture.

On June 14, 1946, the United States, represented by Bernard Baruch, dramatically announced that the only way the nations of the world could choose "World Peace" rather than "World Destruction" would be by submitting to a new international agency, not subject to veto, to be staffed by personnel "with proven competence" in atomic science, and empowered to evoke the "immediate, swift, and sure punishment" of any nation violating its orders. They must do so, Baruch declared, because America is now in possession of "the absolute weapon." No nation would be allowed to have nuclear weapons except for the United States, which would keep producing them until it had "a guarantee of safety, not only against the offenders in the atomic area but against the illegal users of other weapons— bacteriological, biological, gas—perhaps—why not?—against war itself."[13] Here is the culmination of that great fantasy, from the motor bomb of *The Great War Syndicate* in 1889 through the atomic bomb of *Lightning in the Night* in 1940: by wielding the ultimate weapon, the United States could force the world to end war for all time.

Notes

[1]For analysis of the British and European literature, see I.F. Clarke's ground-breaking study, *Voices Prophesying War*. The American future-war literature from 1880 through 1987 is discussed at length in my *War Stars*.

[2]This note to Bess and other evidence of young Truman's insatiable appetite for the fiction in *McClure's*, the *Saturday Evening Post*, and other magazines can be found in Ferrell, *Dear Bess*, 78-79, 126, 157, 161.

[3]See, for example: A.G. Ingalls, "Incomparable Promise or Awful Threat," *Scientific American* 161 (July 1939), 2; "Vast Power Source in Atomic Energy Opened by Science," *New York Times*, May 5, 1940, 1; "Vast Atomic Power Possible If Enough Uranium Is Isolated," *Newsweek* 15 (May 13, 1940), 41; "Atomic Power in Ten Years?" *Time* 35 (May 27, 1940), 44; "Harnessing the Atom," *Popular Mechanics* 74 (September 1940), 402-5. Also see Note 5.

[4]According to *Liberty* (August 24), the novel was written by Fred Allhoff with "the advice and counsel of General Robert Lee Bullard, Rear Admiral Yates Stirling, George E. Sokolosky, and many others."

[5]John J. O'Neill, "Enter Atomic Power," *Harpers* 181 (June 1940), 1-10; R.M. Langer, "Fast New World," *Collier's* 106 (July 6, 1940), 18-19, 54-55; William L. Laurence, "The Atom Gives Up," *Saturday Evening Post* 213 (September 7, 1940), 12-13, 60-63. Also see Note 3.

[6]Campbell 123; Groves 146-48, 325; Brians 7; Brown and MacDonald 203-9; "Drop that Post!" 4.

[7]"Writer Charges U.S. with Curb on Science," *New York Times*, August 14, 1941.

[8]*Newsweek*, August 20, 1945, 68.

[9]For the best account, see Albert I. Berger, "The *Astounding* Investigation: The Manhattan Project's Confrontation with Science Fiction," *Analog*, September 1984, 125-37.

[10]Ferrell, *Off the Record* 53. The prevailing myth about hundreds of thousands of American lives that would be lost in an invasion of Japan ignores several crucial facts: the Japanese home defense forces were already virtually impotent; U.S. air and naval forces were already encountering no resistance in their bombing and shelling of the islands; the invasion was not scheduled until November; the main forces that would be carrying out such an invasion, in the extremely unlikely event that Japan had not surrendered by then, would most probably be Soviet.

[11]Quoted in Sherwin 44.

[12]Ferrell, *Off the Record* 56; Truman, *Year of Decision* 421; Truman, "Radio Report to the American People" 213.

[13]All citations are to the text of *The International Control of Atomic Energy: Growth of a Policy* (Washington: U.S. Government Printing Office, n.d.).

Works Cited

Allhoff, Fred. *Lightning in the Night. Liberty.* August 24, 31, September 7, 14, 21, 28, October 5, 12, 19, 26, November 2, 9, 16, 1940.

Brians, Paul. *Nuclear Holocausts.* Kent, OH: Kent State University Press, 1987.

Brown, Anthony Cave and Charles B. MacDonald, eds., *The Secret History of the Atomic Bomb.* New York: Dial Press, 1977.

Campbell, John W. Jr., *The Atomic Story.* New York: Henry Holt, 1947.

Cartmill, Cleve. "Deadline." *Astounding Science-Fiction.* March 1944.

Clarke, I.F. *Voices Prophesying War: 1763-1984.* London: Oxford UP, 1966.

"Drop that Post!" *Saturday Evening Post*, 8 September 1945, 4.

Ferrell, Robert H., ed. *Dear Bess: The Letters from Harry to Bess Truman, 1910-1959.* New York: Norton, 1983.

———. *Off the Record: The Private Papers of Harry S. Truman.* New York: Harper & Row, 1980.

Franklin, H. Bruce. *War Stars: The Superweapon and the American Imagination.* New York: Oxford University Press, 1988.

Groves, Leslie R. *Now It Can Be Told: The Story of the Manhattan Project.* New York: Harper & Brothers, 1962.

Herken, Gregg. *The Winning Weapon: The Atomic Bomb in the Cold War 1945-50.* New York: Vintage, 1982.

Hollis, Godfrey. *The Man Who Ended War.* Boston: Little, Brown, 1908.

London, Jack. "The Unparalleled Invasion." *McClure's Magazine.* July 1910.

Moskowitz, Sam. *Explorers of the Infinite.* Cleveland: Meridian Books, 1963.

Norton, Roy. *The Vanishing Fleets.* New York: Appleton, 1908.

Sherwin, Martin J. "Old Issues in New Editions." *Bulletin of the Atomic Scientists* 41 (December 1985): 44.

Smith, A. Merriman. *Thank You, Mr. President.* New York: Harper & Brothers, 1946.

Stockton, Frank. *The Great War Syndicate.* New York: Dodd, Mead, 1889.

Szilard, Leo. *Leo Szilard: His Version of the Facts.* Ed. Spencer R. Weart and Gertrud Weiss Szilard. Cambridge, MA: MIT Press, 1978.

Train, Arthur and Robert Wood. *The Man Who Rocked the Earth.* Garden City: Doubleday, Page, 1915.

Truman, Harry S. "Radio Report to the American People, 9 August, 1945," *Public Papers of the Presidents of the United States: Harry S. Truman.* Washington: U.S. Government Printing Office, 1961.

———— *Year of Decision.* Garden City: Doubleday, 1955.

Wells, H.G. *The War of the Worlds* in *The Time Machine and The War of the Worlds.* Ed. Frank D. McConnell. NY: Oxford University Press, 1977.

Sex and Death in Nuclear
Holocaust Literature of the 1950s

Jacqueline R. Smetak

America I've given you all and now I'm nothing
I can't stand my own mind.
America when will we end the human war?
Go fuck yourself with your atom bomb.

(Allen Ginsberg, "America")

History doesn't repeat itself, but sometimes it seems as if it were trying to and the 1980s is a case in point. We were living in a "Red Dawn" world, in danger of imminent invasion by the "Evil Empire" through the "window of vulnerability;" "Amerika" on the verge of collapse or capitulation. It was the panic of the 1950s all over again. But this time around something was missing. There were no fallout shelters, no "duck and cover," and in spite of a concerted propaganda campaign, public opinion polls indicated that the number of Americans who feared communist aggression had dropped to less than one in ten.[1] In fact, opposition to nuclear madness, which had taken over a decade to organize in the 1950s, in the 1980s materialized overnight.

But the tensions created had to go somewhere and they got channeled, overtly, even crudely, into sex. It was the decade of herpes and AIDS, concern over abuse and the abduction of children, and, as Lloyd DeMause documents in *Reagan's America* (1984), a proliferation of sexual imagery. Political cartoons sprouted phalluses the way empty lots sprout weeds. But the power elite seemed confused as to who, or what, they wanted to attack. The desire for war expressed itself in fits and starts: by proxy in the Falklands, by a splendid little war in Grenada. DeMause speculates that we were putting ourselves through these contortions to punish ourselves for the good times of the 1970s, the sexual revolution of the 1960s. Whatever the case, the anxieties of the 1980s expressed themselves in perverse ways as noted by Alexander Cockburn in "Out of the Mouths of Babes" (*The Nation*, Feb. 12, 1990). In the 1940s and 1950s, generalized anxieties had been channeled into a domestic Red Purge and a foreign Cold War. In the 1980s, an attempt to resurrect the Red Purge, Senator Jeremiah Denton's investigation into terrorism, flopped but "society was ripe for a witch hunt nonetheless, and the accumulated energies poised to this end displaced themselves onto the

15

cause of hunting for body-snatchers of the nation's children" (191). The result was the persecution not of Communists but of parents and baby sitters complete with all the Satanic paraphernalia of a sixteenth century ergot poisoning frenzy. If Walt Kelly's Pogo had been correct back then—"We have found the enemy and he is us"—this time the connections were more clearly drawn.

If, as the saying goes, the first time is tragedy; the second time farce, the grotesque exaggerations of farce should enable us to see more clearly the structural lines of the tragedy. And there are parallels. If DeMause is correct, that we elected Reagan because he promised to punish us, there are indications that we were feeling quite as guilty in the years following the Second World War. We had just been through a major depression and a major war, both of which had demanded sacrifice and the submerging of the individual in the group if they were to be survived. After fifteen years of this, post-war prosperity (the term here is relative) finally allowed us the opportunity to indulge. But, as Marshall McLuhan comments, "This, then, is the dilemma...the child of Calvinist forebears who saw not in wealth but in the process of acquiring wealth the surest means of defeating the devil's power over idle hands" (55). Now that we had the wealth, we felt funny about spending it though spend it we did as is illustrated in Thomas Hines' *Populuxe* (1987) which speaks of the fifties as a decade-long romp through kitsch and outrageous disposable junk. But when people such as Wilhelm Reich or Philip Wylie suggested other modes of pleasure, the response was predictable. Reich felt that fascist violence was the inevitable product of a culture which rendered people incapable of genital satisfaction. Reich was jailed for his unorthodox opinions. Wylie, in *An Essay on Morals* (1947), insisted that sexual repression was destroying us. Copies of his book were burned.

Obviously, rampant consumerism was OK; playing in the garden was not. We were becoming an over-organized society as noted in depressing detail by intellectuals such as David Riesman, *The Lonely Crowd* (1950), and William Whyte, *The Organization Man* (1956). Aldous Huxley felt over-organization the inevitable result of over-population but that over-organization could take any of several different forms. In his own *Brave New World* (1931), human beings are reduced to the level of termites by granting them all their desires, but in George Orwell's *1984* (1949), the same is accomplished by granting them none. As Huxley remarks in *Brave New World Revisited*, in Orwell's book "the members of the Party are compelled to conform to a sexual ethic of more than Puritan severity" because the society described is "a society permanently at war, and the aim of its rulers is...to keep their subjects in that state of constant tension which a state of constant war demands of those who wage it" (21). That something of the sort was happening in America was clear. Huxley notes that the traditional American ethic of individualism had been replaced by a social ethic of conformity such that a good citizen was a "standard good mixer" who put his sex life on hold. Quoting from the *Harvard Business Review*, Huxley notes that the ideal wife " 'must not demand too much of her husband's time and interest. Because of his single-minded concentration on his job, even his sexual activity must be relegated to a secondary place' " (20). Apparently the *Harvard Business Review* felt that a constant state of tension stemming from sexual frustration was good for business. It was also, as any student of recent American history knows, good for war: "Hot," "Cold," and "Low Intensity."

Our overt reasons were defending Freedom and stemming the rising Communist tide. Our real reasons seemed to be something else and perhaps we were, as Felix Greene insists in *The Enemy: What Every American Should Know about Imperialism*, (1970) simply grabbing what was grabbable. But literature exists on a different plane. While it connects with the economic and the political, it expresses other concerns which exist not on a rational, empirical level but below the level of reason. As noted by Martha Bartter in *The Way to Ground Zero*, American nuclear holocaust fiction of the late 19th century expressed a variation on the idea of Manifest Destiny, the notion that "America's moral imperative is to impose peace and further trade" (38).[2] That this entailed imposing peace by force on everyone else involved no contradiction. As a people for whom altruism is an important virtue, we seemed ideally suited for the task. But World War II put a different spin on it. We had ended the War by dropping an atomic bomb on people we had originally seen as alien enemies but now saw as victims. Our jubilation was mixed with guilt and fear because now we were as if God. In the words of Robert Oppenheimer, "Now I am become Death, the Destroyer of Worlds."

To become as if God is unsettling: "If we had taken over God's role, it might be up to us to give it back to Him, even if doing so meant destroying ourselves in an atomic war" (Bartter 130). Prior to World War II, we had seen other people as worthy of destruction because of their impiety. Now we began to see ourselves that way. Bartter speculates that our single-minded opposition to Communism may be the result of simple projection. Not only had the Soviets "made" us drop that bomb as argued by Gar Alperovitz in *Atomic Diplomacy: Hiroshima and Potsdam* (1965), but they, as of 1949, had a bomb too. Perhaps the Cold War, with its brinksmanship and hair-raising confrontations, was nothing more than our effort to force them to punish us for what we had done. Perhaps it was a repetition compulsion. The trauma of the Second World War had been such that our anxiety about the looming potential of another expressed itself in a conflicted desire both to avoid war and get it over with, this desire expressed in fantasy enactments which at times were too real. The enactments which were too real do not concern us here, however. We can find them discussed in histories. Those which were clearly fantasy appeared in a number of different forms and the form which will concern us comes under the heading of literature.

In "The Poet and Day-Dreaming," Freud suggests that the function of the poet is to do our day dreaming for us. Works of literature are formalized fantasies, the driving force behind them "unsatisfied wishes" (47). Thus one can use the artifacts of popular culture to speculate about the wishes of those who consume them. The emphasis here is on "speculate;" Freud was cautious about his generalizations, and as John Lenihan points out in his study of Western films, *Showdown* (1980), the relationship between what is expressed in popular culture and what people actually feel is problematic. But problematic does not mean that no relationship exists and the fear of and/or desire for war expressed in nuclear holocaust stories is real. Public opinion polls done immediately after W.W. II indicate that few people thought a third world war a possibility. Three years later, 78% felt such a war either highly likely or inevitable. Empirical studies attempting to explain this change credit either events in Europe and Asia or a propaganda campaign carried out by our own government, but attempts at the time to explain this widespread anxiety show a marked tendency to read the problem in psycho-sexual terms. Paul Goodman, in explaining why we project repressed anger caused by the tension of frustrated desire, put it thus:

The desire for final satisfaction, for orgasm, is interpreted as the wish for total self-destruction. It is inevitable, then, that there should be a public dream of universal disaster, with vast explosions, fires, and electrical shocks; and people pool their efforts to bring this apocalypse to an actuality. (209)

And Allen Ginsberg:

America gone mad with materialism, a police-state America, a sexless and soulless America prepared to battle the world in defense of a false image of its authority. (26-27)

Norman Mailer, in *The White Negro* (1957), posited the sexual rebel, the hipster, as the only properly human response to "the suppressed knowledge...that we might still be doomed to die as a cipher in some vast statistical operation...a death by *deus ex machina* in a gas chamber or a radioactive city" (n.p.). Norman O. Brown, tracing the connections between Capitalism and de-sexualization in his psychoanalytic history, *Life Against Death* (1959), stated that "it also begins to be apparent that mankind, unconscious of its real desires and therefore unable to obtain satisfaction...is hostile to life and ready to destroy itself" (intro x).

While it is up in the air whether these people thought sexual repression the ultimate cause of impending nuclear obliteration, Goodman and Brown apparently did, or that repression was more properly thought of as an effect, it is clear that many felt there was a connection somewhere. Two novels, George Orwell's *1984* (1949) and Aldous Huxley's *Ape and Essence* (1948), focus on that connection. In neither book is repression seen as the ultimate cause. Rather, repression is caused by war and used by those in power to further their own ends, in *1984* to keep the war going.

Although as a nuclear holocaust novel per se, Orwell's book has some problems—he depicted nuclear war as an extension of the London Blitz— it had been a nuclear war which had created the conditions for the grimly totalitarian society of late twentieth century England. Winston has faint memories of "the time the atom bomb had fallen on Colchester" (30). The atomic war, occurring in the 1950s, had created the conditions for perpetual war with three evenly matched and unconquerable super states competing, as is explained in *The Theory and Practice of Oligarchical Collectivism* by Emmanuel Goldstein (a stand-in for Trotsky as Big Brother is for Stalin), for the natural resources and cheap labor of the Third World. The purpose of the war is to "use up the products of the machine without raising the general standard of living" (155) for to do so ensures the continuance of hierarchical systems by permanently frustrating the promise of industrialism (abundance without drudgery), the war guaranteeing that people will deflect their anger toward an external enemy rather than turn it against their own rulers. Sexual frustration merely intensifies the misery caused by material want. That misery, deflected into war, accomplishes in a psychologically acceptable manner the destruction of wealth necessary to maintain a hierarchical society. It's a neat, self-enclosed system reinforced by the propagandistic manipulation of Newspeak. At the end of the novel, Winston, a momentary rebel, finally wins the victory against himself. He comes to love Big Brother.

What Orwell is talking about is something which used to be called "brainwashing," the intent of which was to "change a mind radically so that its owner becomes a living puppet...a mechanism in flesh and blood" (Hunter 285) but ironically, the concept became a "brainwashing" technique as illustrated by Edward Hunter's book about American POWs during the Korean War, *Brainwashing* (1956), advertised as "the true and terrible story of the men who endured and defied the most diabolical Red torture" (from the cover). Obviously, "brainwashing" was something that Communists did to people, not something we were doing to ourselves. This tendency, to assume only those on the "other side" capable of such atrocities, was repeated in the essay, "Brainwashing," from *Brave New World Revisited*. The technique is Pavlovian and is described as a "conversion process." Assuming the victim survived, he or she would "emerge with new and ineradicable behavior patterns" (53).[3] Huxley believed that totalitarian societies worked their people over using the kinds of "mind-control" techniques perfected by Hitler ("Propaganda Under a Dictatorship") but that democracies used "methods of mass persuasion" ("The Art of Selling") and appealed to passion rather than enlightened self-interest ("Propaganda in a Democratic Society"). In other words, the Soviet Union might look like *1984* but the United States was heading toward something more like *Brave New World*.

A real war, as opposed to a "cold" war, puts a different face on it and Huxley explores that in *Ape and Essence* (1948). The story, ostensibly a discarded movie script too avant garde for Hollywood producers, tells of a post-holocaust world in which New Zealand has been spared but the United States has been reduced to a strange place where the descendants of the survivors rob graves for the material goods they are no longer capable of producing. These people have also created a society where sexual manipulation has been raised to extraordinary levels. Radiation poisoning has not only resulted in an excess of birth defects but has radically changed human sexuality. Human beings, unlike other mammals, are capable of sexual activity and response all the time but these people, biologically altered, are subject to the same sort of cycle as cats in heat. But there are suggestions in the novel that the change is perhaps not biological but cultural since a tribe to the north (presumably just as radiated as the one to the south) still do it the old way and the citizens of this odd remnant of Los Angeles live under considerable constraint. They wear patches that say "NO" sewn all over their clothing and educate themselves (the schools are practiced in the art of emotional abuse, subjecting the girls to intolerable humiliation and referring to them as "unclean vessels") to keep their sexual impulses in check until after the Purification Ceremonies of Belial Eve at which point everyone is allowed to engage in an old fashioned orgy that goes on for days. As in *1984*, sexual frustration maintains a hierarchical society, in this case, run by and for the benefit of castrated priests of Belial who spend their free time reading quasi pornographic novels salvaged from old libraries. They've also solved the problem of excess production, not by blowing everything up but by not producing in the first place. Belial, as the Arch-Vicar explains to Dr. Poole, a rather prissy member of the New Zealand Rediscovery Expedition to North America who had been captured by a North American grave robbing team, had "created an entirely new race of men, with deformity in their blood" and "no prospects but of more squalor, worse deformity and, finally, complete extinction" (99). These people are committing race suicide. With that in mind, the refrain from their anthem, "Give Me Detumescence," acquires several layers of significance. Huxley was also, no doubt, playing games with the look of the signature mushroom cloud of an atomic bomb explosion. If it can go up, it can also go down and if there is movement forward, there is also movement back, a repetition in reverse, an anomaly Freud sought to explain in *Beyond the Pleasure Principle*.

In this essay, Freud urges us to abandon our belief in an "instinct towards perfection" but it is clear that he is defining "perfection" in terms of nineteenth century notions of progress, that is, our "instinct towards perfection" has brought us to our "present high level of intellectual achievement and ethical sublimation" (36-7). Writing in the aftermath of the First World War, such ideas, quite naturally, seemed utter nonsense. Kenneth Burke, in *Language as Symbolic Action*, points out the contradiction in that section, for Freud had noted that the "repressed instinct never ceases to strive for complete satisfaction" (qtd. in Burke 17). Such satisfaction is, for Burke, a type of perfection in that Man is defined as "separated from his natural condition by instruments of his own making...and rotten with perfection" (16). Obviously, the societies described in both *Ape and Essence* and *1984* strive toward perfection. In Huxley's novel, the effort is to bring to fruition previously failed attempts at obliteration. Industrialism had poisoned us; world wars had slaughtered us; the demand for unconditional surrender had annihilated us. The function of the survivors of these catastrophes is to bring the whole bloody process to a perfect close. As the

Arch-Vicar points out, no alternative is possible because "the overwhelming majority of human beings accepted beliefs and adopted courses of action that could not possibly result in anything but universal suffering, general degradation and wholesale destruction" (96). In Orwell's novel, the effort is to create a system of perfect control, to evolve a language perfectly suited to make dissent and independent thought impossible. Freud had explained such efforts at self-destruction in terms of a repetition compulsion, an instinctive urge to return to an earlier state which, if taken far enough, means a return to a state of inorganic inertia. In brief, the aim of all life is death. Given that sex counters this by guaranteeing biological survival and that Eros, the life instinct, turns toward pleasure rather than destruction, any society intent on obliterating itself will repress or distort erotic tendencies. It will also repress awareness of whatever, for the sake of its own continued existence, cannot be acknowledged, in this case, its desire to kill itself. The contradiction here is only apparent. If such a society ceased to exist, were dismantled by its own citizens, it would fail in its efforts to destroy itself. It is not the people who wish to die but the political collective, a distinction C. Wright Mills makes in *The Causes of World War III* (1958): "It is not the aggression of people in general but their mass indifference that is the point of their true political and psychological relevance to the thrust toward war" (86).

Thus the other aspect of the Cold War mentality is a loss of affect as well as a loss of eros. Hannah Arendt, in *The Origins of Totalitarianism* (1951), discusses loss of affect as it related to those incarcerated in concentration camps where the effort was to destroy "the moral person in man" by killing "the juridical person." This was done by creating conditions "under which conscience ceases to be adequate and to do good becomes utterly impossible" (424). That this also was done to people who were bombed is the point of John Hersey's *Hiroshima* (1946), a report based on interviews of survivors of the first atomic bombing. His criteria for choosing which survivors would be included seems to have been that they all be ordinary people and that nothing they did or did not do have any effect on whether they lived or died. Hersey notes that "a surprising number of the people of Hiroshima remained more or less indifferent about the ethics of using the bomb" and a survivor recalls that in spite of terrible injuries, no one cried, "they died in silence" (112-3). If for these people, loss of affect was the result of suffering under conditions which rendered that suffering meaningless, Mordecai Roshwald, in *Level 7* (1959), turns it around and makes loss of affect the cause.

In this novel, the Cold War, structured according to the dictates of Mutually Assured Destruction (MAD), has gone on for so long that no one knows, or cares, what it is all about. The countries in question are never identified and we, the readers, do not know if we are reading about them or reading about us. But the distinction is irrelevant: "Each of us wanted to rule the world, or to save it (both formulas amount to the same thing now)" (134). Too clever by half, the rulers of both countries had developed a perfect

MAD. Nuclear weapons are controlled by computers and those who will push the button are chosen because they are unable to feel or connect with other people. Obviously, only a sociopath could blow up the world. These people are housed in level 7 of a mass shelter far underground and forever. Given the conditions of their lives, their inability to feel is an advantage. A normal person would go insane. But by some miscalculation, one person is miscast. X-117 still has a soul and refuses to push the button: "I can't kill my mother!" (96). He is removed and within a matter of hours, the entire world is destroyed; within a matter of days, the population reduced to 2,500 people who will soon die of radiation poisoning. They get to spend the intervening time listening, over the radio, to the people in the levels above them sicken into silence. X-117, tortured by guilt, doesn't wait for the inevitable. He hangs himself.[4]

The issue is conscience. The war had started by accident, was carried out by robots through orders issued to human beings reduced to automatons who could distinguish between "killing with the bare hands and pushing a button" (112). And because they could distinguish, they burned, blasted, and radiated hundreds of millions of people with hardly a second thought. This was the inevitable and logical extension of the age old practice of reducing the "enemy" to non-human status for they not only did this to the "enemy," they did this to their own people.[5] X-117, maladjusted by level 7 standards, simply moved in the opposite direction. He could feel the humanity of the people he was killing and he could sense, in the old Animistic way, the livingness of the earth itself. He could not kill his mother.

What Roshwald is getting at is what Mills explicitly states. It is not the aggression of people which is the issue but their indifference, their refusal to take responsibility. Kurt Vonnegut picks up on this in *Player Piano* (1952), but here, unlike other holocaust stories, the war had gone well. The United States emerges from a third world war in which tactical nuclear weapons had been used not only victorious but powerful, wealthy, and unscathed. The only problem is that in order to win the war, everything had to be centrally controlled and the task had been handed over to a giant computer, EPICAC. After the war EPICAC kept on going. Everyone's needs and desires are taken care of automatically. No one works except the New Class managers who simply watch control panels and live in a fifties era suburban valhalla. This is worker's paradise American style and everyone is bored beyond human endurance. The people of Ilium, New York, for lack of anything better to do, stage a revolt which fails and EPICAC keeps on going. Meanwhile, the barren wife of the main character runs off with one of his colleagues because she's more interested in career advancement than in love (one wonders if, perhaps, she read the *Harvard Business Review* article cited by Huxley) and being the perfect fifties housewife, her career is her husband. The message seems to be that even if a nuclear war were just a minor inconvenience, you are not going to like what you get. The chilling side of the message is that we already have it.

But *Player Piano*, for a holocaust novel, is unusual for it is nuclear without the holocaust. More typical are Pat Frank's *Alas, Babylon!* (1959) and Philip Wylie's *Tomorrow!* (1954). *Alas, Babylon!* seems to have worn better than *Tomorrow!* It has gone through 43 printings (as of 1983) whereas the other has been out of print for at least twenty-five years and is nearly impossible to find. This is likely due to the political specificity of Wylie's story because he wrote it as a propaganda tract, an effort to convince the public of the need for a civil defense program and an adequate system of shelters.[6] He also included in the novel a long diatribe attacking McCarthyites for thinking American Communists were dangerous and ignoring the real danger posed by Communists on the other side of the world. It is highly polemical, interesting as an expression of the Cold War Liberal mindset, and extraordinarily gruesome. Like Nevil Schute's *On the Beach* (1957), with its pregnant woman who won't live long enough to deliver and Mary who will have to kill her baby before radiation does it for her, *Tomorrow!* leaves us with disturbing images of abortion: a gutted woman trying to stuff her fetus back inside or another stumbling over the dragging entrails of a dead baby she won't put down. But, from another angle, the story is odd. It has an element of rape as suggested by the cover of the original paperback edition which shows an attractive young woman running from the blast, her clothing in shreds and strategically torn to reveal the crotch of her panties. Given that one of the positive effects of the bomb (since it leveled the city, the city can be rebuilt, better and brighter than before, the bomb, in effect, "no catastrophe at all, but pure benefit" [286]) is that Lenore Bailey won't have to marry Kittridge Sloan, son of the rich Minerva Sloan, a nasty woman to whom Lenore's father owes a great deal of money. Kittridge is spoiled, drives a red sports car, is perfectly hateful, and dies leaving Lenore free to marry Lt. Charles Conner, all-American boy. The bomb transforms itself into a rape prevention device, purifying the world of Soviet Reds, Kittridge Sloan, people with bad taste in home furnishing, and keeping the all-American girl safe from all of them.

Frank's *Alas, Babylon!* has the same thread, the obsession, less overtly expressed, with purity. In this book, however, the bomb unleashes the forces of darkness rather than eliminates them and the story is about the efforts of the people of Ft. Repose, Florida (against all odds spared both blast and radiation) to keep themselves from being overrun by refugees from Miami all of whom seem to be either red-neck lowlifes or Latinos. Tourists from New York City are more easily disposed of. They accidentally set fire to their hotel and die leaving only good solid middle Americans. The one black character is old, a helpful and self-sacrificing servant who is, sadly, killed by invading red-necks trying to stay alive by stealing. Unlike Wylie's novel, Frank's is not particularly vicious. Frank also understands, as Wylie does not, that the bomb will not give us the opportunity to build a better world. It will, instead, be the beginning of "the thousand year night." That "thousand year night" is picked up in Walter Miller's *A Canticle for Leibowitz* (1959) where a nuclear war flips us back to the Dark Ages and a monastery which has, in saving what it could from the old civilization, provided the seeds of destruction for the new. Some of the books the monks preserved contained the information needed to build another atomic bomb. Here, repetition exists as a Mobius strip but cut for Mrs. Grales' other head comes alive, "a creature of primal innocence" to whom God gave "the preternatural gifts of Eden—those gifts which Man had been trying to seize by force again from Heaven since first he lost them" (318).

This, then, is perhaps the common theme, the effort to grasp the Second Coming, the "preternatural gifts of Eden." We move toward death, or regress to the womb, conflate the two but, as McLuhan notes, "womb, tomb, and comfort have always been interchangeable symbols" (101). Perhaps this interchangeability cannot adequately explain why we are engaged in this course of action but it does explain the stories we tell.

Notes

[1]Refer Michael Parenti, *Inventing Reality* (1986), citing New York *Times* polls (93, 137). These are consistent with Gallup and Harris polls done later in the decade.

[2]According to Bartter, the earliest example is Frank Stockton's *The Great War Syndicate* (1889).

[3]Bruno Bettelheim questioned the effectiveness of "brainwashing" based on his own experience as an inmate at Dachau. Those prisoners who kept themselves informed about how they felt, who knew exactly how far they were willing to let themselves be de-humanized and deprived of choice and who, past a certain point, would not comply survived. Those who surrendered completely did not emerge with new patterns of behavior. They simply died. Refer *The Informed Heart: Autonomy in a Mass Age* (New York: The Free Press, 1960).

[4]X-117 had exhibited signs of trouble early on. He had developed a paralysis in his right hand. The narrator attributes it to X-117's ability to love; X-117 insists that it is because he fears "punishment from 'above' for his readiness to push buttons and destroy the world." (50) The staff psychologist, however, has a tidy Freudian explanation. His mother had caught him masturbating, had punished him, and the repressed trauma of this experience is expressing itself in hysterical symptoms. Bruno Bettelheim, in *Freud and Man's Soul* (1982), criticized Americans for misusing Freud, for "jargonizing" his work in an attempt to avoid self-knowledge. Roshwald has provided the perfect example.

[5]Isabel Moore's long out of print *The Day the Communists took over America* (1961) is a good example of this kind of dehumanizing propaganda. It qualifies as a nuclear holocaust story in the same sense as the TV mini series, "Amerika," in that the simple threat of nuclear war causes the United States to decide "better Red than dead" and the country surrenders to the Soviet Union. Communists are depicted as inhuman monsters totally devoid of normal feelings. Sex is mere physical release having nothing to do with love and one of them, on discovering that his mistress is pregnant, pushes her down a flight of stairs. Her injuries not only cause her to miscarry, they render her permanently sterile. The root cause of the downfall of America is a loss of virility. American men are more interested in television than they are in sex. Oddly enough, the book also attacks American Conservatives, dismissing them as half-baked quasi-fascists and echoes a common tactic of the 1950s. Liberals discredited both Radicals and Conservatives, as can be seen in Harry and Bonaro Overstreet's *The Strange Tactics of Extremism* (1964), an expose

of the John Birch Society, by collapsing them into each other. In this Moore parallels some of the odder ravings of Philip Wylie.

[6]In 1949, Wylie helped persuade Senator Brien McMahon to urge President Truman to build the H bomb and in 1950 was an advisor to Gordon Dean, Chairman of the Atomic Energy Commission. From 1949 to 1954, he was a special consultant to the Federal Civil Defense Administration.

Works Cited

Alperovitz, Gar. *Atomic Diplomacy: Hiroshima and Potsdam.* New York: Vintage, 1965.

Arendt, Hannah. *The Origins of Totalitarianism.* New York: Harcourt Brace Jovanovich, 1951.

Bartter, Martha A. *The Way to Ground Zero: The Atomic Bomb in American Science Fiction.* New York: Greenwood Press, 1988.

Bettelheim, Bruno. *The Informed Heart: Autonomy in a Mass Age.* New York: The Free Press, 1960.

———. *Freud and Man's Soul.* New York: Vintage, 1982.

Brown, Norman O. *Life Against Death.* Middletown, CT: Wesleyan University Press, 1959.

Burke, Kenneth. *Language as Symbolic Action.* Berkeley: University of California Press, 1966.

Cockburn, Alexander. "Out of the Mouths of Babes." *The Nation.* 12 February 1990.

DeMause, Lloyd. *Reagan's America.* New York: Creative Roots, Inc., 1984.

Frank, Pat. *Alas, Babylon!* New York: Bantam, 1959.

Freud, Sigmund. *Beyond the Pleasure Principle.* trans. James Strachey, New York: W.W. Norton & Co., 1961.

Ginsberg, Allen. "Poetry, Violence, and the Trembling Lambs." *A Casebook on the Beat.* ed. Thomas Parkinson, New York: Thomas Y. Crowell, 1961.

Greene, Felix. *The Enemy: What Every American Should Know About Imperialism.* New York: Vintage, 1970.

Goodman, Paul. *Growing Up Absurd.* New York: Vintage, 1956.

Hersey, John. *Hiroshima.* New York: Bantam Books, 1946.

Hine, Thomas. *Populuxe.* New York: Alfred Knopf, 1987.

Hunter, Edward. *Brainwashing.* New York: Pyramid/Farrar Strauss & Cudahy, 1956.

Huxley, Aldous. *Ape and Essence.* New York: Harper & Row, 1948.

———. *Brave New World and Brave New World Revisited.* New York: Harper & Row, 1960.

Keefer, Thomas F. *Philip Wylie.* Boston: Twayne Publishing, 1977.

Lenihan, John H. *Showdown.* Urbana: University of Illinois Press, 1980.

Mailer, Norman. *The White Negro.* San Francisco: City Lights, copyright 1957 by Dissent Publishing Associates.

McLuhan, Marshall. *The Mechanical Bride: Folklore of Industrial Man.* Boston: Beacon Press, 1951.

Mills, C. Wright. *The Causes of World War III.* New York: Ballantine Books, 1958.

Moore, Isabel. *The Day the Communists Took Over America.* New York: Wisdom House, 1961.

Orwell, George. *1984.* New York: NAL, 1949.

Overstreet, Harry and Bonaro. *The Strange Tactics of Extremism*. New York: W.W. Norton, 1964.

Parenti, Michael. *Inventing Reality: The Politics of the Mass Media*. New York: St. Martin's Press, 1986.

Roshwald, Mordecai. *Level 7*. New York: Signet Books, 1959.

Shute, Nevil. *On the Beach*. New York: Harper & Row, 1957.

Vonnegut, Kurt. *Player Piano*. New York: Dell, 1952.

Wylie, Philip. *Tomorrow!* New York: Popular Library, 1954.

A Flash of Light:
The Evolution of Anti-Nuclear Consciousness
in an Alternative Literary Journal
(*Samisdat,* 1973-1990)

Merritt Clifton

For members of a generation raised in the shadow of the atomic bomb, a shadow presenting the ever-present possibility that at any moment we might be as old as we ever would be, we young writers and artists who founded *Samisdat*[1] back in 1973 were very slow to take notice of nuclear war. Our early issues were dominated by stories and poems of young people dealing with the concerns of young people, most notably mating and discovering self-identity.

This isn't to suggest we were politically unconscious. As with most alternative publications that emerged from the Vietnam War era, and most especially from heavily politicized Berkeley, California, the war was a constant backdrop, along with racial unrest. Because founding fiction editor Tom Suddick was a Vietnam veteran, from the first we published veterans; because founding poetry editor D.G.H. Schramm is gay, we were also uncommonly accepting of gay literature. Both veterans and gay writers were a constant presence from Volume I, #1 in June, 1973, through to our last regular issues, 17 years and 220 numbers later.

Nuclear war, however, didn't surface until our fifth issue, our first of 1974; and even then, the reference in my own story "In Command" was faint. "For a minute or two," I wrote, "we both look out the windows, staring over the bleak straw hills and barren, once wooded crests. Even the blackened stumps are near gone now." I could have been describing the aftermath of a forest fire, or conventional warfare. I made no reference to nuclear radiation. I envisioned "Abandoned houses and outbuildings...some surrounded by broken cars and equipment." But because I was the author, I know my 'Road Warrior'-like post-apocalyptic scenario did depict the distant aftermath of nuclear war, as I envisioned it from ninth grade civil defense exercises, from popular fiction such as Walter M. Miller's *A Canticle*

"A Flash of Light: The Evolution of Anti-Nuclear Consciousness in an Alternative Literary Journal" appeared in *Samisdat* Volume 56, no. 1. Essay and excerpts reprinted by permission of *Samisdat,* Merritt Clifton, editor.

for Liebowitz, and from having recently read accounts of Hiroshima as it looked 25 years after the blast.

In December, 1973, when I wrote the story as a 20-year-old college senior, I had no more concept of nuclear war than I did of sex, which I also had yet to experience. And I was the only one of the editorial board, which soon dwindled down to just me, whose work acknowledged the possibility of nuclear war at all.

Yet nuclear war was perhaps the strongest motif of that fifth issue, whose most distinguished contribution was an excerpt from Scott Sanders' then unpublished novel *Warchild*. (I have no idea if it ever was published, but Sanders did shortly win the Phillips Exeter fellowship to help him complete it.) Writing in the satirical, surrealistic mode of the films *Catch-22* (based on Joseph Heller's novel of the same title) and *M.A.S.H.*, Sanders presented Big Jake, a John Wayne caricature who traveled through time on the big screen at a military base movie house, waging war for America as an everyman secret conscientious objector named Ransome watched. At last "Big Jake plumped down in August, 1945, month of Ransome's birth." Big Jake was bombardier on the Enola Gay. "When the bomb struck all the audience cheered and Ransome cheered with them, cheered Big Jake's bravery, cheered the scientists who had made the bomb, cheered the industry that had constructed the airplane, cheered the flag on the wings, and cheered themselves. Ransome was overwhelmed with a sense of belonging.... Here was his place, here were his buddies.... He would sleep in his flight jacket, he would learn to swagger like a pilot, he would smoke and swear and race all night in customized Chevrolets.... But the camera would not leave the smoking ruins. At zero point, the very center of the firestorm, there was nothing but stone and dust, everything wooden or human turned to vapor, steel girders half a mile away slithered into heaps of snakes, the shadows of pedestrians darkened pavement scorched white by the blast, and still the camera would not leave the city alone.... On every side there were charred bodies, or cinders that might have been people.... Ransome fought for air amid the stink of burnt flesh." Escaping the theatre at last, Ransome cannot escape the "twisted bodies of a thousand generations of mutants, each of them calling to him Pilotman O Pilotman come drop your bomb, come sow your radioactive seed in our enemy flesh, come warchild come."

Thus from our first notice of nuclear war, *Samisdat* offered two parallel but opposing themes I would see recurring in related literature both here and elsewhere. On the one hand here was nuclear war as cleanser, as planetary purification ritual, prelude to a simplified, anarcho-fascistic world most resembling the Dark Ages. As a literary device, nuclear war as cleanser was and is used most often to clear the stage of complications as prelude to a morality play in prose—the usual theme of which concerns sexuality. In retrospect, an entire sequence of post-nuclear apocalypse stories I wrote and published in *Samisdat* were actually about the consequences of feminism. It says a lot about male confusion and insecurity that I subconsciously equated female social equality with nuclear war, even as I consciously and editorially embraced the idea (to the point of adopting the pseudonym Robin Michelle Clifton for editorial essays.) My stories "Onward, Christian Soldiers" (volume 4, #3, 1974), "Maid Of Fortune" (volume 6, #3, 1975), "The First Stone" (volume 8, #3, 1975), "The New Way" and "What A Man Is" (released as the chapbook *Two From Armageddon*, volume 10, #3, 1976), and "Tarzan Of The Apes" (volume 14, #4, 1977) all dramatized male/female conflicts in the context of complete destruction of the twentieth century social fabric. "Christian Soldiers," "The First Stone," and "Tarzan" each envisioned religion re-emerging as in the Dark Ages to restore some semblance of order, at cost of individual freedoms and rights of moral judgment. They might be described as the darkest side of *A Canticle For Liebowitz*, with hope emerging only through the triumph of sexuality whenever young men and women managed to find each other outside the constraints of the new theocracy. These stories might also be fairly assessed as a young former Seventh Day Adventist's expressions of apprehension as the Jesus Freaks of the early 1970s—mostly college-aged ex-drug abusers—merged into the more traditionally fundamentalist Born Again movement that surged into political power with the 1976 election of "born again" Baptist Jimmy Carter to the U.S. presidency. But even though most of the stories made superficial reference to nuclear war, they can't really be said to have addressed it squarely as an issue or threat. None ever acknowledged nuclear war as anything more than a distant past event that somehow erased history while leaving people behind who, for the most part, thought and acted just like 20th century members of the counterculture—from loving flower children to the Manson Family.

What I was writing was not unique. *Samisdat* published similar visions from others, whose references to nuclear antecedents tended to be even weaker than my own. Comparable stories still appear regularly in science fiction fanzines, and had been a staple of popular science fiction ever since The Bomb was invented. The *Road Warrior* movies merely project the genre onto the screen. Nuclear war in this genre is nothing more than a means of implying "Once upon a time," or as the Star Wars motion pictures put it, "In a galaxy long ago and far away." Call it The Bomb as cue for suspension of disbelief, or The Bomb as Acid, vehicle for journeys into surreality. In this genre The Bomb emphatically isn't real. Whether it isn't real because the usually young authors simply don't comprehend the totality of the threat, or because they ignore it, I still don't really know. I know that in my own case it was a little of both.

On the other hand there are the writings of people like Sanders, who strive to wake us up, to bring us face to face with the real Bomb and all it means, to send each of us running into the street like Ransome, out of the theatre to do something, anything, to insure no more bombs will ever be detonated.

Miriam Sagan, now a nationally noted poet but then a Harvard undergrad still unpublished anywhere else, contributed our first anti-nuclear war poem in *Samisdat* volume 2, #4, dated winter 1974. Her poem, "Fallout," has become an anthem of the anti-nuclear and peace movements, and has never been out of print since, appearing in numerous other magazines, chapbooks, and broadsides:

> The land is dry; nothing
> grows here but frozen rose
> gypsum, lava, and white sand.
> The uranium miners descend,
> no lights strapped to their foreheads.
> They descend into a golden light.
> Daughters-of-Radon disintegrate
> into radium and burn.
> They wash off thumbprints, the roadmaps
> of lifelines.
> In the bones irradiated cells forget
> their borderlines and devour the marrow.
> Half-life, like a summer afternoon's
> half-light, suffocates the heart.
> The uranium miners descend.
> Turn the pages in the Book of Clouds.
> Clouds in a blue sky, page one.
> Clouds in a black sky, page one thousand.
> The constellations are nailed to the sky.
> On the Southern Cross there are light years
> from wound to wound.
> The uranium miners climb out slowly
> past the stalagmites growing
> drop by drop.
> On the white desert they glow,
> skin golden, transparent, radioactive.
> Inside the cave of their chests
> their lungs flutter like waking bats,
> then constrict. The delicate
> airways of the lungs labyrinths
> where breath is lost at every twist.
> The uranium miners tightrope-walk
> the white horizon strip
> as the sky breaks open like an egg
> and pours out unhatched stars and
> galaxies spinning their great burning arms.

No matter how often I re-read and retype it, I never cease to marvel at how much Miriam encompassed: the great nuclear furnaces we call stars, the devastation of the New Mexico desert (where she now lives, in Santa Fe, a short drive from Alamogordo), the nuclear fuel cycle that powers both bombs and civilian reactors, the impact of nuclear development upon families, communities, and individual workers. The marvel is not only the marvel inherent in the achievement of any exceptionally gifted image-maker, but also that Miriam, at 19, was the youngest contributor to that issue, and yet addressed one of the most complex, threatening issues of our time more comprehensively, more memorably than almost anyone since.

At any rate, Miriam set the standard, not that *Samisdat* consciously chose the direction toward protest, away from fantasy, until mid-1978, approximately one year before the near-meltdown of the Three Mile Island reactor in 1979 suddenly revived public interest in nuclear issues of all sorts. The evolution of consciousness was slow. My own first poem on nuclear war (in *From the Golan Heights, Samisdat* volume 3, #4) could be read as rationalization, a reflection of the typical Middle American view that, well, yes, The Bomb is terrible, but we only used it because we had to, and anyway the Japs had it coming:

> *Trade*
>
> The Enola Gay dropped anchor,
> riding at rest
> in orange seas swamping Hiroshima.
> Ship and crew sailed on.
> The image remains,
> goods delivered in four short years
>   from Pearl Harbor.
>
> Looking up, from the bridge,
> one still sees the parachute,
> pale premonition
> of incoming mushroom
>   —suspended, that the plane might pass.
>
> Looking down, from the bridge,
> one notes paled cement,
> pink earth,
> twisted buildings.
> At Pearl we saw sailors, tombed alive.
>   In Washington, cherry trees.

Contrast this affirmation of faith in my government with my outrage five years later, when "R.I.P." appeared in *Samisdat* volume 19, #1, 1979:

> Six minutes from launching,
> submarine-fired cruise missiles
> could strike the heart of the continent.
> Ashes to ashes, dust to dust returneth.
>
> We can rest assured,
> the Pentagon tells us,
> that all possible has been done
> to insure continuity of government.

In the interim *Samisdat* had become much more militantly radical than in our Berkeley years, as I myself evolved from an environmentally aware anti-war Republican into an outspoken Gandhian anarchist. Though the sources of my disillusionment and of *Samisdat* radicalism were much more personal than political, leading in 1977 to self-imposed exile from California to Quebec province, Canada, the nuclear arms race nonetheless epitomized everything I saw wrong with a political system whose primary business was and is perpetuation of self rather than helping people and caring for the planet.

My newly expressed rage and disillusionment wasn't really new at all. It lay unrecognized just beneath the surface of my motivation for founding *Samisdat* in the first place, had already bubbled out in the sociopathy characterizing most of my own early stories and most of those I accepted, was basis of my alliance with disaffected Namvets, militant homosexuals, feminists, and, increasingly, with Native Americans, Blacks, Hispanics, and animal rights activists.

My rage and disillusionment also weren't newly applied to nuclear war; rather, this focal point was rediscovered as I became increasingly politically aware in all directions. Further, what I was doing, I believe, is what the activist portion of my generation was doing, evolving out of generalized anti-establishment attitudes formed during the late 1960s and early 1970s, into less flamboyant but much more effectively directed grassroots activism that characterized the 1980s.

Finally, though I know no way to prove it, I think Three Mile Island became the landmark event between the passive later 1970s and the activist 1980s not because it was the greatest outrage to attract public attention— there were, after all, bloody and irrational U.S.-supported wars underway in Latin America, acid rain falling, etcetera—but because Three Mile Island more than any other outrage recalled our worst childhood fears. We didn't grow up afraid of death squads or ecological collapse; we grew up practicing to hide beneath our desks when and if the Russians nuked us. The Three Mile Island near-meltdown in effect appealed to an archetypical fear etched into the racial memory of all of us born after Hiroshima.

I had acknowledged this archetypical fear in my autobiographical first novel 24X12, initially published as *Samisdat* volume 6, #1 in mid-1975, reprinted by Mudborn Press, now defunct, as a quality paperback in 1980. 24X12 was the record of my life as I lived it through 24 critically difficult hours at age 12, the writing of which commenced in September, 1966, when I was barely 13. In the concluding pages I recalled my earliest fantasy of nuclear war as cleanser, a fantasy entertained in bed at night when stress kept me from sleeping: "I wished I'd be with a girl when the warheads hit, embracing, the heat melting us into a single ball. There was something comforting about contemplating destruction in this manner. Even my own.... An airliner shrieked overhead, engines thundering away the predawn still. For a moment I thought this was it. I counted the seconds to doom, neither happy nor sad, resigned and ready for the initial pain.

But the din tapered off as the plane cleared the hills, moving on. No explosion came. I cried a little, disappointed."

According to Walter Cummins, English Department chairman at Fairleigh Dickinson University, my narrator in "yearning for the release of a nuclear apocalypse" is "unlike any other twelve-year-old in fiction" (3). I wouldn't know about that, but enough friends have confessed having had the same fantasy as children, including one lady raised in West Germany, well away from my immediate cultural influences, that I imagine it does have some universality.

> Lo, we made a joyful noise unto the Lord.
> The flash made brilliant the early morning sky,
> Over a hundred thousand square miles.
>
> —Ron Crowe, from "Faith In The Atomic Age";
> *Samisdat* volume 8, #3, January 1976.

There was certainly gathering anti-nuclear and anti-nuclear war momentum long before Three Mile Island, evident in *Samisdat* as well as elsewhere. Throughout the latter 1970s I received an ever-increasing volume of submissions with nuclear themes, more and more of which were in the warning mode. Crowe was the first of many to equate our nuclear accomplishments with hubris, and to echo Percy Shelley's "Ozymandias" in warning of the consequences:

> Like the enigmatic sphinx
> these unwanted gifts will live
> long after the reasons are gone,
> waiting squat and crouched on the desert floor,
> with no place to go,
> guarded by coyotes and darkling beetles.
> Through the faith alone
> shall you be saved,
> and these are its monuments.

Interestingly enough, Crowe anticipated by almost a decade the U.S. Department of Energy's proposal to mark nuclear waste storage sites with Stonehenge-like monoliths, to be maintained through the next 10,000 years by "nuclear priests."

Another dramatic early anti-nuclear vision came from Wisconsin librarian Don Dorrance, who mailed me his longpoem *Morituri* (published as *Samisdat* volume 9, #2, 1976) about an hour before he shot himself. Without once mentioning or referring to nuclear war in specific, *Morituri* records the deaths of one hundred million civilians in wars of all types during the first three-fourths of the twentieth century. Only in concluding did Dorrance suggest the prospect of nuclear holocaust, yet his final words do give unmistakable warning:

We have not
learned that children must not be killed.
This must
be our safety, our only hope: to know we are all
children and sacred, all of us, and must understand
that we kill ourselves in the machines our century
has created.

Paradoxically, former Strategic Air Command fighter pilot H.R. Coursen Jr. made only one reference to nuclear war in his chapbook *Walking Away* (volume 16, #1, 1977), which nonetheless almost entirely concerns preparations for same: "The swept-wing version of the Republic F-84...carried an atomic bomb and was ready to fly low-level missions over Russian in case someone in Washington decided it was time for Judgement Day."

I didn't notice it at the time, but looking back, the most remarkable aspect of *Walking Away* is Coursen's complete lack of conscientious introspection about the meaning of his aerobatic adventures. Consciousness was dawning, yet even I, as concerned editor, was still not all that far removed from the adolescent boy who glued together model military aircraft as unrecognized symbols of penis-power.

I'm embarrassed to admit that it was my fascination with military aircraft that inspired the 1971 first draft of "Heritage," now occasionally taught in classes devoted to nuclear war literature. But very vague misgivings kept it in a folder, unpublished, until *Samisdat* 18, #2, 1978, our turning point. The catalyst for us was Mark Phillips' short story "On The Brink," set on the Sunday of the 1961 Cuban missile crisis. Phillips' autobiographical central figure, Jack, is obliged to attend Sunday school despite the danger of being outdoors if bombs are dropped. On his way, he rescues an abandoned kitten, but an outraged and superstitious Sunday schoolmarm confiscates it, then throws it into the furnace. Phillips' message was that the mindset permitting a nuclear war is widely distributed among us, that the difference between one kitten burning and the world burning isn't great so long as moral symbolism means more than compassionate deeds. Disturbed, I finally pulled out "Heritage," added the subheads and middle stanza, and ran it as a companionpiece:

I. Endangered Species

The Consolidated-Vultee B-36 Condor,
nine bomb bays, four turrets,
range 8,000 miles, could drop to death
twenty-one tons from 40,000 feet.
Phased out in '58, it never saw combat.

II. Drop Shot

Europe would fall in ten short days,
Britain holding out through 40 nuclear hits.
Suffering 80 percent losses,
air crews would mutiny. Half America might die.
Yet war would remain war
as mankind has always known it.
We would win.

This plan was scrapped with 230-foot wingspans,
ten engines, three pilots, three gunners,
two navigators, & two anesthetized bombardiers.

III. Detente

Consolidated-Vultee became Convair,
dinosaur birds yielding to the B-58A Hustler.
It hit Mach 2.1 in level flight,
the fastest Western bomber ever deployed,
yet with a three-man crew & 55-ton load,
was obsolete by 1960.

Abandoned on Mojave sand and mud,
squadrons point like silver arrows
alternately toward Los Angeles & Las Vegas.

The editorial in that issue at last declared our support for "immediate, unilateral nuclear disarmament." When the local newspaper, the Sherbrooke *Record*, ridiculed our position as naive, I responded with a short essay, "Disarmament Works," which recounted how I prevented a potentially deadly gangfight in Berkeley, 1969, by allowing one of the leaders of the opposing gang to hit me, repeatedly, for over an hour, neither flinching nor taking my hands out of my pockets, but taking care to avoid getting hit anywhere vital. My opponent eventually ran away in tears, his gang melting into the night behind him in confused silence. Oddly enough, I had never before accorded that incident political significance, although I was well aware of the power of passive resistance when it happened. Phillips' story had awakened my recognition that nuclear war is not just a distant, if ominous problem dealt with by world leaders: it is in truth an extension of how we see ourselves in relation to the world and one another.

The *Record* didn't print my little essay. Then-editor James Duff also found it naive, though he hired me as a reporter about then. But the *Record* did typeset it, and it did appear in my essay collection *Freedom Comes From Human Beings*, published as *Samisdat* volume 26, #3 in 1980. By then *Samisdat* had also declared overt opposition to nuclear power, as of volume 21, #1, 1979. Our subscription flyers and rejection slips proclaimed "We say to hell with Big Brother and his threat of nuclear apocalypse," making political opposition to the nuclear war machine not only editorial policy but also a rallying point to attract other readers and writers.

Awareness of nuclear war continued threading itself through most of our publications, even those not overtly addressing the issue; and the awareness was increasingly pessimistic. Some of the most memorable examples came from poets well entrenched within the middle class, with children, property, and little history of militant political action.

From Ottawa housewife Rita Rosenfeld's chapbook *Bound Books* (volume 21, #3, 1979):

> We construct our days with care under an
> oppressive fear of nuclear fury
> searing like a hungry star....
>
> We pretend,
> absorbed with the
> fantasy of living, secure in the belief
> that no one would unleash
> that hell.
> But reality is a tower of Babel—
> an empty wind bellowing through
> diplomatic corridors.
>
> Reality is
> grains bending
> to the rain of radioactive death.

Easthampton, Massachusetts, schoolteacher Gary Metras contributed a second example, much reprinted, in his chapbook *The Yearnings*, published as *Samisdat* volume 22, #4 in 1980; though specifically inspired by Three Mile Island, it deliberately is ambiguous enough to suggest war's aftermath as well.

> *After the Disaster*
>
> Fertilizing will not bring back the grass,
> receding a foot a year from
> the concrete domes
> and silos. Wildflowers
> are hopeless, roots scorched, and seeds
> not dropped as if in kindness
> to the future. Trees have long abandoned
> leaves, refusing, themselves,
> to fall, memory alone alive. Worms
> have elapsed from the soil, its taste
> bitter even to simple mouths.
> Only ants bask in some dream of joy,
> building sand to towers, each grain
> lifted to strange, heat-thrilling winds.

Birds fly in wide
arcs of avoidance; their eggs,
if laid at all, are wrong-
colored, and the shells, too thick
in a too-quick adaptation,
as fetal muscles and beaks recall
the old way of birth. The buried alive
scratch the coffin lid: no air,
no air, no one there to sing to,
just hardened footprints that point
to the glow in the horizon.

Metras, like Coursen, is an Air Force veteran—a former flight controller
at a base in Turkey, where medium-range fighter bombers were poised
specifically to wait for nuclear war.

Career activist W.D. Ehrhart likewise linked the nuclear power and
nuclear war threats, which in fact are closely related, inasmuch as the
plutonium for making nuclear weapons is a by-product of power-generating:

Sunset
　　Dresden Nuclear Power Station
　　Morris, Illinois

Late afternoon: in the stillness
before evening, a car on the road
between cornfields surrounding
Dresden Station raises a plume
of dust, and a light wind
settles the dust gently over the corn.
Power lines over the cornfields
audibly sing the power of cities
beyond sight, where neon lights flash
tomorrow, laughter and dreams.
Deep within Dresden Station,
human beings tamper with atoms.

Dresden: say it, and the air
fills with the wail of sirens,
thin fingers of light
frantically probing the clouds,
red bursting anger, black thunder,
the steel drone of the bombers,
dry bones rattle of falling bombs:
　　deliver us from fire;
　　deliver us from the flames;
　　Lord, have mercy upon us.
135,000 human beings
died in the flames of Dresden.

The air to the west is on fire.

> The lake to the west burns red
> with the sun's descending fire.
> The sky rises out of the lake gold
> to copper to deep blue, falling
> gently away, black, to the east.
> Deep within Dresden Station,
> human beings tamper with atoms.
> Light wind rustles the cornstalks,
> the sound like the rustle of skirts
> on young graceful women.

"Sunset" appeared in *Samisdat* volume 24, #1, a collection of four chapbooks in one entitled *The Samisdat Poems of W.D. Ehrhart*, who even then was perhaps the most prominent poet to emerge from the Vietnam War.

Our analysis was fast becoming more sophisticated, even if our leaders and much of the public still didn't listen.

> That guy laughed at me

wrote Florida schoolteacher Margaret Key Biggs in "Twice Told," from her chapbook *Swampfire* (volume 24, #3, 1980),

> when I tried to talk to him
> about Three Mile Island
> and Crystal River.
> "You remind me of my old dad;
> he said when they dropped the bomb
> on Hiroshima that that was it—
> the end of the world."
> He laughed all over himself.

Even as we had come to recognize the potential imminence and overwhelming consequences of nuclear war, so I personally began to see new reasons why it might not ever happen, reasons rooted not in politics but in ecology and insight into the human condition. I began to believe we would not extinguish ourselves because preservation and perpetuation of our species is engineered into our very genes; ultimate destruction isn't. Further, as an ecologist and environmental journalist by profession, I tended to suspect that, as in every other aspect of human endeavor, we overrated ourselves when it came to our potential for destruction. Nuclear war might annihilate ourselves and all like creatures, but I felt certain it would not end life on earth, that instead it would create new niches for new and different creatures who would evolve out of whatever microbes and lichen endured. Finally, I recognized the threat of nuclear war as a form of blackmail, rationalizing the continued existence of the military industrial complex. I greeted 1980 (volume 23, #4) with an editorial not anticipating doom but offering the hope of a new age, when our maturing baby boom generation would look into the mirror and recognize each and every one of us as our own messiahs—and then act upon that opportunity. This editorial was written specifically to counter a doom-and-gloom prophecy by Val Ross of the Canadian national news magazine *Maclean's* (28-30). Val, a friend of mine, anticipated nuclear war within the decade. Whether it didn't happen for the reasons I saw, or simply because so many of us joined the Nuclear Freeze and other protest campaigns, we'll never know—and it doesn't really matter. Either way, it did not happen, and either way the rise of consciousness helped make us more responsible people.

I went farther with my analysis of the nuclear threat in my editorial opening *Samisdat* volume 25, #2, 1980, tracing the history of the Cold War in light of a re-reading of Machiavelli. That issue was specifically an anti-war issue, addressing the Iranian crisis and also the many other brushfire wars underway around the world with U.S. support. We reprinted a memo from an active-duty officer in the Strategic Air Command as an anonymous found poem:

> My former opinion on opposition
> to the Soviets is weakening,
> because I am beginning to suspect
> that the Western leaders are in collusion with them
> manufacturing a fake antagonism much as
> the Republicans and Democrats do.
>
> I'm not yet convinced,
> but I have doubts.

We also reprinted the late William Wantling's prescient "Cold War," from his 1967 chapbook *San Quentin's Stranger*:

> today i saw a strange sight
> i saw a set of mutant ugly siamese twins
> joined from hip to shoulder—
> they were hissing, snarling, sneering
> each mouth spoke hate for the other
> and the one with a right hand
> waved a dagger at the one with a left hand, who
> also waved a dagger...

His own daughter Mona dying of leukemia, Quebecois poet Real Faucher prayed for children who might love "the glory of total war" enough to insure a future in which

> none will be
> left
> to teach hatred to
> or simply grow up.

Self-described Vermont ridgerunner (hillbilly) D. Roger Martin described a couple of his neighbors leaning on a pickup truck, watching high school girls picketing a nuclear site, whether military or civilian doesn't matter:

> "She's had an abortion," Judd says. . . .
>
> "What kind of person would do that, Ward?
> Destroy an unborn child?"
> Bill Ward looks hard at Old Judd,
> as if he's seeing the old man for the first time,
> then gazes back at the construction site.
> With a trace of apprehension, Bill replies,
> "I don't know, Judd.
> But I've often wondered."

The theme of nuclear war as a particular threat to children, hence to the future, became increasingly prominent. In *Samisdat* volume 26, #1, also from 1980, Kentucky photographer Syd Weedon envisioned a post-nuclear "Brave New World":

> *Clone Clone #7*
>
> I saw you—
> your skin was smoother;
> no one had ever broken your nose;
> you missed the signature of time.
> You walked the starship hall;
> my spine chilled in eerie recognition.
> We feared our own hidden fertility,
> and shot our semen into glass—
> the tube could be predicted;
> irradiated wombs could not.

Saluting aged radicals Tom McGrath and James Cooney an issue later (volume 26, #2, 1980), W.D. Ehrhart wondered:

> In the age of the MX missile and the Trident
> nuclear submarine and the 20-megaton bomb
> multiplied by a couple of thousand or so,
> what are the odds I'll ever see
> the same age you are now?
>
> Did it seem so bleak in 1940?

Our attention to nuclear war probably peaked with publication of Ernest Robson's Nagasaki Portfolio in volume 27, #1, 1981. I met Robson in a San Francisco television station that January. He was there to be interviewed about his anthology of mathematical poetry, *Against Infinity*, by the late Todd Lawson, while I was there to discuss *Samisdat*. Over supper Robson mentioned that he'd been a Marine Corps photographer during World War II, and that he'd been parachuted into Nagasaki with two other men to take pictures just three days after the bombing. He still had some photos that had never been published, to the best of his knowledge, and would I like to use them?

The six photos appeared, with Robson's brief memoir of Nagasaki, behind another of my editorials advocating unilateral nuclear disarmament and again explaining the utility of the threat of nuclear war to politicians and industrialists getting fat from the status quo. My cynicism seemed to be catching. Offered Dan Silverberg, a reclusive back-to-the-earther from northern California:

Education

There were two boys in the yard as we idled,
minding themselves within earshot.
Gary, the six-year-old, spent the afternoon
guarding his pocket.
Now he had a pipe and a rock
and little David spellbound under the almond tree:
  "See this?"
He cupped his hands as though showing a lizard.
  "See this? It's 'tomic."
  "Is not."
"Yes it is. See, if I put it in this pipe and hit it
the whole world will blow up."
  "No it won't."
  "Yes it will. Wanna see?"
  "No!"
  "Hey, get over here closer."
  "No. I don't like the world blow up."
  "You can't stop it. If you run away
  I'll do it anyway... You'll never get home!"
  "No No No Maaaaaaaaaaaa—"
Hey, David, for Chrissake pipe down you two.
  "Maaaaaaaaaaaaaaaaa—"
And he was off as though trailing bees,
throwing open the screen door and swarming
into his mother's lap.
We laughed and laughed,
and Frank went out to take the cartridge
from his son, explaining in dark tones.
A precocious boy, even in his thefts.

By that time we were again less leading anti-nuclear war consciousness than responding to it. We had assumed a leadership role in consciousness-raising almost by default; we relinquished it as others rallied to the cause, with fresh energy and often more resources. Anti-nuclear war poems and stories of all the above genres continued flooding in; I continued publishing occasional examples of each. But now many other magazines, both big and little, were devoting considerable page space to nuclear issues. In addition, specifically anti-nuclear anthologies were appearing. Nina Langley and Betty Shipley issued *Meltdown: Poems From The Core* as a project of the Cimarron Reactors affinity group of the Sunbelt Alliance of Oklahoma. Mark Melnicove produced *Vote Yes On September 23rd: An Anthology By Maine Artists For A Nuclear-Free Maine*. And Morty Sklar of *The Spirit That Moves Us* edited perhaps the finest of them in *Nuke-Rebuke*, featuring 65 writers, poets, artists, and photographers, including Hiroshima survivor Hayashi Kyoko. At the moment the first atomic bomb fell, Kyoko had been backed into the junction of two brick walls and was about to be raped by two men at the factory where she worked. She prayed for deliverance and the nuclear flames incinerated them; the walls saved her. The episode seemed to me testimony in itself that nuclear war might serve an ecological purpose if ever waged, that my old view of The Bomb as cleanser might not be entirely as naive as I'd later supposed.

In any case I made an editorial decision to de-emphasize nuclear war in *Samisdat*, since others were now addressing the issue, and instead tried to raise consciousness in other directions. Only one poem concerned nuclear problems in *Samisdat*, volume 28, #1, and that, by Vermonter Cathy Young Czapla, spoke specifically of a nuclear waste disposal site proposed for the corner of the state called the Northeast Kingdom:

> They dump their loads of canisters
> and roar off down the dirt
> road like banshees,
> shaking us out of our nightmares
> in which the water glows
> but the moon does not.

Still, Czapla's chapbook *Heirloom* (volume 28, #4, 1981) was more than half devoted to anti-nuclear war poems. The cover, by her husband John, was drawn from one of Robson's Nagasaki photographs. Czapla's father also was part of the American observation team assigned to Nagasaki. She memorialized him in the title poem to her next collection, *Genetic Memories* (volume 35, #3, 1983):

> A leatherneck in Japan,
> my father walked in
> to Nagasaki like a blind man,
> stumbling past the ruined temples,
> sifting through the ashes
> for a mirror that might reflect
> the enormity of his survival.
> He refused to see the walking
> wounded wailing around him like ghosts.
> He refused to be

haunted by those bitter consequences.

Years later in his own hills,
between the sawmills and the trees,
he forgot why his hair fell out.
Six children grew from his irradiated
genes like six new houses
built of sinew and bone, and he believes
they were the reason behind the cataclysm.
He turned away from their nightmares
when they woke up shouting
that the trees were in flames.

There were still occasional new themes emerging from the threat of nuclear war, and *Samisdat* did explore them, even as I tried to refer submissions repeating the old themes to other publications, where they might reach readers as yet unawakened. For instance, the threat of imminent death often acts as an aphrodisiac. I have often wondered if the "free love" fervor of the 1960s was a direct response to having grown up in the shadow of the bomb, and more particularly, coming of age with the risk of the Vietnam War draft. Whether that was true or not, The Bomb as sexual stimulant emerged in volume 32, #3, 1982. Wrote Sally Ehrman:

Before It Happens

You would do well to hold me now,
before the bombs fall,
one last blast from technology
that has developed itself
right out of this world.

You would do well to kiss me
before my lips melt into my skin,
sticking to dripping plastic
as the cup collapses in my hand.

You would do well to love me
before your heart bursts through your chest
from impact
and bleeds down your trousers.
You would do well to hold my hand,
interlacing fingers
so that when it happens
at least our bones will break together.

Note the parallel to the concluding portion of *24X12*, earlier quoted. Echoed W.D. Ehrhart in the same issue:

The girl in the green cotton dress

> purses her lips
> and grinds her hips on the chair,
> imagining love and hoping
> someone will notice her breasts:
> she didn't have them last year. . . .
>
> At any moment in the world,
> nuclear missiles are ready to plunge
> into the heart of the future.
> Submarines patrol the seas,
> and bombers flown by family men
> prowl the dark over Canada.

Longtime anti-nuclear activist Robert Head's *I Once Was Alive* (volume 29, #3, 1982) commenced a series of three collections pondering various dimensions of both the arms race and civilian nuclear development. Head followed up with *The Enriched Uranium Poems* (volume 35, #4, 1983) and *In Praise Of Caveman: The Atom Bomb Poems* (volume 40, #1, 1984). Credited by Louisiana Power and Light president E.A. Rodrigue with having almost single-handedly blocked construction of three nuclear reactors in 1975, Head offered little new insight. His work consisted mainly of random quips and musings, and though I took on the three chapbooks in respect of his political accomplishments, I began to wonder if anti-nuclear literature hadn't already rapidly combusted all the fuel available and burned itself out. I had similar feelings about a Duane Davis collection, *Bang Up Futures*, issued as volume 35, #3, 1983.

As the freeze movement peaked, there were also signs public concern was waning, that we were all beginning to have greater faith in humanity and in ourselves, no matter how warmongering our politicians. Wrote Daniel Silverberg in "Peace March," from volume 33, #3, 1982:

> The jets left before dawn,
> climbing the northeast run...
> I must be getting old.
> I wished them hot coffee,
> faithful wives and
> yet another snapshot
> of themselves
> returning.

W.D. Ehrhart also reconsidered the men carrying the weapons in "Waiting For Word From Alaska," volume 34, #3, 1983:

> We were always
> the closest of the whole family.
> The time I fell through the ice
> he carried me home in his arms.

Even American intervention in Indochina
couldn't intervene—though for me it meant
the end of a military career,
while for him it was just the beginning:
we danced with the difference for years,
laughing, pretending it wasn't there,
like two high-wire artists balanced
above the dazzled crowd—

until the night American bombers
leveled Bach Mai Hospital in North Vietnam:
I could hear the screams of the patients
trapped in their beds, years later,
as we argued on a Cascade camping trip,
the difference between us
tumbling finally to earth;
he said the bombers didn't exist,
shut me out like a bomb bay door
closing after a high-speed run,
and disappeared into the Arctic waste
to wait for Russian missiles.

I could endure a hundred arguments,
each one fiery orange and hot as napalm
scorching the heart of an Asian afternoon.
I could endure anything
but this vast silence
lying between us
like ice.

In dreams I imagine him standing alone
in the Arctic twilight, pointing north
at the sky, his last
words to his waiting brother:
"Look, there! What did I tell you?
Missiles. You have fifteen minutes
to live."

So after five years of ardent, ever-intensifying activism, the arms race was still underway and we all were tired. My editorial in that issue critiqued the confrontational aspects of the freeze campaign, urging peace activists (and activists of other varieties) to establish strong mainstream credentials and identities, so as to gain the confidence of an anxious and suspicious Middle America. Contrast that advice with my own confrontational stridency at the outset of the campaign. If activism failed, we could always laugh at the threat, as Scott Cramer did in his send-up story "The Button," highlight of volume 36, #3, 1983. Cramer postulated bums being hired at minimum wage to watch over The Button at the underground wartime White House in White Sulphur Springs, Virginia. As it's a boring job, the bums pass their hours drinking wine, doing dope, quarreling, and reveling with a local sexual thrillseeker who eventually urges one of them to push The Button just to see what will happen. That sort of prelude to nuclear disaster, I could well imagine. Intelligent people wouldn't start a nuclear war under any circumstances, but suppose responsibility were delegated to morons while no one was looking?

A similar start to nuclear war popped up shortly in the hit film *War Games*, wherein the missiles are nearly launched by an adolescent computer hacker who thinks he's playing with a video simulation. And suddenly the freeze movement went mainstream. That image, the public could accept. That didn't require complete reappraisal of morality, the basis of our political and economic creeds, the reasons we had nuclear weapons in the first place. There was another hit anti-nuclear war film, *The Day After*, most of which I missed because I was cuddling and consoling a young lady who had somehow reached her 19th year unaware that The Bomb could mean she might be vaporized at any moment, that there might be no warning and no survivors on whole continents. Feeling old, at 31, I recalled my own naivete when I'd been her age, when I'd begun writing my post-nuclear Apocalypse stories. And I was not surprised when soon afterward I was deluged with a whole new generation of such stories by other young would-be writers, whose evolution to understanding was just getting started.

"What happened/to the last 20 years?" asked W.D. Ehrhart in "Warning To My Students"; volume 39, #1, 1984. Ehrhart turned for reassurance to a wife as much younger than he as that unnerved coed had been younger than I. At least in the poem the reassurance comes from the faith Ehrhart feels as she sleeps that her innocence protects them both. I had felt something similar with the 19-year-old: that if the threat wasn't recognized, it wouldn't be real. Once recognized, however, it felt incumbent upon me to somehow hold The Bomb at bay, back in the bays of the missile-launching aircraft. Writing of his own inability to sleep, Ehrhart evidently felt much less reassured than he claimed. He wanted to be reassured. He wasn't, really.

Robert Hentz considered the gulf in awareness with "Silos, A Generation Gap," volume 41, #1, 1984:

> There were silos then,
> when I was young,
> monuments to Vishnu,
> standing tall and bounteous
> above midwestern plains,
> granaries of life and preservation—
> not at all like those
> we have now,
> monuments to Shiva,
> lying low and ominous
> below midwestern plains,
> granaries of death and destruction.

And Michael Hemmingson had at the awareness gap in *Nowhere Is Safe*, issued as volume 42, #2, in 1985, the last *Samisdat* title explicitly addressing nuclear war, apart from broader contexts. Again, as with the Head and Davis chapbooks, I had the feeling I'd covered the same ground more memorably before, that I was only repeating an old lecture for the benefit of an audience too young to remember the vivid urgency of the first one.

In 1985 *The Bulletin Of The Atomic Scientists* moved the Doomsday Clock on their cover to two minutes before midnight, or nuclear holocaust. Responded Jennifer Hecht in her poem "Two Minutes To Midnight," volume 42, #4, 1985,

I guess the pink-headed, drugged-out
tattoo babies who strut the streets
with their spastic
marionette style
are trying to break the glass face
and fuck up the numbers
and dent the gold casing
and bend the hands
so that those who don't think
to put the watch to their ears
won't miss the message.
But (now here's the problem)
after the time of the mutilated, broken watch
what time will it be?

Meanwhile, warned Gretchen Nielsen in volume 46, #1, 1986,

Hell's Getting Ready

to be lit
with missiles
built by robots
programmed with misconceptions
while ridiculed into silence,
the wise watch wordless.
Bombs are bought and sold
by parents
still not knowing what they're doing
'til the children they have nurtured
scream in fiery beds.

Responded Robert Schlosser in "It's The Atom, Bob," volume 46, #3, 1987,

Yes, we know
as sirens blow
and our carefully constructed plans

flop like trout
yanked out of fresh water...

Again exhaustion, frustration, and despair seemed to bring cynicism. Marc Munroe Dion presented "16 Reasons To Have A Nuclear War" in volume 49, #1, 1987:

For the noise,
the fierce light.
To loot,
and kill the lawyers
in the chaos.

To usurp God
and shut the senators up.
As a toy
and to break every window at once.

Because summers are too long,
the Russian is evil.
Because Kennedy is dead and Marciano.
To get rid of the poor.

To stop worrying
and end the poet's holy blather.
To make a harder world
and see if we are heroes.

Two pages later, one of our oldest poets, G.W. Sherman, likened the arms race to a duel neither principal attends, leaving only seconds to stand perplexed. Apparently we weren't going to have a nuclear war after all, not immediately, leaving the whole issue in suspense for yet another decade, maybe a generation.

Anti-nuclear war themes virtually vanished from *Samisdat* during our last three years of publication. Perhaps, jaded, I simply rejected everything of that nature that came in. More likely, most poets now concur with Jim Banks, who opined in "Open House," volume 54, #3, 1989,

I do not believe we will all be exploded...
I know all the doors won't open,
but just enough can widen slightly,
just enough air and light can enter,
for us to dodge the big bullet,
for us to, just barely,
within an inch of our lives,
squeak by.

But I don't know how.

Though "how" and even "if" remain open questions, it is clear to me that many of my most memorable anti-nuclear war contributors are finding personal answers in other life-affirming pursuits, no longer "just saying no" to death, but also doing small individual bits to create a world that doesn't want or need military/industrial complexes, superpower confrontations, or even superpowers. W.D. Ehrhart, Mark Phillips, Miriam Sagan and I remain committed activists; we have also become parents, feeling new optimism, rational or not, despite our acute consciousness not only of nuclear war but also of acid rain, global warming, topsoil loss, toxic wastes, overpopulation, loss of species, drug abuse, racial conflict, and poverty. If the anti-nuclear war theme in *Samisdat* has any resolution, it is that living under the shadow of The Bomb, the nuclear sword of Damocles, has not defeated us. We have discovered it, contemplated it, turned it round and round, tried every form of petition and prayer to make it go away, failed, and managed to go on living. We have rekindled hope for the future because the future has kept on coming, day after day, no matter what the clock on the cover of *The Bulletin Of The Atomic Scientists* says. We have arrived at Voltaire's conclusion, from the last page of his 1759 satirical novel *Candide*, that no matter what calamities might happen, for the time being we must tend our gardens.

Neither is this a cop-out. In the late 20th century context, a context of intense ecological consciousness, tending our gardens includes combatting the many environmental problems enumerated above. Further, from an ecological perspective, nuclear war may be seen as a theoretical problem, something that can happen, maybe, whereas the others are clearly and definitely happening now. Though nuclear war if ever waged would be the ultimate man-made eco-disaster, in the present context it is mainly a needless diversion of economic resources. If we cannot stem the diversion of tax money and political energy into the war machine, at least we can redirect our own time, money, and energy into the other areas requiring most immediate attention.

W.D. Ehrhart has concentrated his attention on peace issues ever since returning from Vietnam in 1968: first ending the war, then fighting for veterans' rights, against reinstated draft registry, and against nuclear war as a logical extension of his other work. His recent focus, yet another logical extension, has been leading opposition to U.S. support of anti-democratic forces in Latin America.

Mark Phillips since the middle 1980s has been most involved in grassroots campaigns against toxic waste dumping near his homestead in New York's Southern Tier (a mountain chain extending west from the Adirondacks, along the Pennsylvania border.)

Miriam Sagan moved into feminist activism, got into holistic health, and continues working on a variety of fronts. Her most recent major poem, *Aquecia Madre*, concerns water rights in the desert near her home in Santa Fe.

For my part, in late 1978 I began a series of newspaper and television exposes of asbestos pollution near my home in rural Quebec. Then in mid-1979 I published the first major newspaper expose of the impact of acid rain upon rural Quebec. Even as anti-nuclear war consciousness was peaking in *Samisdat*, my personal attention was more and more devoted to environmental causes of greater local urgency. During the middle 1970s *Samisdat* had been my primary economic pursuit; but as I began to make more of my living—and a much better living—through locally focused environmental journalism, my careers as editor and as author/citizen increasingly diverged. By the time global problems again became my foremost concern, in the late 1980s, I had become news editor of *The Animals' Agenda*, a slick monthly subtitled *the international journal of animal rights and ecology*, and my expressions were no longer literary.

Literature, as voice of the imagination, is also often voice of the politically voiceless—including the young. Approaching or entering middle age, with access to mass media and growing political influence, the *Samisdat* generation of activist authors is no longer voiceless. It remains to be seen whether in our new incarnation as enfranchised, responsible citizens we can remain as conscientious as we hoped we would be when younger and disenfranchised; but I think, many years from now, we shall look back upon Jim Banks' poem above as historically accurate prophecy. There are already signs, in the dismantling of missiles and the Berlin Wall, that the conditions that kept us so close to nuclear war for so long are changing, perhaps because those of us who turned toward other causes have gradually helped convince world leaders that environmental damage and economic injustice are greater threats to our health and stability than the other society on this planet most like our own.

Whether *Samisdat* actually helped bring about the present optimistic scenario is something else we can't know, and will probably never know. We do know we tried, with our crude printing and paid circulation never topping 300. As editor, publisher, and printer for most of 17 years, I often consoled myself, when everything was going wrong, with a Biblical story, one I repeated to the young lady who freaked out over *The Day After*, about how Sodom and Gomorrah might have been spared for the presence of even a few righteous citizens.

I also contemplated an American Indian myth, which explained the evening flights of bats:

And The Least Shall Save Us

The buffalo folk remembered
that when smoking Death shrouded the Great Spirit
the mice grew wings,
boiled out from underground caverns
and nibbled until the sun shined through.

The buffalo folk are gone,

and so are the buffalo,
but in underground caverns,
behind wired consoles,
the mice nibble on.[2]

We too were mice, chewing at the wires to keep the missiles grounded, encouraging other mice to chew with us.

Notes

[1]All subsequent *Samisdat* citations are identified in the text by volume, issue and year.

[2]*From Angel of Their Human God*, by Merritt Clifton, published as *Samisdat* volume 54, #2, 1989.

Works Cited

Cummins, Walter. "War Zone." *Small Press Review*. April 1976: 3.

Langley, Nina, and Betsy Shipley, eds. *Meltdown: Poems From the Core*. Edmond, OK: Full Count Press, 1980.

Melnicove, Mark, ed. *Vote Yes On September 23rd*. Hull's Cove, ME: Dog Ear Press, 1980.

Miller, Walter M. Jr. *A Canticle For Leibowitz*. Philadelphia: Lippincott, 1959.

Ross, Val. "Tightrope Decade." *Maclean's*. 7 Jan. 1980: 28-30.

Sagan, Miriam. *Aquecia Madre*. Northampton, MA: Adastra, 1988.

Samisdat. 1.1-54.4 (1973-1989).

Sklar, Morty, ed. *Nuke-Rebuke*. Iowa City: Spirit That Moves Us, 1983.

Wantling, William. "Cold War." *San Quentin's Stranger*. San Francisco: Second Coming Press, 1973.

The Days After Tomorrow:
Novelists at Armageddon

Michael Dorris and Louise Erdrich

Faced with extinction, we imagine reprieve. The 19th-century Paiute prophet Wovoka postulated that through the revitalization of ancient beliefs and through the newly begun practice of the Ghost Dance, military defeat, slaughtered buffalo herds and cultural genocide could be exchanged for a utopia guided by traditional values of cooperation and moderation. The devastating history of European invasion and dominance were, these Indians desperately theorized, but a test of their faith, a punishment for assimilation, a catalyst through which the past might become the future. For both the individual and the tribe, hope of continuity was an antidote to annihilation, and there was a dream life accessible beyond the apparent destruction of the familiar world.

Living with the menace of instant, global, nuclear war, many people today feel vulnerable to an analogous threat of extinction. But ours is still an abstract apprehension; we do not rely upon exhaustion-induced trances to see past the immediacy of our fragile mortality and connect with prospective alter egos and descendants. In the years since Aug. 6, 1945, writers of fiction have repeatedly and variously attempted to conceive a future beyond an Armageddon which, if and when it comes, is guaranteed to exact casualties on a scale beyond precedent, beyond comprehension. In a range that parallels the theoretical grapplings of scientists and the machinations of politicians, these novels as a group are a curious mixture of facile hopefulness and utter nihilism of myopia and experimentation.

Some of the earliest work displays a curious fascination of the inconvenience that middle-class Caucasians may suffer in the war's aftermath. There is a touch of *The Swiss Family Robinson* in the resourceful, determined postattack inhabitants of Pat Frank's *Alas, Babylon!* (1959). As short supplies and broken communications are countered with backwoods folklore, a little girl must wait to flush her toilet after every use until the pump of the artesian well is hooked up to an improvised generator. A Westchester maid is forced to stand in food lines at a suburban supermarket in Judith Merril's *Shadow on the Hearth* (1950). War seems awful not so much because of massive anonymous death tolls heard on emergency frequency broadcasts, but, because the tidy structure of a "Leave It to Beaver" world is disrupted, women may take charge of governments or repair a gas leak, while men find it impossible to contact their brokers.

Adversity, however, sometimes cleanses. Since the breach between yesterday and tomorrow in these books is only a millisecond of fission and fusion, materialistic preoccupations seem to melt in the firestorm's blast, and a core of red-white-and-blue basics solidifies. Characters experience loss, but after the smoke clears, husbands return or widows are provided with new mates. Only unadaptive, greedy people or faceless urban masses actually perish.

The Last Day (1959) by Helen Clarkson and *On the Beach* (1957) by Nevil Shute are distinctive in their rejection of cozy survivalist endings. Their scale is personal, their gaze unblinking. Protagonists mourn the death of their own children, and thus the symbolic extinction of humanity. They have the vision of no vision, imagine a world empty of human consciousness. Slow, inexorable radiation sickness, like the invisible societal psychosis that led to war in the first place, terminates all plucky short-term solutions, and the world ends in a sea of old newspapers blowing down deserted streets.

In 1987, Carolyn See's *Golden Days* continued this before-and-after convention, but with greater optimism. In a New Age view of female toughness and regeneration, Ms. See creates a heroine, Edith Langley, who has battled sexism to achieve financial security and identity, and damn well isn't going to roll over and die just because of atomic holocaust. She hunkers down, literally embodies her past by encrusting herself with her own jewels, and changes everything except her own resolve. Her recollections become protectively selective and she endures. "What if," she offers, "we tried to remember John Donne and the Rolling Stones and driving the car with the radio on, and lying on clean sheets with perfect bodies looking out at palm fronds, and the clean blue of the biggest ocean, what if we only remember *California*?" (181).

In *Warday* (1984), Whitley Strieber and James Kunetka's mock-documentary novel, two friends travel the country, bearing witness to the social and environmental fallout of a small-scale war. The authors meticulously detail a United States in which law exists only in isolated pockets and where the fabric uniting the disparate factions of the country has eroded beyond recognition. The narrators encounter feudalism, anarchy and decline in most sectors, a landscape predicted by a 1987 M.I.T. computer simulation in which the loss of fossil fuel following a limited nuclear exchange soon results in worldwide famine and a Middle-Ages level of subsistence.

Other controversial but chilling warnings are even more drastic. Studies have recently forecast that in an atomic attack, a nuclear electromagnetic pulse might well render useless all electric-powered technology, and the atmospheric dust of destroyed cities might create a nuclear winter severe enough to eliminate agriculture for centuries to come.

Yet in spite of all this, a majority of postnuclear war novels of the last 25 years are irrationally optimistic, if only in their lack of true realism. Often degraded, mutated and dazed, human beings—or some facsimile of them—*do* survive to tell the tale.

Why now, when the lethal consequences of ultimate weapons are understood and when the means of their efficient delivery exist in greater numbers, are there fewer writers with the bleak vision of a Nevil Shute or a Helen Clarkson? Perhaps the very naivete of the 1950s made the concept of annihilation tolerable. Perhaps some of today's younger authors, born and raised in the context of nuclear threat, fallout shelters and evacuation plans, have become anesthetized by the crossed fingered wishfulness of Deterrence.

Perhaps the postnuclear landscape has simply become a part of contemporary consciousness. Our children learn what to expect by perusing the J.C. Penney Christmas catalogue, which features in its toy section pages of Transformer robots, hybridized machines and medieval-futuristic figures called Visionaries, set in rocky ruins meant to resemble our increasingly familiar dystopia. In popular films, white knights and punk outlaws cavort, not in the burned and bloodied everyday clothing of Hiroshima's witnesses, but in chic leather duds and studs. Mad Max retains his spiked hair, his white teeth, and has the strength to tote heavy souped-up machinery as he quests for fuel and adventure in a rough-and-tumble Australian outback, the opposite of its lifeless, untitillating counterpart in *On the Beach*.

As we acquire a sense of living in the Before, and take for granted fantasies of how the new A.D. (after detonation) will look and feel, the blighted future becomes for some writers almost an actual place, a shadowland that exists an instant away, a wretched but intriguing playground for the literary and semantic imagination. Though characters survive, the novels are deeply anguished and sardonic in their views of a devolved and ailing humanity.

The narrowed perimeters of this imaginary terrain, simultaneously ordinary and alien, are used as a philosophical and linguistic proving ground retaining elements of language and custom, but with a shuffled detritus. Commencing with Walter Miller Jr.'s *Canticle for Leibowitz* (1959), and continuing through Angela Carter's *Heroes and Villains* (1969), Russell Hoban's *Riddley Walker* (1981), Bernard Malamud's *God's Grace* (1982), Denis Johnson's *Fiskadoro* (1985) and Paul Auster's *In the Country of Last Things* (1987), we hear the voices of victims—paranoid, comic, agonized, suspicious, adrift in dangerous neocivilizations. These are cultural orphans, uncertain even of the rules of languages altered as drastically and carelessly as the rearranged topography.

"Entire categories of objects disappear," says Paul Auster's Anna, "flowerpots for example, or cigarette filters, or rubber bands—and for a time you will be able to recognize those words, even if you cannot recall what they mean. But then, little by little the words become only sounds, a random collection of glottals and fricatives, a storm of whirling phonemes, and finally the whole thing just collapses...Your mind will hear it, but it will register as something incomprehensive, a word from a language you cannot speak" (89).

The monks of the Albertian Order of Leibowitz dedicate their lives to copying and preserving pre-conflagration fragments in *A Canticle for Leibowitz*, though all referential meaning is lost. These texts, so meticulously saved on bits of paper, have no bearing on the e capacity to understand blueprints, circuit designs, memos and racing forms.

Angela Carter's dysphoric young protagonist, Marianne, studies dictionaries, which contain "innumerable incomprehensible words she could only define through their use in other books, for these words had ceased to describe facts and now stood only for ideas or memories." In Ms. Carter's vision, humans are no longer capable or deserving of Adam's task; and when her characters can no longer identify the ceaseless variety of natural forms, they lose their primal link with nature, that of words. With the loss of civilization, they are not returned to a pastoral state of union with the cosmos; rather, they are unmoored, shaken to the core. "Losing their names...things underwent a process of uncreation and reverted to chaos, existing only to themselves in an unstructured world where they were not formally acknowledged, becoming an ever-widening margin of undifferentiated and nameless matter." Bereft of the ability to name, to control, to describe human vocabulary becomes a pattern of arcana referring to an antique lexicon.

In *God's Grace*, the last human survivor in the world, Calvin Cohn, teaches chimpanzees to speak. "God was Torah. He was made of words," (104) Cohn remembers. In attempting to preserve language, he seeks to endow his primates with idealized reason, but his failure, or theirs, is grim and farcical. His half-human offspring is cannibalized by renegade members of the group, and Cohen's agonized protest—"We have a functioning community and are on the verge of an evolutionary advance, if not breakthrough" (229) is to no avail. Cohen joins the rest of his species, a burnt offering.

The actual texts of *Riddley Walker* and *Fiskadoro* mirror a universe whose structure is barely recognizable. Both books feature invented pidgins that reflect a collapsed social order degenerated because of disease yet energized by exotic orthographies and folklores. Riddley Walker's dialect is the most extreme, a richly decomposed English, mixing elision and whimsey. He speaks of "fizzics" and the Puter and Power Leat, the Eusa folk and those "who ben bernt out after Bad Time all the clevver is bernt out with all the clevverness." The protagonists of both novels are adolescent boys who embark on coming-of-age quests after the deaths of their fathers. In *Fiskadoro*, utterance is a mixture of Spanish, English, and static. The war is still going on, somewhere; its artifacts and idioms are curiosities in the isolated, superstitious, cancer-ridden fishing village where the narrator lives.

Erstwhile brand names and the flotsam of a former world linger like fallout, ludicrous, out of context—Jimi Hendrix sings on "Cubaradio," the god Bob Marley is revered, and the solemn gift of a half-pint bottle of

Kikkomon soy sauce, "never opened," is a treasure. In *Canticle for Leibowitz*, a sacred relic is solemnly preserved, a hand-scribbled note: *"Pound pastrami, can kraut, six bagels—bring home for Emma."* A Punch-and-Judy show in *Riddley Walker* becomes quasi-religious, sinister. What trash survives by luck, becomes endowed with mana.

Riddley Walker's quest, pursued through a maze of tortuous clues, ends in an acting out of Nietzsche's idea of eternal recurrence. Gunpowder is rediscovered, and the first explosion since "Bad Time" is ugly and sensational. "I minim they wer men and the nex they wer peaces of meat nor it wernt done by knife nor spear nor arrer nor sling stoan it were clevverness done it and the 1 Big 1. That old chard coal berners head took off strait up like a sky lark only parbly not singing. Up it gone and down it came thwock on a poal and ripe for telling. Goodparley sitting there dead with a stoan pounder in his skul. You myt say after all them years of looking for that 1 Big 1 it finely come in to his mynd" (209).

Two of the most provocative recent novels offer a more drastic and a more benign forecast for future humanity. Extrapolating less from immediate cultural fact than from fantasy or theory, they suggest that true change can only come about through a drastic reorganization of our species, or the radical shift of our deepest values.

Galapagos (1985), Kurt Vonnegut's satire about "The Nature Cruise of the Century" on the "new Noah's ark," projects a million years hence the results of today's international strife. Though in fictional Guyaquil the incendiaries are "dagonite," "the latest advance in the evolution of high explosives" (212) rather than thermonuclear, the calamitous results are the same: the population of the world is wiped out except for a few expatriate castaways, and no precedent of recuperation is applicable. "What humanity was about to lose...was the ability to heal itself. As far as humanity was concerned, all wounds were about to become very permanent, and high explosives weren't going to be a branch of show business any more" (233).

Devolution, as opposed to learning from mistakes, insures that, with the shrinkage of "big brains," there is no second opportunity at global suicide. "As for human beings making a comeback, of starting to use tools and build houses and play musical instruments and so on again: They would have to do it with their beaks this time. Their arms have become flippers in which the hand bones are almost entirely imprisoned and immobilized" (185).

Reading Ursula K. LeGuin's *Always Coming Home* (1985), a less bizarre but equally original version of a projected postcatastrophe world, one encounters an eventual emanation that rectifies elements of the present. Though there are mentions of chemical contamination zones and "a congenital degenerative condition affecting the motor nerves...evidently related to residual ancient industrial toxins in soil and water," (476) the book is mute on the particular causes—be they nuclear war or another disaster—of the previous society's collapse.

The Kesh, members of the novel's central community, are described, through a myriad of perspectives, internal and external to society, as relentlessly and stubbornly gentle, connected by webs of kinship and respect for nature. The entrapments of technological violence and sexual inequality have been revealed, the lessons have been internalized, and unlike the neighboring aggressive, patriarchal Condor people, the Kesh have achieved enduring balance.

Always Coming Home more than even the most sanguine books discussed in this essay, finds the seeds of a superior, less dangerous revitalization in the treasury of culture's traditional values. Its perspective is as nostalgic as a memory of childhood—filled with straightforward simplicity and clarity of choice. The insights gained *in extremis* or after the fact in other fictional creations have reached fruition here, and even *with* "big brains," there is no chance that this branch of humankind will elect to reinvent weapons capable of its own destruction. This is Wovoka's ghost dance, culturally generalized and come true in the most enriching sense: a return of abiding peace, of sanity, a movement from the brink, a test passed, a logical conclusion averted forever.

Works Cited

Auster, Paul. *In the Country of Last Things*. NY: Viking, 1987.

Carter, Angela. *Heroes and Villains*. NY: Viking, 1969.

Clarkson, Helen. *The Last Day*. NY: Torquil, 1959.

Frank, Pat. *Alas, Babylon!* Philadelphia: Lippincott, 1959.

Hoban, Russell. *Riddley Walker*. NY: Summit Books, 1981.

Johnson, Denis. *Fiskadoro*. NY: Knopf, 1987.

LeGuin, Ursula K. *Always Coming Home*. NY: Harper and Row, 1985.

Malamud, Bernard. *God's Grace*. NY: Farrar, Straus & Giroux, 1982. NY: Avon, 1983.

Merril, Judith. *Shadow on the Hearth*. Garden City: Doubleday, 1950.

Miller, Walter Jr. *Canticle for Liebowitz*. Philadelphia: Lippincott, 1959.

See, Carolyn. *Golden Days*. NY: McGraw-Hill, 1987.

Shute, Nevil. *On the Beach*. NY: Morrow, 1957.

Strieber, Whitley, and James Kunetka. *Warday*. NY: Warner/Holt Rinehart & Winston, 1984.

Vonnegut, Kurt. *Galapagos*. NY: Delacorte, 1985.

Psychic Numbing, Radical Futurelessness, and Sexual Violence in the Nuclear Film

Jane Caputi

Much of the danger of radioactivity is mental.
—Richard Gerstell, in his government-sponsored publication,
How to Survive an Atomic Bomb (qtd. in Boyer 315)

In a series of books and articles, psychologist Robert Jay Lifton (Lifton and Falk) has consistently focused analytic attention on the nuclear psyche: the mental state, individual and collective, produced by the new fact of nuclear technology. He writes:

We are just now beginning to realize that nuclear weapons radically alter our existence....nothing we do or feel—in working, playing, and loving, and in our private, family and public lives—is free of their influence. The threat they pose has become the context for our lives, a shadow that persistently intrudes upon our mental ecology. (3)

Some of the effects Lifton ascribes to this all-pervasive, if shadowy, nuclear influence include: a new ephemeralism which tends to undermine interpersonal and family relationships; a sense of radical futurelessness due to an expectation of annihilation in our lifetimes; widespread fundamentalism; and a stance of near worship of nuclear weapons. Above all, he contends, those same weapons which have so totally changed our world characteristically act to stagger our minds into numbness, confirm a sense of helplessness, and profoundly impair our capacities to come to terms with the realities of nuclear weapons. In short, a "psychic numbing" prevails as one of the hallmarks of consciousness in the Nuclear Age.

If many of our feelings about nuclear technology are numbed or repressed, what is repressed nevertheless inevitably returns and these wide-ranging feelings consistently appear in various symbolic and metaphorical forms in the popular arts. Critics such as Marshall McLuhan, Susan Sontag, Michael Wood, and Robin Wood all have claimed that the American popular cinema provides something of a window on the collective subconscious and that

A shorter version of this article was printed in *JPFTV*, under the title "Films of the Nuclear Age." Reprinted with permission of the Helen Dwight Reid Educational Foundation. Published by Heldref Publications, 4000 Albermarle St., N.W., Washington, D.C. 20016. *Journal of Popular Film and Television* Volume 16, no 3: Fall 1988. 100-107.

popular movies function as cultural ritual, giving symbolic shape to cultural concerns unnamed elsewhere (sometimes conjuring, sometimes neutralizing, these). Since Sontag's germinative article, "The Imagination of Disaster," it has become commonplace to interpret the giant insect/space invader/ human mutation science fiction films of the 1950s as metaphorical expressions of nuclear anxiety. As she noted: "One gets the feeling...that a mass trauma exists over the use of nuclear weapons and the possibility of nuclear wars. Most of the science fiction films bear witness to this trauma and, in a way, attempt to exorcise it" (220). But that attempted exorcism resulted in, Sontag argued, films which were essentially "in complicity with the abhorrent," for in most cases these films expediently and climactically neutralized the terror they initially invoked. In one frequent scenario of the nuclear film, for example, the monster unleashed by some nuclear effect or device is ultimately vanquished by some even more awesome nuclear effect or device. In another, most of the world's population is wiped out by nuclear war, but a new "Adam and Eve" emerge to begin the world anew.

Although we recognize this group of science fiction films from the 1950s as constituting a subgenre of "nuclear films," and although the "mass trauma" Sontag referred to has only deepened in the last two decades, there has been little continued analysis of subsequent productions which could be similarly classified.[1] There is, of course, a clear grouping of films (mostly science fiction and thrillers) which overtly deal with nuclear technologies, weaponry, war and holocaust. These have been critiqued quite extensively (e.g., Shaheen; Cumbow). But perhaps more significantly, there also exist many other more subtle cinematic expressions of nuclear consciousness, a number of genre-spanning productions which, although not explicitly about nuclear technology, nevertheless metaphorically reflect the configurations and concerns of the nuclear mind and culture. Like their counterparts from the 1950s, many of these movies also enter into that "complicity with the abhorrent," promoting nuclearism or attempting to ritually transform or contain its threat, e.g. *Star Wars*, George Lucas 1977 (Caputi, "Seeing Elephants"). Still, a significant number of contemporary films both critique nuclear weaponry and illuminate the nuclear psyche. In this space I will be unable to address adequately the great number and variety of nuclear films. My purpose here will be to identify two, frequently complementary, strains of the nuclear film: those which cross over, eyes open, into the horrific terrain of the psychically numbed; and those which unerringly name the relationship between the twin terrors of sexual and nuclear violence.

The Living Dead

The question so often asked, "would the survivors [of a nuclear war] envy the dead?" may turn out to have a simple answer. They would not so much envy, as, inwardly and outwardly, resemble the dead.

Robert Jay Lifton and Kai Erikson (278)

People are pods.... They have no feelings. They exist, breathe, sleep. To be a pod means that you have no passion, no anger, the spark has left you.

Don Siegel, discussing Invasion of the Body Snatchers (Kaminsky 77)

Sometimes I think it would be a lot easier being dead.
Clarissa, a character in River's Edge

The zombies are us.
George Romero, discussing Night of the Living Dead (Peary 277)

Since its release in 1968, George Romero's *Night of the Living Dead* has endured as a cult horror classic, inspired two sequels and numerous imitations, and gained a respectable critical reputation. Several analysts of the film have pointed to its revision of the vampire myth, its implicit critique of the capitalist/consumer society (Wood 1979), its "open-eyed detailing of human taboos" (Dillard 15) and its utterly unconventional refusal to resolve the fears it evoked "in any way that does not sacrifice human dignity and human value" (Dillard 27). As R.H.W. Dillard continues, with *Night of the Living Dead*'s assault on government, family, individual identity, and reason: "The film as a whole undercuts most of the cherished values of our whole civilization" (28). This wholesale refusal to resolve fear or to hold sacred traditionally cherished social myths, heroes, and institutions, is itself a primary attribute of the radical nuclear film (e.g. *Kiss Me Deadly*, Robert Aldrich, 1955). However, before delving into this more abstract component, let us first trace out some of the more concrete ways in which *Night of the Living Dead* reveals its ties to Nuclear Age consciousness.

The story is of a night when the world turns upside down. The dead mysteriously reanimate, roam the Earth, and seek to devour living human flesh. A grab bag of types—a lone black man, a young white woman who has seen her brother killed by a ghoul, a triune white nuclear family, and a pair of young white lovers—hole up in an abandoned farmhouse. All of their efforts to escape from the ghouls fail. The lovers are roasted, when their truck blows up and they are graphically consumed by the zombies; the explosive nuclear family ends up eating itself; and the young woman is carried off by her undead brother. The black man, who alone survives the night, is mistaken for a ghoul by a roving posse, shot in the head, and dumped on a pile of the dead. The living dead themselves are depicted in a distinctive style. They look most terribly ordinary, move slowly and clumsily through the frame and, except when motivated by desire for flesh, appear to wander aimlessly.

Although there are no explicit references to nuclear technology in *Night of the Living Dead*, one conventional element points to its kinship with other nuclear films. In horror, there always must be some reason given for the sudden appearance of the monster and, dating back to the giant bug films of the 1950s, a classic rationale is some effect of nuclear technology.[2] In *Night of the Living Dead*, the explanation for the reanimation of the dead is a "beam of radiation" directed at the Earth by a Venus probe. Alerted by this conventional reference, we can tap *Night of the Living Dead*'s imagery for its nuclear bases.

In an essay, "Nuclear War's Effect on the Mind," Robert Lifton and Kai Erikson attempt to imagine the psychological condition of survivors of nuclear war. To gain some understanding, they refer to conditions experienced at Hiroshima:

...survivors...had a sense that *everyone* was dying, that "the world is ending." Rather than panic, the scene was one of slow motion—of people moving gradually away from the center of the destruction, but dully and almost without purpose...most felt themselves to be so much part of a dead world that...they were "not really alive." (275)

Lifton has described this mental deadening as part of a complex of phenomena he calls "psychic numbing"—the partial shutdown of mental facilities and emotional responses, denial, repression and apathy in the face of disaster— a condition he contends affects all of us living under constant nuclear threat. For survivors at Hiroshima and Nagasaki, this numbing was a necessary defense mechanism as no one could have responded with full emotions to the devastation around them and remained sane. Those survivors, referring to themselves, "used such terms as 'walking ghosts'.... People were literally uncertain about whether they were dead or alive." Extrapolating from this, Lifton and Erikson hypothesize about the postnuclear world:

The landscape is almost moonlike, spare and quiet, and the survivors who root among the ruins seem to have lost contact with one another...survivors will remain in a deadened state, either alone or among others like themselves, largely without hope and vaguely aware that everyone and everything that once mattered to them has been destroyed.... Virtually no survivors will be able to enact that most fundamental of all human rituals, burying their own dead. (277)

If this scenario is posed as a likely one for a world following nuclear war, we might also recognize it, right down to the impossibility of burying the dead, as the ambiance of *Night of the Living Dead*. The female lead, Barbara, after encountering a ghoul and seeing her brother killed by him, remains in a catatonic state throughout most of the rest of the movie. But the psychic numbing she so obviously manifests is only a token, pointing toward that psychic state which is more subtly and powerfully represented by the ghouls themselves.

The ghouls of *Night of the Living Dead* bear some resemblance to the traditional vampire in that they too are the undead who seek sustenance from living bodies. There is, nonetheless, a key distinction. The vampire is not only intensely individuated (as opposed to the mass, ordinary, and interchangeable ghouls), but the disturbance at the heart of the vampire myth is one of emotion, sexuality, desire. The ghouls, however, show no emotion whatsoever, only the hunger for flesh. Moreover, unlike the vampire, the ghoul cannot be dispatched with a stake through the heart. Rather, they can be destroyed only with a blow to the head. "Kill the brain and you kill the ghoul," gloats the beefy sheriff at the film's end. The disturbance represented by the ghouls is a *mental* one. They bespeak a monstrosity of consciousness and, finally, *Night of the Living Dead* offers not only a symbolic description of the landscape of a postnuclear world, but provides a powerful metaphor for the psychic numbing which characterizes general consciousness in the nuclear age.

If the ghouls of *Night of the Living Dead* resemble yet diverge from the vampire, they are, however, direct descendants of the "pod people" of Don Siegal's classic *Invasion of the Body Snatchers* (1956). In this film, seed pods with the ability to exactly replicate any form of life drift down to Earth from space. While humans sleep, the pods take over, replacing them with true-to-form, but emotionally blank substitutes. Some humans notice, but are unable to explain the psychically-numbed pod people in their midst. A psychiatrist (who might or might not be a pod at this point) dismisses the phenomenon as a bizarre though harmless mass neurosis. When pressed by the hero to explain what causes it, he shrugs, "Worry about what's going on in the world, I guess." Later the hero himself attempts to explain the monstrosity. "So much has been discovered in the past ten years," he muses. Indeed.

Invasion, like *Night of the Living Dead*, is explicitly a horror film, yet these themes recur in other works outside that genre, most notably *River's Edge* (Tim Hunter, 1987). Vincent Canby proclaimed that this movie, while not actually of the genre, was nonetheless: "... the year's most riveting, most frightening horror film. Metaphysics has nothing to do with *River's Edge*, although, like *Dracula*, it's a tale of the undead" (25). The "undead" in this film are not cannibalistic ghouls, but a group of ordinary North American high school students. The film is based upon a true incident in Milpitas, California, where a high school student raped and killed his girlfriend, bragged about it to his friends, and, when they showed disbelief, escorted them to the corpse to see for themselves. Later, still more students came to look. For two days, no one reported the crime and the gang of friends casually broke that most sacred of Western taboos: neglecting to bury the dead. In *River's Edge*, as in *Night of the Living Dead*, *Dawn of the Dead* (George Romero, 1979), and *Return of the Living Dead* (Dan O'Bannon, 1985), it is an image of the unburied dead that fills the screen as the camera insistently returns to scan the naked corpse of the murdered girl. If that cold body is the screen emblem of psychic death in life,[3] it is the gang of aimless, unfeeling, and anomic teenagers who—either through hyperkineticism (in one case) or generalized dullness—truly embody the emotional state of the undead. David Denby writes that *River's Edge* succeeds in getting at: "... a phenomenon that has haunted the twentieth century the way Satan haunted the Middle Ages—affectlessness, indifference, the inability to feel what we think human beings should feel" (91). *River's Edge*, then, can be understood as a filmic exploration of the emotional borders of the "Numbed State,"[4] one inhabited by those who manifest the paradigmatic consciousness not exactly of the twentieth century, but more precisely of its second half, the nuclear age.

Like *Night of the Living Dead, River's Edge* is not manifestly concerned with nuclear issues, but it too suggests the underlying connections through conventional references to things nuclear. The killer, Samson, tells another character:

Me. I get into a fight. I go fucking crazy, you know. Everything goes black and then I fucking explode, you know, like it's the end of the world.... I mean the whole world is going to blow up anyway. I might as well keep my pride.

He also reveals that although he wasn't "even mad really" at the moment of murder, he soon reached a peak of hitherto inaccessible emotional intensity: "It all felt so real. It felt so real. She was dead there in front of me and I felt so fucking alive." Samson is so numb that only inflicting death can and does enliven him. Of course, the killer's mindset is not so readily distinguishable from his cohorts. Rambling around the river's edge, one of them remarks:

You got to make the best of it while we're still alive because any day now—boom—and we're dead. Somebody could just murder you, you know; or Russia could send up a whole batch of nuclear bombs.

Apparently, screenwriter Neal Jimenez means to connect the mental state of his characters with the psychological exigencies of nuclear living. Although no critics I know of have pinpointed this link, many do speak of the film in apocalyptic terms. Canby, for example, writes:

Mr. Jimenez has written a screenplay that has the effect of a surreal comedy, about a society that's reached the absolute end of commitment to—or interest in—anything, set in a time without moral obligations, when the quick and the dead have at long last achieved the same body temperature. (25)

Canby's pithy assessment bizarrely evokes Dan O'Bannon's comedy/horror film, *Return of the Living Dead* (1985) for in this movie precisely that situation occurs.

In one striking scene from *Return of the Living Dead*, paramedics are examining two men who have inhaled a chemical toxin and are suffering very grave effects. After taking their vital signs and conferring, the medics tell them:

You have no pulse. Your blood pressure is zero over zero. You have no pupillary response. You have no reflexes. Your temperature is 70 degrees.... Technically you're not alive except you're conscious...and moving around.

Here the differences between the quick and the dead *have* literally collapsed.

The story is that these two workers in a medical supply warehouse, Frank and Freddie, have tampered with some sealed containers mistakenly shipped to them, containers holding corpses pickled in a chemical agent which when activated can reanimate the dead. While fooling around with the containers, Frank and Freddie inadvertently open them, releasing a gas which not only causes them eventually to turn into the undead, but also unleashing a chain of events which leads to global death/undeath.

Return of the Living Dead takes its viewers into deep cinematic space. Before showing him the containers, Frank asks Freddie if he has seen the movie, *Night of the Living Dead*. Sure he has. Frank then tells him that it was based upon a true incident, a collaboration between the U.S. Army and Dow Chemical which resulted in a chemical agent to reanimate the dead. After their fatal fumble, a corpse stowed in the warehouse is reanimated. Frank, Freddie, and now Burt, owner of the warehouse, try to kill the ghoul "as they did in the movie"—with a blow to the brain. But it doesn't work this time. Nothing, even vivisection, which they try next, kills the undead, so in desperation they call upon a mortician, Ernie, to burn the still motile, though dismembered, corpse in his crematorium. As the dangerous corpse burns, they sigh with relief. But the fumes from the burning body go up into the night sky and immediately a heavy rain begins to fall, sending the chemical agent right back down to the Earth. It falls on Freddie's friends, a crowd of punk anomic kids (descendants of those in *Rebel Without A Cause*, Nicholas Ray, 1955, and *Badlands*, Terrence Mallick, 1973 and precursors of those in *River's Edge*). The kids complain that the rain has a stinging, burning feel, "like acid rain." The burning rain also falls on the ground, seeping into graves and resurrecting the buried dead. These newly risen, 1980s ghouls not only cannot be stopped with the old bullet to the brain, but they actually feed on human brains. "Brains, brains," they wail, running through the frame as they hungrily assimilate the mental centers of the living.

Nearly twenty years after Romero's nuclear parable, *Return of the Living Dead* poses an even grimmer, more apocalyptic vision, imagining not only psychic numbing, but also vividly miming the lethal procession of chemical/nuclear contamination through the environment. Nothing can stop the ghouls. Burning doesn't work; it just spreads the contamination and, as with nuclear waste itself, burial is no permanent solution. By the end of the film—just as the now fully ghoulish Freddie is about to feast on the brains of his girlfriend and just as the survivors of the terrible night await with hope the proverbial arrival of the cavalry—the army carries out a surgical nuclear attack on the embattled area. A hydrogen bomb blows away Louisville, Kentucky, and the officials sigh with relief thinking that they have contained the problem. But in the last few minutes, we see a thundering rain begin to fall and news reports inform us that residents claim the rain to have a "stinging" quality. What next but apocalypse as the undead rise to completely take over the world.

In *Return of the Living Dead*, as in *River's Edge*, we follow the action through a band of alienated youth. Here they are played to the hilt—in leather and chains or orange hair (although a few conspicuously normal/nice types are included to mock even that stereotype). The band hangs together in a car with "suicide" written across the hood; they listen to a constant music which tells of death, partying, suicide, and endings. The nihilism of the characters matches, of course, the general philosophy of the film. The exploitation horror movies, *Night of the Living Dead* and *Return of the Living Dead*, are free within their genre (certainly since the 1960s) to loudly suggest apocalypse. The more mainstream *River's Edge*, however, takes two baby steps back from the brink by having one of its scariest characters, a twelve-year-old budding psychopath who will do anything to be accepted by Samson and his gang, put away his gun and succumb to brotherly love at film's end. This token resolution of horror aside, these films by and large reflect the fear which underlies the larger nuclear nightmare, the fear that does not respond to the quickie kill, the monster that will not/cannot be put to rest. Indeed, *Return of the Living Dead* brazenly mocks the expedient solutions of the 1950s films. Not only are its ghouls "immortal," but the nuclear explosion at its end only acts to further spread the contamination, ensuring doom.

These films, moreover, with their grotesque and overt violation of taboos—the presence of the unburied dead, sexual murder, intrafamilial violence, the shattering of the child-parent bond, cannibalism, etc.—point to an absolute end time. All vividly express that component of nuclear consciousness—radical futurelessness—the conviction that there will be no biological continuance, a conviction attended by a breakdown of traditional morals and institutions. All also project that most insistent conclusion of nuclear technology—the annihilation of human society, if not the world itself. As such, these films do not expediently calm nuclear fears, like much of the science fiction of the 1950s. Nor do they symbolically celebrate, and even sacralize, nuclear technology as do contemporary productions such as *Star Wars* (George Lucas, 1977), *Raiders of the Lost Ark* (Steven Spielberg, 1981), or *Ghostbusters* (Ivan Reitman, 1984) (Britton). Rather, these productions, with all due horror, relentlessly, if often subliminally, reveal and critique that paradigmatic half-life of the nuclear mind.

Safer Than Sex?

I wish you were the town of Hiroshima and I *la bomb atomique pour tomber dessus*
  —the master of ceremonies to a female performer in an Athens
  nightclub, 1945 (qtd. in Boyer 246)

Nuke The Bitches
  —slogan on a male counter-demonstrator's T-shirt at the Women's
Encampment for a Future of Peace and Justice, Seneca, New York, 1984

Nuclear Energy—Safer than Sex
  T-shirt slogan on a woman's pro-nuclear group, S.A.F.E. (Society
  for the Advancement of Fusion Energy), 1979.

River's Edge not only offers a meditation on psychic numbing, but, like many other nuclear films, suggests a relationship between nuclear and sexual violences. When the bomb-like Samson finally "fucking explodes" into rape and murder, the target he aims toward is a female body. In the equation which identifies the killer with a nuclear bomb, the body of his female victim can be understood as signifying the corpse of "Mother" Earth. This suggestive paralleling of sexual and nuclear assaults is by no means unique to *River's Edge* (Caputi, *Age of Sex Crime*; Caputi, "The Metaphors of Radiation; Cohn). Indeed, this recurrent metaphor vividly illustrates the validity of the feminist insistence upon a gender analysis of nuclear technology. Briefly, many feminists argue that the arms race is rooted in the values of a male supremacist culture, particularly its promotion of a domineering phallic sexuality (Caldicott; Russell *Exposing Nuclear Phallacies*). As Diana E.H. Russell ("Sexism, Violence, and the Nuclear Mentality") writes: "at this point in history the nuclear mentality and the masculine mentality are one and the same" (74). Though it is beyond my scope here to more fully explore this argument, I will point to several popular films that recurrently link one modern manifestation of phallic sexuality— serial sex murder—to nuclear mass murder.

It was Charlie Chaplin who, in *Monsieur Verdoux* (1947), made perhaps the first explicit cinematic connection between mass sexual murder and nuclear megadeath. From 1915 on, Chaplin, through his much beloved character of Charlie, the Little Tramp, had come to be the quintessential symbol of the "common man," innocence, survival, and the soul or spirit. His star persona was set and Chaplin carried these associations into every other role he assumed. In 1936, Chaplin abandoned the Tramp character, soon playing Hitler himself in *The Great Dictator* (1940). Some years later, in *Verdoux*, Chaplin played a bank clerk who, having lost his job due to economic depression, matter-of-factly began a new career—marrying wealthy widows or spinsters and then murdering them. As Roger Manvell has remarked, this film was "wholly alien to the public's conception of Charlie and was his least successful production" (206). The public, apparently, did not want to hear Chaplin's message that the common man no longer had much of a soul, was no longer an innocent but had become a mass murderer. Many critics, too, expressed distaste for *Monsieur Verdoux*, especially for the last scene where Verdoux, having allowed himself to be caught, makes a courtroom speech explicitly analogizing his serial murders of women to those mass killings so recently accomplished by the atomic bomb:

As for being a mass killer, does not the world encourage it? Is it not now building weapons of destruction for the sole purpose of mass killing? Has it not blown unsuspecting women and little children to pieces and done it very scientifically? As a mass killer, I am an amateur by comparison.

Some years later, Stanley Kubrick released his morbid comedy, *Dr. Strangelove; Or How I Learned to Stop Worrying and Love the Bomb* (1963). In this film, the madman militarist who triggers world nuclear holocaust is named after the archetypal sex murderer, Jack the Ripper. *Dr. Strangelove's* General Jack D. Ripper, obsessed with what he sees as a worldwide communist plot to pollute his "purity of essence" through fluoridation of water, decides to wipe out the Soviet Union on his own initiative. He instructs airborne bombers to launch a nuclear attack, a move ultimately resulting in the detonation of the Soviet's "doomsday machine." The film thus ends with the end of the world, but before doomsday, General Ripper elaborates on his ideas to his captive, Colonel Mandrake:

Mandrake: Tell me, Jack, when did you first become, well develop this theory.
Ripper: Well, I first became aware of it, Mandrake, during the physical act of love— yes—a profound sense of fatigue, a feeling of emptiness followed. Luckily, I was able to interpret those feelings correctly—loss of essence. I can assure you, it has not recurred. Women, women sense my power and they seek the life essence. I do not avoid women, Mandrake, but I do deny them my essence.

The naming of the crazed General, however much a potshot it seems, is actually one aimed with deadly accuracy. General Ripper's criminal namesake, the infamous "Jack the Ripper," killed and mutilated five prostitutes in London in 1888. He did not rape his victims and his actions therefore were not immediately understood as sex crimes. Soon, however, with the conceptual aid of Freud and Krafft-Ebing, the knife (as well as every other weapon) was understood to be a symbolic penis, and public opinion apprehended that, although the killer did not rape his victims, "the murderous act and subsequent mutilation of the corpse were substitutes for the sexual act" (Krafft-Ebing 58-59). Like his prototype and namesake, *Dr. Strangelove's* General Jack D. Ripper finds his ultimate satisfaction in violent assault, one using a sexualized weapon in place of his penis. In the General's case, however, the mutilation sex murder takes the form of an all-out nuclear attack and the victim is the planet Earth.

Yet another popular film spells out the connections between sexual and nuclear violences—*The Dead Zone* (David Cronenberg, 1983), based on the best-selling novel by Stephen King. The story concerns a man, John Smith (played magnificently by Christopher Walken), who, after suffering a car accident and remaining in a coma for five years, awakens to find that he is able to envision the future of anyone he touches. In the course of the film, Smith is called upon first to solve and then to prevent two modern forms of mass murder. The first is the serial sex killings of young girls in a small Maine town; the second is world nuclear war.

To solve the first, Smith identifies Maine's "Castle Rock Killer" as Frank Dodd, a trusted member of the local police force. As the novel makes clear, Smith then finds himself somewhat unaccountably attending political rallies, seeking out opportunities to shake the hands of politicians. Smith soon realizes that he has unconsciously connected the "patterned destructive madness of Frank Dodd" (King 296) to some parallel madness he senses in the political arena. He confirms this intuition when grasping the hand of rising demagogue, Greg Stillson, and receiving a nightmare vision of that man as future president "pushing the button," initiating world nuclear war, and going down as the "greatest mass murderer in history." Now understanding Stillson to be what he calls "the political equivalent of Frank Dodd," (297) Smith sets out to stop him. Attempting to assassinate Stillson at one of his rallies, Smith misses his shot. But Stillson, trying to protect himself, snatches a baby out of its mother's arms and uses its body to shield his own. Although Smith is shot and killed by Stillson's goon, before the psychic dies he has one last vision. In it, a thoroughly undone Stillson sits suicidally contemplating an issue of *Newsweek* magazine. The cover shows a photograph of Stillson cowering behind the body of the baby. The headline reads: "No Future for Stillson." He takes out a gun and blows out his brains.

The world, then, is saved, at least for now. Actually, *The Dead Zone* could be criticized for providing too facile a solution to the threat of nuclear holocaust: kill one madman. Moreover, our hero has to end up as a self-sacrificial victim. Nevertheless, the film largely transcends these conventional trappings as it powerfully depicts the overcoming of psychic numbing and the efficacy of committed awareness. Smith is, of course, at first literally comatose. Even after awakening, he does not want to use his psychic gift to help anyone; he just wants to be left alone, refusing even the plea of the Castle Rock sheriff to help solve the serial sex killings. After finally agreeing to help, Smith travels to the town and there undergoes a qualitative change in attitude. A murder has just taken place. Going to where the teenaged girl's dead body lies, Smith has a horrifying vision of the murder as it happened, only he also sees himself on the scene just standing by and watching passively as it occurs. Coming out of his trance, Smith is able to identify the murderer, but he also is shaken and repeats helplessly and with self-recrimination: "I just stood there. I stood there and watched him kill the girl. I did nothing." This experience galvanizes his responsibility and prefigures his later decision to intervene against the potential nuclear mass murderer, Stillson. Another event contributes to this as well. Sometime after the Castle Rock incident, Smith envisions the death of a young friend; he is able to warn the boy in time, saving his life. At this juncture, Smith realizes that not only can he "see the future, I can change it."

The Dead Zone offers a vision of a potentially vital future amidst the diminished expectations of the nuclear age. If the nuclear-crazed Stillson has "no future," then there is hope for the future of the world. Moreover, the film validates individual power and responsibility and provides a powerful metaphor for a nemesis of psychic numbing in the perceptive mind of the psychically sensitive John Smith. That name, of course, indicates that this character is meant to be "everyman" and thus promises that all of us have the potential to prevent the non-future of nuclear annihilation. This is a heartening message; still, the conventional use of a male character as the focus of audience identification here is problematic. Not only has it been women who have been at the forefront of the anti-nuclear movement, but, as *The Dead Zone* itself suggests, albeit subtextually, the nuclear mass murderers are the political equivalents of misogynist sex killers. *The Dead Zone* would have been far more radical and powerful, had it placed an "everywoman" at its center and, moreover, had that central female figure survived.

All of the films discussed here represent but a sprinkling of contemporary films which, however subtly, deal with nuclear concerns and/or reflect facets of nuclear consciousness. Manifestly, much of the elucidation of the nuclear mindset and much of the debate over nuclear technology is taking place not only in public forums, but in the dark of the theater. Here, the messages are coded into the shadowy forms of "just entertainment" or the symbol and metaphor of genre. In such films we can find in profusion propaganda for and criticism of nuclearism. Equally, we encounter explorations of facets of nuclear consciousness—its connection to teenage alienation and patriarchal sexuality—which have barely begun to break the surface in public discourse. For those who seek to discern the effects of nuclear technology on consciousness as well as for those who aim to break the grip of the nuclear mindset through naming and analysis, we might, then, keep watching the screens.

Notes

[1] See Jack G. Shaheen, ed., *Nuclear War Films* (Carbondale: Southern Illinois University Press, 1978); Robert C. Cumbow, "Survivors: The Day After Doomsday," in *Omni's Screen Flights/Screen Fantasies: The World According to Science Fiction Cinema*, ed. Danny Peary (Garden City, NY: Doubleday, 1984) 35-42. Also, since writing this essay an excellent study by Andrew Britton, "Blissing Out: The Politics of Reaganite Entertainment," has come to my attention. Here, Britton discusses themes of "nuclear anxiety" in several contemporary films.

[2] For example: radiation in *Them*, Gordon Douglas, 1954; some alteration in the environment caused by nuclear testing in *The Beast from 20,000 Fathoms*, Eugene Lourie, 1954; and, somewhat later, contamination from nuclear waste as in *The Horror of Party Beach*, Del Tenney, 1964. For additional commentary on this, see Stephen King, *Danse Macabre* (NY: Everest House, 1981) 154-158.

[3] "Death in life" is Robert Lifton's phrase to describe psychic numbing. See his *Death in Life: Survivors of Hiroshima* (NY: Simon and Schuster, Touchstone, 1967).

[4] Mary Daly in *Pure Lust: Elemental Feminist Philosophy* (Boston: Beacon, 1984) 347. See also Mary Daly with Jane Caputi, *Websters' First New Intergalactic Wickedary of the English Language* (Boston: Beacon, 1987) 213.

Works Cited

Boyer, Paul. *By the Bomb's Early Light: American Thought and Culture at the Dawn of the Atomic Age.* NY: Pantheon Books, 1985.

Britton, Andrew. "Blissing Out: The Politics of Reaganite Entertainment." *Movie* 31/32 (1980): 1-42.

Caldicott, Helen. *Missile Envy*. NY: William Morrow, 1984.

Canby, Vincent. "Into the Dark Heartland," *New York Times* 14 June 1987, Section H:25.

Caputi, Jane. *The Age of Sex Crime*. Bowling Green, OH: Bowling Green State University Popular Press, 1987.

_____. "The Metaphors of Radiation: Or, Why a Beautiful Woman is Like a Nuclear Power Plant." forthcoming in *Women's Studies International Forum*.

_____. "Seeing Elephants: The Myths of Phallotechnology." *Feminist Studies* 14 (1988): 486-524.

Cohn, Carol. "Sex and Death in the Rational World of Defense Intellectuals." Russell 127-159.

Denby, David. "Our Gang." *New York*, 18 May 1987: 90-92.

Dillard, R.H.W. "*Night of the Living Dead*: It's Not Like Just a Wind That's Passing Through." *American Horrors: Essays on the Modern American Horror Film*. Ed. Gregory A. Waller. Urbana: University of Illinois Press, 1987.

Gerstell, Richard. *How to Survive an Atomic Bomb*. Washington, D.C., 1950.

Kaminsky, Stuart M. "Don Siegel on the Pod Society." *Science Fiction Films*. Ed. Thomas R. Atkins. New York: Monarch Press, Simon and Schuster, 1976. 73-83.

King, Stephen. *The Dead Zone*. New York: The Viking Press, 1979.

Lifton, Robert Jay, and Erikson, Kai. "Nuclear War's Effect on the Mind." Lifton and Falk 274-278.

Lifton, Robert Jay, and Falk, Richard. *Indefensible Weapons: The Political and Psychological Case Against Nuclearism*. New York: Basic Books, 1982.

Manvell, Roger. *Chaplin*. Boston: Little, Brown and Co., 1974.

Peary, Danny. *Cult Movies*. New York: Dell, 1981.

Russell, Diane E.H., ed. *Exposing Nuclear Phallacies*. New York: Pergamon Press, 1989.

_____. "Sexism, Violence, and the Nuclear Mentality." Russell 63-74.

Sontag, Susan. "The Imagination of Disaster." *Against Interpretation*. New York: Dell, 1966.

Wood, Michael. *America in the Movies*. New York: Dell, 1975.

Wood, Robin. "Apocalypse Now: Notes on the Living Dead." *The American Nightmare*. Ed. Andrew Britton, et. al. Toronto: The Festival of Festivals, 1979.

_____. *Hollywood from Vietnam to Reagan*. New York: Columbia UP, 1986.

Post-Nuclear Holocaust Re-Minding

William J. Scheick

The serious novelist who describes the post-nuclear holocaust world faces a curious situation. If his or her work proves untrue, it "dies" in the future, where it might be dismissed as mere fantasy; if it forecasts correctly, it also "dies" in the future, where its potential readers have expired. What use can such a book have in either world? Perhaps such fiction might be constructed only as a timeless aesthetic artifact, a work of serious art designed by its author to endure forever; but its subject matter,[1] so urgent and apocalyptic, presses hard against this objective of aloofness. Its subject matter would perhaps expose any purely aesthetic objective in this instance as callous, as if the artist were merely remotely musing upon his species' proclivity for self-destruction; and its subject matter would certainly expose this aesthetic objective as patently irrelevant in a predicted future without the capacity for the passive enjoyment of such rarefied expressions of art.

As a result, fiction treating the post-nuclear holocaust world might be better constructed as self-consuming artifacts (Fish 1972). Self-consuming artifacts transfer the reader's attention away from the aesthetic nature of the work itself and toward its effects in that reader's mind, which ideally is challenged to confront and change its sense of what is normal. If it succeeds, this kind of post-nuclear holocaust novel would technically no longer be needed and so might also "die," just as if it were a mere document that proved correct or incorrect; but at least the novel which is a self-consuming artifact would have played a role in "making the world safe" for a future aesthetics of life and of art.

Such self-consuming artifacts have a deconstructive feature. They are (to apply Roland Barthes' terms) narratives of bliss (*jouissance*) rather than texts of pleasure. That is, apropos language, they unsettle the reader's values and memories, and they challenge the reader's historical, cultural, and psychological assumptions (Barthes 1975, 14). These post-nuclear holocaust novels are like the shattered world they describe, for their portrayal of a profound unmitigated loss fractures any conventional expectations of comfort the reader might seek in the structure of reading. Their thought-defying picture of the total or near-total loss of human life occasions a disorientation of the reader's familiar sense of the known, particularly in such axiological matters as values. The ideal reader (in Iser's sense) experiences a crisis at some level of his or her mind, which cannot fathom such worldwide

71

destruction and which registers a sense of complicity in this devastation. This deconstructive experience of crisis is necessary before reconstructive thought can begin. In the best nuclear holocaust fiction of the 1980s, this aimed-for sense of crisis, suggesting the need to replace one set of social values with a new perspective, is generated not only through a horrifying depiction of the end of the world (Rabkin 1983, x, xv), but also through a specific disorientation of the implied reader's normal sense and valuation of language, time, and reality.

Language

Several of these contemporary novels suggest that the average reader unconsciously believes in a firm relation between language (the experience of shared denotative meanings) and reality (the experience of shared temporal eventuation). Sometimes, moreover, recent authors of post-nuclear holocaust fiction indicate that language, as the fundamental expression of the human mind, lies at the heart of the nuclear threat in the reader's world. Their fiction suggests that language not only cloaks ideological and other biased agendas (cf. Hilgartner 1983), but also conceals its own arbitrariness in fashioning our unsafe world. To most people, at least in their day-to-day lives, language seems readily to signify the signified. However, like Barthes (1975, 28), some contemporary authors of nuclear holocaust fiction sense how conventional language can authoritatively repress all alternative discourse.

This point is made in David Graham's *Down to a Sunless Sea* (1981), which specifically notes how the language of all political ideologies is pernicious to human survival, and in Denis Johnson's *Fiskadoro* (1985), which argues for the transformation of the language of both political and religious ideologies into a mythic discourse capable of furthering a better dream of life. Similarly, Michael Swanwick's *In the Drift* (1985) is especially grounded in the problem of ideology.

Set in the east coast of America, where a nuclear accident has created a radioactive no-man's-land called the Drift inhabited by mutants, Swanwick's novel demonstrates how language serves as a tool of repressive governmental forces. The word *drift*, designating the zone of genetically mutated outcasts, functions to sharpen ideological boundaries and to justify a lack of compassion toward others in general, most particularly toward deformed humans in the Drift, who are treated like slaves and even killed at random. Moreover, the governmental application of the word *drift* keeps from common knowledge the fact that during the last century the zone has slowly spread across previously uninfected areas. Even more subtly, the distinction implied by the word *drift* conceals from the average citizen in the novel the fact that all life has become hellish: in the Drift, where life-expectancy is a mere twenty-two years, and outside the Drift, where a harsh militaristic organization called the Mummers patrol the borders of the badlands and try to keep Philadelphia a "safe haven from all that lay behind" (10). Such a slogan reverberates with echoes of a similar use of language in the reader's world of the 1980s.

In Swanwick's novel this alleged safe haven is dominated by males, whereas in the Drift a female vampire, a Joan-of-Arc figure, emerges as a sacrificial leader. Similar to such other novels of this decade as David Graham's *Down to a Sunless Sea*, Poul Anderson's *Orion Shall Rise* (1983), David Brin's *The Postman* (1986), Whitley Strieber's *Wolf of Shadows* (1986), and Paul Theroux's *O-Zone* (1987), Swanwick's story urges as part of its agenda the idea that women must have a more central place in any effort to reform human sensibility in a post-nuclear holocaust world. Like Hélène Cixous, some of these novelists of post-nuclear holocaust fiction suggest that it is essentially *male* authoritarian discourse that asserts its dominance over another, possibly transformative language.

Two contemporary post-nuclear holocaust novels written by women indicate that women will have a more central role in the future, but caution about the limits of suggesting that women might readily derive a viable alternative discourse. In *The Shore of Women* (1986) Pamela Sargent describes a post-nuclear holocaust world in which women live separately from men, who are kept in a state of barbarity by the fear-inducing "wicked spell" of delusive female discourse (154). In this novel, as in Brin's *The Postman*, women wage war against men, and even if their cause is to end the era of male aggression, they are nonetheless engaged in the same activity. Brin seems unaware of this problem in his book, but Sargent sees it clearly. She makes the point that an ideal rapprochement between the sexes can only occur when each recognizes that though their natures indeed differ, yet "there is something of us in them and something of them in us" (468). If Sargent emphasizes the need to expand the discourse of love to include genuine friendship and to transcend all gender discourse by means of a "worship...[of] life itself" (413), Sheri Tepper wonders in *The Gate to Women's Country* (1988) whether the articulation of love will be possible at all in the post-nuclear world, a "Hades" where "there's no love" because love leads to betrayal between the sexes (315). Although the women in Tepper's novel are slowly breeding gentle males, a practice unknown to the men who live separate warrior lives outside women's country, her protagonist ends in silence, her final discourse not a specifically female alternative to male language, but only silent tears of grief over the sorry state of affairs.

That language, whether assessed from gender or ideology, is indeed an agent in the prevalence of the nuclear threat informs James Morrow's *This Is the Way the World Ends* (1986). In Morrow's novel an American assistant secretary of defense, on trial by the post-apocalyptic unborn, protests hotly: "Can't you use a goddamn metaphor any more without being dragged into court?" (156). But, as the novel shows, metaphors have been at the bottom of the disaster. The assistant secretary asserts that "your missiles must send the right message" (194), but as a Pentagon arms controller, also on trial, unwittingly complains, "It's a real pain arriving at certain definitions" (185). Missiles convey a message, for they are powered by the language of the human mind. However, the real message they convey points not to endurance (the strength to deter nuclear destruction) but to the essential instability of the meaning of our life and of our interpretations (language) of life. That the final authority for meaning, in life and in language, resides in us is the main message of serious nuclear holocaust fiction. This fiction is (to apply Jacques Derrida's comments on the metaphor of nuclear holocaust) a missile-like missive (language) returned for deconstruction to the sender, who is humanity, its only authorizing author.

Time and Memory

This missile of the post-nuclear holocaust text sends its message through the deconstruction of the reader's normal sense not only of language (as we have seen) but also of time. The post-nuclear holocaust novel records the characters' past, which paradoxically remains the reader's future. This paradox amounts to a disorienting coalescence of the reader's sense of the past and the future. Such an erasure of distinctness of time periods corresponds to the assault in these novels on a distinctness of concrete denotative meaning in language.

Collapsing past and future, several of these works represent a disorienting linguistic timefold similar to the holocaustal rip in time literally described in the plot of some of these novels. Tears in time occur, for example, in John Varley's *Millennium* (1983), in which a small group of contaminated individuals in the dying Last Age try to start civilization over again by going back in time to rescue select people from airplanes which are known to have crashed in the past. In Morrow's *This Is the Way the World Ends*, too, George Paxton learns that "time is ruined," that "one of the many effects of nuclear war that nobody quite anticipated" was the annihilation of fundamental particles so that "time gets twisted and folded" (93).

In post-nuclear holocaust fiction, this literal and linguistic timefold suggests that time, like the nature of all language (metaphor), is not fixed, but is always an arbitrary present moment rife with unseen alternative possibilities. As the metaphoric timewarp in these books describe and represent, there is an instability in the fabric of the seemingly fixed material world and its language. These works, as self-consuming artifacts, emphasize this instability in order to challenge the average reader's comfortable sense of material reality. However, this destabilization intimates more than a threat of dissolution. The destabilization of time, like the decentering of the fixed meaning of language, also suggests the openness of human experience to potential change for the better.

To elicit a sense of this possibility, these novelists focus on memory, the faculty which uses seemingly fixed language to record seemingly fixed time. If, as we have noted, language is the subtle tool of political, religious, gender and cultural ideologies, so too is the sense of time as documented by human memory. This relationship between memory and political control is evident in the process of selection, for memory (as unstable as are the language and time comprising it) is always selective. It privileges this; it brackets that. Just as language is an instrument of the authoritative domination of people (by whatever forces), so too is memory. As Michel Foucault has observed, "Memory is actually a very important factor in struggle.... If one controls people's memory, one controls their dynamism.... It is vital to have possession of this memory, to control it, administer it, tell it what is must contain" (Jordin 1975, 25, 26).

So, finally, serious authors of contemporary post-nuclear holocaust fiction emphasize their characters' past (memory) as the reader's future to conflate time palindromically to give the reader a sense of *déjà vu*, which possibly makes this reader reassess his or her own memory. These writers, to apply Foucault's point, struggle for control over their reader's memory, the reader's sense of the past that will shape the direction of the human future (the authors' characters' past). In Whitley Strieber and James Kunetka's *WarDay* (1984) we are told that "words like *history* have lost their weight. They seem as indefinite as memories and as unimportant" (511). But this is only a minority report in post-nuclear holocaust fiction during the 1980s.

Johnson's *Fiskadoro* at first seems similarly to suggest that since "memories...make you crazy," the remnants of humanity might try to avoid "waking up and remembering the past and thinking it's real" (217); perhaps such an erasure of the past, as if merely forgetting a bad dream, might allow a new possible mode of human existence. So Fiskadoro suffers a severe memory loss, from which he never recovers. The narrator of Johnson's novel, however, clings to bits and pieces of past lore, as typically do the narrator of Russell Hoban's *Riddley Walker* (1980), who writes "in memberment" (204) and the narrator of Kim Stanley Robinson's *The Wild Shore* (1984), who writes, in imitation of an old story-teller, "to hold on to the part of the past that's of value" (289). Finally, as these three characters indicate, memory is critical to human mental evolution, whether distorted, collaged memory, or new post-destruction current memory (like Fiskadoro's). As the palindrome of reader future and character past in these timefold novels suggest, memory is for their authors as important a means of access to their readers as Foucault notes it is a crucial means of political control over people.

Hoban's and Robinson's protagonists are pessimistic about the ability of their narratives to achieve anything. But behind the pessimism of each of these narrators hides their respective novelist's hope in the possibility that his characters' memory might serve as a reminder of the reader's choices for the future. Just as Robinson's protagonist, despite his despair, continues to contemplate the duplicitous selfishness of humanity even in the post-nuclear holocaust world and just as Hoban's Riddley accepts how his ongoing pursuit of the meaning of human existence, which he "parbly...won't never know," is "jus on me to think on it" (204), the ideal reader of these two books, and many others in their genre, is left *in medias res*, in the midst of contemplating human nature.

Put another way, there is a profound subtextual question lurking in the presentation of the reader's future as a narrative past: can humanity finally develop a "deep *memory*" (Amis 1987, 118), value "painful memories" "with a bite" (Morrow 1989, 110, 174), recover "those things not so much lost as unremembered" (Tepper 1989, 81), and learn from the past, even a fictional past in a fantasy about the future? Is humanity, so "capable of anything," able to learn to value an evolution of mind, not merely to crave the survival of body even in a hellish world (Amis 1987, 123, 142)? Can such a reminding (a character's memory) provide an opportunity for a re-minding (a reader's future), a revision/re-vision in human consciousness? When reminding/re-minding is experienced by the ideal reader, through the destabilization of that reader's perspective of time and language, the post-nuclear holocaust novel manifests its potential as a writerly (*scriptible*) text, defined by Barthes in *S/Z* as a work which displaces the mere consumer of fixed meaning with the reader who produces meanings; or, in a related sense, it manifests its potential as a self-consuming artifact, defined by Fish as a work which transfers the reader's attention from the aesthetic nature of the work itself to the challenge in the reader's mind to conventional notions of what is normal. Then it urges the reader not to be a mere consumer of fixed meaning (prevalent values) but to be a producer of new meanings (alternative values) in his or her sense of both the temporal world and the language which gives that world actuality.

Reality: Characterization

This destabilization of reader perspective through a revision of comfortable notions of language and time includes for many contemporary post-nuclear holocaust novelists a break from mimetic representation of the sort typical of realistic fiction. These authors use the vehicle of fantasy, if not entirely then at least to a degree, as an assault on their reader's complacent sense of the concreteness of their experience of reality, especially as expressed in the conventions of realistic fiction. Fantasy provides these writers with a freedom to use language, unmoored from the demands of mimesis, to communicate an urgent message about alternative possibilities. Like a missive missile (in Derrida's sense), this message must break through the reader's defense systems, the defense systems of fixed (culturally or politically determined) signified meaning; for a re-minding requires an explosion of the conventional—not only in presentations of language and time, but also in presentations of characterization and setting.

It is true that a character presented mimetically can be a companion in consciousness for the reader. Mimetic characterization serves as a mirrorlike reflection of the reader, or at least of some features of the reader. The reader, consequently, might find a character's voice comfortably recognizable, and might find him- or herself readily seduced to companionship by this sense of familiarity. Identifying oneself with post-nuclear holocaust characters might generate sympathy, ultimately self-sympathy, but can it communicate the need for a radical re-vision as forcefully as sensing mere fragments of recognizable human sensibility in bizarre characters? Mimetic characters, I think, tend to support the status quo because they keep the reader interiorized, locked within the self and the given values of that self's sense of reality, whereas bizarre characters with only the rudiments of human sensibilities potentially force the reader to confront an *Other* outside the reader's valorized self. Such characters contribute to the work of fantasy, which as a polysemous genre departs from consensus reality, suggests the mutability of the present, and provokes intensity of engagement by circumventing verbal defenses (Hume 1984, 20-21, 103, 194-96). Such fantastical characterization forces a dual perspective upon the ideal reader, who looks within him- or herself sympathetically and at the same time looks outward at him- or herself as a monster.

If, as Hélène Cixous notes (1976), mimetic characters convey a sense of the present as everlasting, then fantastic alternatives to such characters might more successfully defy the reader's impression of the firmness of his or her sense of the present. When George Paxton discovers, in *This Is the Way the World Ends*, that his daughter is really an android, a rupture occurs for him and the reader between signifier and signified—such an explosion of expectations that the very nature of reality (in our world, in our memory [mind], and in our language) is called into question.

Consider, as well, Martin Amis' *Einstein's Monsters* (1987), the five stories of which evince a progression from mimetic to fantastical characters. In this book, accounts of how average lives reflect the threat and violence endemic to a world defined by a nuclear referent steadily give way to a post-nuclear holocaust reality in which a sacrificial puppy (with more consciousness than many people) transforms into a human form; and an eight-feet-long, four-feet-wide, five-legged, crimson-eyed mutated dog is fed Queers (human defectives); and an allegedly single immortal man, clearly insane, laments the fact (to an audience dying before his eyes) that humanity "will all be gone and I will be alone forever" (149). This shift from mimesis is informed by Amis' conviction that a post-nuclear holocaust world would be as fantastical a version of hell as ever conceived of by humanity, that such a world would in its non-human nature be almost beyond imagining. This shift from mimesis to the fantastical also, and more importantly, conveys Amis' recognition that if there is to be a re-minding, his readers must see themselves outwardly as Other, as "terrible mutations," as well as inwardly as Self, as "human beings" (58). As the title of his book indicates, we are "energetic actors, vivid representations of the twentieth century—Einstein's monsters" (51). Similar to Tepper's intimation in her abiding metaphor of role playing in *The Gate to Women's Country*, Amis reveals that we are not *only* what we appear to be on the surface. We could be more or we could be less, as both Tepper and Amis suggest. In Amis' book we, whatever our outward features, are like actors with a hidden conflicted nature below the surface. We are, on the one hand, potentially the very human descendents of Einstein, that symbol of our capacity for transformative thought; we are, on the other hand, potentially degenerative monsters sub-humanly perverting our Einstein-like capacity for thought (re-minding).

Reality: Setting

If fantastical characters like the alleged Immortal in *Einstein's Monsters*, the Joan-of-Arc vampire of *In the Drift*, the ghosts of the unborn in *This Is the Way the World Ends*, the apparently psychic dogs in *Riddley Walker*, the clairvoyant servitors in *The Gate to Women's Country*, and the cosmic overseer in *Millennium* typically represent assaults on the reader's comfort in mimetic characterization, the descriptions of reality itself in post-nuclear holocaust fiction can equally thwart the reader's desire for mimetic representation and thereby potentially provoke a revision of reality. A thoroughly mimetic presentation, *War Day* depicts in unforgettable detail what nuclear devastation might be like, but it also is enmeshed in the status quo insofar as it emphasizes human limitations and evades the question of how or what changes in human sensibility might occur.

In contrast, Denis Johnson's *Fiskadoro* supplants mimesis with dream reality (the fantastical). Johnson's narrative technique suggests that life at any moment exists as if in a dream. Just as a person tends to forget his dreams upon awakening, so too can the race forget its past as humanity evolves out of the holocaust and forms new memories. In this way the human race might yet redeem itself from the hell it tends to make out of life; this process is the Romantic hope implied in the closing words of Johnson's novel: "And in her state of waking, she jerked awake. And from that waking, she woke up" (221). The *ands*, and the successive wakings from a preceding dream state these *ands* connect, imply a potentially regenerative process which goes on and on.

But Johnson is no starry-eyed optimist. In *Fiskadoro* he implies that in the long run the post-holocaust new life-dream-story might not be any different than the pre-holocaust one. Johnson has Mr. Cheung say, "Some of us are aligned with a slight force, a frail resistance that shapes things for the better" (122-123). Fiskadoro is slight and frail, and he does indeed bring change. But the words "slight" and "frail" hint at the precariousness of the possibility for an improvement in the human condition. And this suggestion is supported later in the novel when a minor character ponders how "everything came to an end before. Now it will happen again. Many times. Again and again" (219). Maybe post-holocaust humanity will merely recapitulate the pattern of pre-holocaust humanity; maybe the human mind is so insistent in its hell-making self-destructive force that the slight, frail resistance in that same mind will be overpowered. Still Johnson (like Robinson and Hoban) posits the reality of this resistant force, and he hopes for the small chance, which seems to exist, for its emergence from the myth-engendering human mind and for the possibility for a better dream (life) to which this emergence could give rise.

In post-nuclear holocaust fiction similarly characterized by the nature of dreams, the reader cannot tell what is dream and what is actual in the narrative. This confusion makes the point—a point H.G. Wells insisted upon throughout most of his career (Scheick 1984)—that life is like a dream, that life is not a fixed immutable reality but an open-ended series of alternative possibilities. Humanity is "living in a dream world" replete with nebulous "frail memor[ies]" (Morrow 248, 260); human life, as aptly imaged by Amis, is "a gorgeous and dreadful dream, the two states—panic and rapture—welded as close as the two faces of a knife" (106). And, as we have noted, the characters in this *mise en scene*, replete with fantastic possibilities, may be outlandish caricatures, insane immortals, psychic dogs, mutant vampires, clairvoyant servitors, bizarre aliens, or unborn ghosts. Such characters are appropriate to a dreamlike setting. If revision/re-vision in the reader's future, if an emphasis on possibility, rather than an emphasis on limitation, is the goal of the post-nuclear holocaust novel, then the fantastical past of the fictional character's memory should ideally distort or breach usual mimetic representations of the commonplace. Such disorientation in the reader might lead to revisionary thought.

Deconstruction/Reconstruction

The assault on mimetic representations of language, time, and reality for the purpose of provoking thought in the disoriented reader[2] is essentially a deconstructive feature of the post-nuclear holocaust novel of the 1980s. As the narrator of Sargent's *The Shore of Women* learns, "Doubt can show us how we might make things better" (32). But in these works deconstruction is not merely a measure of reality, but also a means of encouraging reconstructive mental patterns. In contrast to the sense of *aporia*—the sense of an infinite regress of meaning that denies any possible "outside" perspective of an ultimate truth (Barthes 1967; Smith 1988), the authors of serious post-nuclear holocaust fiction suggest that there is one external ultimate fact we all indeed know to be true: death.

With death there is no problem of *difference*, the deferment of presence with a sign which is not the thing itself. Death is non-being, the nothing at the end of life. Death is, to adapt Wallace Stevens' line, the "Nothing that is not there and the nothing that is" (54). Reminding the reader of the "outside," fixed, and real referential fact of death requires not only the re-minding that is a devastating missile-like message destroying the ideal reader's conventional sense of things (the deconstruction of conventional sense of language, time, and reality), but also the re-minding that is a possible re-creation (reconstruction of new world possibilities). Grounded in the singular reality of death (non-being or nothing), this fictional re-minding becomes a potentialist discourse, as J. Fisher Solomon cogently suggests in *Discourse and Reference in the Nuclear Age*.

Post-nuclear holocaust fiction uses the fantastical in a way that conforms with a post-structural reading of humanity's subjectivization and relativization of reality; but even while conceding that reality, in an ontological sense, is not ultimately knowable, it insists upon a single empirical potentiality, the potential external reality of death. The death of the post-nuclear holocaust text itself (as we have seen) is at issue, but essentially the possible extinction of the reader's life, perhaps of all life on Earth, by nuclear destruction serves as a limiting "objective" referential ground (*épistémè*) for subjective belief (*doxa*) and action because it can be projected or calculated through our experience of probability, propensity, or regularity. Indeed, for these novelists, as for J. Fisher Solomon, the most urgent instance of the propriety for such a potentialist metaphysics is the nuclear threat of our time.

This threat can be defined as an empirical potentiality: a predictability of human extinction which has objective reality because the possibility of nuclear holocaust bears within itself real propensities for probable development. So, for Solomon and these novelists, as for writers in the field of nuclear criticism,[3] the nuclear referent is not merely the fantastical product of our imaginations that requires a suspension of belief (as Derrida seems to contend), but it is also something extrinsic to us, something with *real* extra-conjectural, extra-interrelational, extra-linguistic dispositional potentialities. In a world which is like an open-ended dream for authors of post-nuclear holocaust fiction, the nuclear referent is a subjective dream and *at the same time* something extrinsic to us, something utterly *real* in its dispositional potentiality to kill the dreamer. The only chance the dreamer (humanity) has for survival in the nuclear age lies (according to serious nuclear holocaust novelists) in his or her ability to dream into "external" existence a "fantastical reality" of alternative potentialities.

In this sense, appearances at once fictionally deceive and factually tell the truth, for everything is the product of the dream-capacity of the human mind. This faith in the protean ability of the human mind counters, anxiously to be sure, the pessimism of such post-nuclear holocaust visions as Robinson's *The Wild Shore* and Varley's *Millennium*. In Neal Barrett, Jr.'s *Through Darkest America* (1986), the father of sixteen-year-old Howie Ryder says, "What you see on the outside's not near as important as the part you can't see"; "it's not what you call something that makes it what it is" (28, 49). Howie learns this lesson about the deceptiveness of appearances and language in painful ways, and the force of his discoveries suggests a rather pessimistic conclusion and outlook. Nevertheless, at the periphery of Howie's main experiences are several little disclosures which abrade a solely pessimistic reading of his encounters. These marginal revelations include the fact that, contrary to popular opinion, some members of the black race have survived the holocaust, some species of animals are reappearing, and (most important of all) "once and a while a ship comes in to port" on the coast of California even though "there weren't supposed to be any" other "places in the world" after the War (250-51).

These intimations of possibilities for regeneration are reinforced by Howie's response (his last words in the novel) to the remark that "there ain't nothin' up that way you can do." Howie replies, "I got to go see if that's so" (p. 256). Informing Howie's uncertain comment—he is not even sure he says it aloud—is a deep sense of the lesson he has learned (as stated by his father) about the deceptiveness of appearances. If, as his encounters indicate, appearances in the world deceive, then even the pessimistic impression they suggest collectively might itself also deceive. Before he accepts the conclusion that he can do nothing at all, he wants to *see* for himself.

Howie's final words in the book, however uncertain, amount to a commitment to search (as he does in the sequel *Dawn's Uncertain Light* [1989]) below the composite appearance of things to discover whether there is in fact nothing he can do to change his world. Implied readers of such post-nuclear holocaust fiction presumably should be left with the same thought: that we should resist a pessimistic capitulation to forces seemingly out of our control and should press on with a commitment to life (cf. Sargent 1986), even if only tentatively against the seemingly great odds suggested by the appearance that nothing can be done about the threat of the nuclear destruction of our world.

Resisting the pessimism of several post-nuclear holocaust works is a tentative hope in alternative appearances, dreams, fictions that might become fact. If one subjective dream (the nuclear referent of the 1980s) could become an objective reality, then possibly alternative dreams could become a new human reality. As is suggested in the assault on language and memory, fact is fiction, and fiction is fact in the repository of the human mind, not only in art but also in the dream that is life. This belief informs the subjective visions of the stories serious post-nuclear holocaust novelists tell. In these timefold works, the fictional memories of future humanity coalesce with the seemingly factual memories of present readers in the 1980s because reality is always the objectification of dream possibilities emanating from the human mind. Post-nuclear novelists deconstruct the language, time, and reality of our present version of the world, a dream reality *really* characterized by the nuclear referent, in the hope that an alternative reconstructive story might somehow emerge. They believe in the fantastical power of stories, of art, to make a difference because all reality, including memory, is only an artistic dream. In this sense, the nuclear reality we now know, albeit real in its propensity for extinguishing all life, is only the product of a mind-invented story.

In Robinson's *The Wild Shore* Old Tom tells stories "to hold on to the part of our past that's of value" (289), and the narrator Henry resolves to continue to contemplate the meaning of life through his writing. In Brin's *The Postman* Gordon Krantz exchanges stories and songs for food (31), and his fictional works salvage something factual from the past. Laissa in Sargent's *The Shore of Women* records from the outside previously outlawed stories, legendary amalgamations of fact and fiction. These narratives infect the barbarous men, seemingly so immune to thought. As Sargent's narrator says, "I had triggered a flood of words and an orgy of self-examination among the men. They told their stories, listened to others, and reflected on their lives; this was something new for most of them" (444). In her hope that these "stories can be powerful in time" (454), that they might also cause the civilized women to think and thereby change too, Laissa expresses the aim of Sargent's use of fiction to urge upon her readers to reflect upon some deep truths about the nuclear age of the 1980s.

The protagonist of Hoban's *Riddley Walker* similarly ponders "what the idear of us myt be" (7) by recording stories with a mythic and allegorical undercurrent. When Lorna says to Riddley, "there ain't never ben no strait story I ever heard" (20), Hoban means that human accounts are as "crookit" (fallen, devious, distorted) as is every postlapsarian post-nuclear holocaust person; that these accounts are, like Riddley's and like human history, non-linear, or disorderly, in their eventuation; that these accounts are allegorical rather than straightforward; and that these accounts are fiction. Indeed, Robinson, Brin, Sargent, and Hoban make the point that whereas in the pre-holocaust world alleged factual accounts presented fictions as truth, in the post-holocaust world fiction preserves some truths, although these truths might well remain elusive to even such sensitive survivors as Henry, Krantz, Laissa, and Riddley. By presenting in their own "crookit" fictions, allegories of truths, about the perilous direction of twentieth-century crooked humanity, Robinson, Sargent, Brin, and Hoban use fiction, not a *straight*forward mode, to reach a not-straight humanity, and in doing so align themselves with the superior role and value of post-holocaust storytelling.

Like Robinson's, Sargent's, Brin's and Hoban's novels, Johnson's *Fiskadoro* posits the immense value of the embodiment of deep truth in fiction, particularly in the post-nuclear holocaust world of his book. The stories told in Robinson's book are heightened embellishments; those told in Sargent's and Brin's books are legendary; those told in Tepper's book are ritualistic; those told in Hoban's book are allegorical; those told in Johnson's book are anthropologically mythic, especially the central story of the book itself that is rendered by a first-person narrator (never identified) who "like[s] to tell stories" (12). If these authors share the view that fiction is a useful vehicle for truth, the difference among them is not only the degree of increasing value attributed to story-telling from Robinson's embellishments, to Sargent's and Brin's legends, to Tepper's rituals, to Hoban's allegories, to Johnson's mythic patterns. Beyond this difference of degree, and perhaps explaining it, is Johnson's implication that fiction, like dreamwork (art, memory, and life), has the capacity to heal, renew, and redirect human endeavors, if not in the twentieth century, then perhaps in a post-nuclear holocaust age when everything is so levelled that healthy mythic patterns might once again be evoked from the human mind.

Johnson and other authors of post-nuclear holocaust fiction portray a future for the reader that is simultaneously the past of the narrator in the hope that this fictional projected memory might result in a different projected future than the one predictable in the present world, a dream reality, defined by the fantastic yet utterly real nuclear referent. In deconstructing our comfortable reliance on the nature of language (denotation), time (memory), and reality (mimesis), they create fantastical fiction as self-consuming artifacts designed to disorient and then to provoke reconstructive thought in their readers. As spent, self-consuming textual missiles, post-nuclear holocaust fiction indicates that humanity will either die through a failed reminding or live through a successful re-minding.

Notes

[1]Studies of thematic patterns in and philosophic implications of nuclear holocaust fiction include Ketterer (1974), Wagar (1982), Rabkin (1983), Brians (1987), Dowling (1987), Scheick (1988), Weart (1988), and Franklin (1988).

[2]Pertinently, Rabkin (1976) notes how fantasy reverses certain narrative features, and Osteen (1990) specifically notes how the frustration of closure in a novel can reflect commentary on an age with a nuclear referent.

[3]On the nature of nuclear criticism, apropos ethical criticism (Siebers 1988; Booth 1988), see Scheick (1990).

Works Cited

Amis, Martin. *Einstein's Monsters.* NY: Harmony Books, 1987.

Anderson, Poul. *Orion Shall Rise.* NY: Timescape Books, 1983.

Barrett, Jr., Neal. *Dawn's Uncertain Light.* NY: Signet, 1989.

——. *Through Darkest America.* Toronto: Worldwide Library, 1988.

Barthes, Roland. *The Elements of Semiology.* Trans. A. Lavers and C. Smith. London: Jonathan Cape, 1967.

——. *The Pleasure of the Text.* Trans. Richard Miller. NY: Hill & Wang, 1975.

——. *S/Z.* Trans. Richard Miller. NY: Hill & Wang, 1970.

Booth, Wayne C. *The Company We Keep: An Ethics of Fiction.* Berkeley: University of California Press, 1988.

Brians, Paul. *Nuclear Holocausts: Atomic War in Fiction, 1895-1984.* Kent: Kent State University Press, 1987.

Brin, David. *The Postman.* New York: Bantam Books, 1986.

Cixous, Hélène. "The Laugh of the Medusa." *Signs* 1 (1976): 875-93.

Derrida, Jacques. "No Apocalypse, Not Now (Full Speed Ahead, Seven Missiles, Seven Missives)." *Diacritics* 14 (1984) 20-31.

Dowling, David. *Fictions of Nuclear Disaster.* Iowa City: University of Iowa Press, 1987.

Fish, Stanley. *Self-Consuming Artifacts: The Experience of Seventeenth-Century Literature.* Berkeley: University of California Press, 1972.

Franklin, H. Bruce. *War Stars: The Superweapon and the American Imagination.* NY: Oxford University Press, 1988.

Graham, David. *Down to a Sunless Sea.* NY: Simon & Schuster, 1981.

Hilgartner, Stephen, Richard C. Bell, and Rory O'Connor. *Nukespeak: The Selling of Nuclear Technology in America.* NY: Penguin Books, 1983.

Hoban, Russell. *Riddley Walker.* NY: Summit Books, 1980.

Hume, Kathryn. *Fantasy and Mimesis: Responses to Reality in Western Literature.* NY: Methuen, 1984.

Iser, Wolfgang. *The Implied Reader: Patterns of Communication in Prose Fiction From Bunyan to Beckett.* Baltimore: Johns Hopkins University Press, 1974.

Jackson, Rosemary. *Fantasy: The Literature of Subversion.* London: Methuen, 1981.

Johnson, Denis. *Fiskadoro.* NY: Knopf, 1985.

Jordin, Martin (trans.). "Film and Popular Memory: An Interview with Michel Foucault." *Radical Philosophy* 11 (Summer 1975): 23-27.

Ketterer, David. *New Worlds for Old: The Apocalyptic Imagination, Science Fiction, and American Literature.* Bloomington: University of Indiana, 1974.

Morrow, James. *This Is the Way the World Ends.* NY: Ace, 1989.

Osteen, Mark. "Against the End: Asceticism and Apocalypse in Don DeLillo's *End Zone.*" *Papers on Language and Literature,* 26 (Winter, 1990): 143-63.

Rabkin, Eric S. *The Fantastic in Literature.* Princeton: Princeton University Press, 1976.

———. et al. *The End of the World.* Carbondale & Edwardsville: Southern Illinois University Press, 1983.

Robinson, Kim Stanley. *The Wild Shore.* New York: Ace, 1984.

Sargent, Pamela. *The Shore of Women.* New York: Crown, 1986.

Scheick, William J. "Continuative and Ethical Predictions: The Post-Nuclear Holocaust Novels of the 1980s." *North Dakota Quarterly* 56 (1988): 61-82.

———. "Nuclear Criticism: An Introduction," *Papers on Language and Literature,* 26 (Winter, 1990), 1-11.

———. *The Splintering Frame: The Later Fiction of H.G. Wells.* Victoria, B.C.: University of Victoria, 1984.

Siebers, Tobin. *The Ethics of Criticism.* Ithaca: Cornell University Press, 1988.

Slusser, George. "Fantasy, Science Fiction, Mystery, Horror." *Shadows of the Magic Lamp: Fantasy and Science Fiction in Film.* Ed. George Slusser and Eric S. Rabkin. Carbondale & Edwardsville: Southern Illinois University Press, 1985. pp. 208-30.

Smith, Barbara Herrnstein. *Contingencies of Value.* Cambridge: Harvard University Press, 1988.

Solomon, J. Fisher. *Discourse and Reference in the Nuclear Age.* Norman: University of Oklahoma Press, 1988.

Stevens, Wallace. *The Palm at the End of the Mind.* Edited by Holly Stevens. New York: Vintage, 1972.

Strieber, Whitley. *Wolf of Shadows.* New York: Fawcett Crest, 1986.

———. and James Kunetka. *War Day.* New York: Warner Books, 1985.

Swanwick, Michael. *In the Drift.* New York: Ace, 1985.

Tepper, Sheri S. *The Gate to Women's Country.* New York: Bantam, 1989.

Theroux, Paul. *O-Zone.* New York: Ivy Books, 1987.

Varley, John. *Millennium.* New York: Berkley, 1983.

Wagar, W. Warren. *Terminal Visions: The Literature of Last Things.* Bloomington: Indiana University Press, 1982.

Weart, Spencer R. *Nuclear Fear: A History of Images.* Cambridge: Harvard University Press, 1988.

The End of Art:
Poetry and Nuclear War

Jan Barry

Since the atomic bombing of Hiroshima and Nagasaki in 1945, artists and writers have grappled with imagining nuclear war. The American imagination of nuclear holocaust has been greatly shaped by novelists, filmmakers and journalists through a searing bombardment over the decades of such cultural explosions as *On the Beach, Doctor Strangelove, The Day After,* and over 40 years of crisis-driven news coverage and editorial speculations on the Cold War.

Nuclear war, or something as dreadful, has stalked the stage in Samuel Beckett's bleak, enigmatic *Endgame.*

But where are the poems of the nuclear age?

Poets have addressed the subject. But poetry in America has had dwindling cultural impact since 1945. Besides the massive shadow cast on most other arts by movies, television and rock music (the electronic triangle which defines American culture in the nuclear age), another possible factor in the loss of cultural impact for modern poetry has been national attitudes toward nuclear war—that the "unthinkable" is a topic in which speculation is best left to experts or Hollywood's cinema chamber of horrors, that the underlying temper of the times is too terror-filled to be "poetic," that the end of our era could well be disaster beyond words.

What could poets, whose baliwick in the popular perception has been to compose light verse or sentimental ballads, what could these moody dreamers add to the heart-churning reality of space age inventions spinning out of the trillion-dollar technology of the nuclear arms race, technology with the power of God to create a world-destroying Doomsday of nuclear holocaust? This is visual, eye-popping stuff—flame-spewing missiles, cities turned into hell in an instant—made for the giant silver screen and eagle's eye-view of television.

The nature of nuclear war may have brought great pause to poets, as well. Perhaps poets sensed better than others knew that nuclear Armageddon would mean the death of art, that nuclear war contained the power to destroy art's illusion of immortality.

Imagining Doomsday, Hollywood mythmakers assumed that after the dust settles something like the Death Valley desert and feuding Wild West (or *Star Wars*) characters would still survive, providing comforting continuity to audiences raised on gunfighter westerns. Novelists and journalists and television writers' scenarios also assumed a fierce struggle among survivors after nuclear apocalypse, not much different from the heroic stories of survivors of civilizations devastated in World War II.

Perhaps poets weighed the literal weight of the words in the Cold War patter about nuclear war: "the end of the world." What if there *were* no one left to admire the breathtaking warnings of the world's end? What could a poet, whose canvas is the human soul, whose passion is casting lines of words to hook immortality—what could the poetic mind facing total extinction—do with such a hopeless vision?

In any case, when I edited a collection of poets' responses to the Vietnam War and the nuclear age,[1] published in 1981, I found it difficult to find many memorable poems imagining nuclear war.

What I did discover was a fierce, nearly underground wave of poetry on waging peace to prevent nuclear war. And I found some bleak, Beckettian images of nuclear holocaust—in poetry that had seldom reached American audiences—conveying a Biblical, stark, lyrical power.

"After the Bomb"

There was a sadness in the land
And silence.
The northern birds had ceased to sing
And blue fire had grown in the east.

From the depths of hell blood welled
And spewed across the valleys and the plains.
Vipers came when the blood had dried
And slithered through the dead, gray grass.

Hearts were sick with longing for the color green,
but it was gone, covered in rust red and gray.
They cried out in their grief...
Lord, have mercy on us! We have seen the pit!

LORD, WE DID NOT UNDERSTAND.
LORD, IF WE HAD ONLY KNOWN.
Lord, let the birds sing. We will listen.
Lord, let the grass grow. We will see.
  (Joseph M. Shea)

Several other poets included in the anthology recovered startling images from accounts of the atomic bombing of Hiroshima to warn of humanity's likely outcome.

"On a Bridge at Hiroshima"
a flat black shadow
etched into the solid
stone had arms outflung
and feet running forward,
as welcome to our future.
                    (R.B. Weber)

And exactly now, across the world,
behind a plane, the *Enola Gay*,
there falls a thin tube
with a small fuse at one end
that will fire one of two parts
into the larger part at the other end
and explode this filament
with a light brighter than the sun. Below,
in the wooden city Hiroshima
can it not be that a man
has just rolled back
one of his living-room shutters
and is looking out on his garden, thinking,
The morning glories on their bamboo sticks,
the blue sky,
how beautiful everything is! Let me enjoy it . . .
          (from "August 6, 1945" by Millen Brand)

Can we speak of the flesh falling from bones
the roaring of matter torn
as loud as the horror screams
deep into the ears
of a hundred thousand burning souls?
The flash, the river, the blast, the storm,
and the sickness
the long slow radiating pain
that will stalk a thousand hallways
into now
and lie in the cribs of the future.
The horror of 8:15
will tear at a billion dreams
               (From "Enola Gay" by Don Ogden)

Other poets wrote biting, icily ironic, appalled responses to the proliferating nuclear arsenals and global battle plans during the depths of the Cold War.

Mrs. Smith, old widow
with her television loaded
with big colored pictures
of grandchildren—

burn her up.
This is the national defense.

It is necessary. History
forced our hand. Our honor
is at stake, our national place.

Michael Grady Maxwell,
fourth grade shortstop
with knee patches and
a d-plus in math,
cremate him alive,
an acceptable loss.

Diplomacy and wealth,
the day-to-day feeling
that we are unsafe,
seeing our beliefs pushed
too long and too far
into the mud.

The Umanoff family,
the father a leather worker
wife a brick mason,
six children in steps
with wide trusting smiles,
reduce them to ash

. . .

Dmitri in his crib,
eight weeks old,
learns to use his eyes
and gurgles.
Bring his internal organs
to a rapid boil.
Simmer them midair
out of his skin.

All the earth contaminant,
Christ and Marx done proud.

Big brave athletically accomplished men
with clear minds and in a time of peace
figured this out and decided it was best.
          (from "Pax" by Tom Hawkins)

Neither you nor I nor children
nor the unborn nor the aged nor
the ill nor the lilies of the field
nor the fish of the sea nor

harvest nor planting nor skies
nor seasons nor
the works of Shakespeare
or Dante of Picasso nor the
blood of martyrs
nor the tears of exiles...
...None of these
not one is safe nothing is safe if
their plans are consummated if their
weapons are lit if mischance
occurs they would declare god a
nonentity...
                    (from untitled poem by Daniel Berrigan)

As I gathered these and other poems together, the aftermath of nuclear war acquired tragic shapes unimagined in the Pentagon or the Kremlin or Hollywood. Some prescient poems foreshadowed subsequent warnings by scientists in the mid-1980s that dense smoke from global firestorms from nuclear war could create "nuclear winter," blocking sunlight possibly long enough to extinguish life on earth.

It is night; the bomb
has fallen.
Here was our mistake:
we marched, but not
to the arsenals.

We never went in, tools in hand,
to dismantle what should never
have been built.
In Russia, it will always
be night.
Tomorrow, our own lights
go out...
                    (from "Dead Wrong" by Shel Horowitz)

"The Last Day"
Night drifts coldly into dawn
    . . .
Terror and alarm, confusion,
fire, death, apocalyptic change—
all these we imagined.
In the darkest alleys of our minds
we covered every possibility.

No one thought of this.

The sun climbs in the east;
still the streets and roads
are empty. No one moves;

each is locked forever

in a dream.
        (W.D. Ehrhart)

The images of nuclear war in American poetry composed during the Cold War are chilling. The chill is deepened when one realizes that most of these poems appeared only in an American form of *samizdat*, the underground Soviet literature. Most of the works cited in this essay were circulated only in manuscript, or had appeared in obscure publications, when I sought poetry for the anthology which I published in a small press venture in partnership with W.D. Ehrhart.

Perhaps these images of nuclear war were too naked, too much like seeing our own bones exposed by a nuclear flash, to appeal to many Americans. It was a terrible subject for poets to grapple with, as well. Once the horror of nuclear holocaust had been held up—like a handmade sign warning that the road ahead is washed out—what more was there to say to a society which kept speeding past all warning signs?

Most of my own poetry has been inspired, and I've been spiritually sustained, by the work of other poets. But poetry on nuclear warfare inspired in me only despair. I found dreaming my own death too difficult to deal with, let alone imagining the death of the world. Editing this anthology, I gained a great admiration for those poets who could convey their horror of nuclear war in poetry.

But the apocalyptic vision was just a part of what I discovered about poetry on the nuclear age. Beyond some memorable poems in a retrospective of Vietnam War protests, the works in *Peace Is Our Profession* that appealed to the widest audience were impassioned, yet practical calls to not just abhor nuclear war, but work to prevent it.

Beneath the dangling sword
the nations rage and snarl and starve
while inept men debate the means of peace.
. . .

That mounting fire,
the coming stench,
like vapors from the deep
assail the nations,
transcend their borders
and rise to debase the nostrils of our God.
He abhors our wars,
our hate,
our violence.
It's not just hating war,
despising war,
sitting back and waiting for war to end.
It's not just loving peace,

wanting peace,
sitting back and waiting for peace to come.
Peace, like war, is waged.
(from "The Peacemaker" by Walker Knight)

This poem, which first appeared in *Home Missions*, a publication of the Southern Baptist Convention, was quoted by President Carter at the signing of the Israeli-Egyptian peace treaty in Washington in 1979, and was prominently cited in a news account of the historic event in *Time* magazine.[2] As I sought to put together a new literary vision of war and peace in the nuclear age, "The Peacemaker" provided the central motif of the anthology—greatly helping to change the thrust of the book from war protest to war prevention.

In a subsequent review of *Peace Is Our Profession*, a *Time* critic[3] called attention to the theme of waging peace thread through the anthology, quoting a Muriel Rukeyser poem:

Peace the great meaning has not been defined.
When we say peace as a word, war
As a flare of fire leaps across our eyes.
We went to this school. Think war;
Cancel war, we were taught.
What is left is peace.
No, peace is not left, it is no canceling;
The fierce and human peace is our deep power
Born to us of wish and responsibility.

I had included a trio of Rukeyser poems in the anthology in a section designed to show the context of protests of the Vietnam War, waged in the midst of the continuing nuclear arms race. But these and other protest poems by well-known and unknown poets were scarcely part of the popular culture; indeed, they were difficult to discover. Poetry reflected the passion of the '60s and '70s peace movement. But (with the singular exception of Allen Ginsberg's coining of "flower power"), it did not provide the rebellious slogans and fiery phrases that helped to fuel the protest.

The Vietnam War was followed by a much different era of peace activism: working to prevent future wars. As I began seeking poetry on war and peace in the post-Vietnam era, Walker Knight and other poets were offering a new vision of peacemaking. Allen Ginsberg made a spectacular effort to change national consciousness about the nuclear age with "Plutonian Ode," a Whitmanesque sweeping song of the times which he chanted like a New Age mantra at nuclear weapons protests and college poetry readings in the late '70s.

Poems on waging peace created by a number of poets inspired many Americans who worked to help prevent nuclear disaster, in a groundswell of public reaction to belligerent calls by the Reagan administration to prepare to wage and win nuclear war, in the 1980s.

One of the most effective poems was Wendell Berry's "To a Siberian Woodsman"—a lifeline of poetry shooting out across the Cold War to the Russians, the people of Pushkin, which the Fellowship of Reconciliation printed on posters with photos of Soviet people, that were hung on walls in churches and schools across America in the desperate years of prodding the Reagan administration to respond to Gorbachev's peace initiatives.

Lines from Berry's poem hanging on church walls were cited by a Soviet editor of a Moscow-based news magazine as one of the most impressive things he discovered in a visit to small-town America.[4]

Grappling for solutions beyond protest, seeking a path to prevent war, other poets hit upon the same theme of reaching out to enemies and estranged strangers to wage peace. Some American poets and peace activists were profoundly influenced by the unexpected, hardy humanism of Vietnamese writers, who reached out to us despite the destruction of their nation by our military machine.

> We will invite the youth
> Who bear on their bodies
> And in their minds and hearts
>   the sounds of war
> The brothers from the Chinese border
>   to the Gulf of Thailand.
>
> We will invite our friends
>   from the West
>   Those whose fathers went
>   and never returned
>   Those whom the war has taken
>   their loved ones.
>
> We will invite our friends
>   from north and south Korea
>   From east and west Germany...
>
> From behind the mushroom
>   columns of smoke
> of Hiroshima and Nagasaki...
>
> We will say new words
>   Our hearts filled with human love
>   And a new language
>   For those who were the enemy.
>   (from "Invitations" by Hai Ha)

The most profound poet on waging peace in the nuclear age I encountered in compiling *Peace Is Our Profession* was Millen Brand, who died shortly before the anthology was published. In 1977, at age 71, he traveled to Japan and joined a marathon peace march from Nagasaki to Hiroshima;

and in the fashion of ancient Japanese poets, he recorded the journey in a volume of poems, titled *Peace March*, acutely attuned to the country and culture he was passing through.

Each day of the journal of his journey he entered an insightful poem on the interaction of Japanese and Americans, the shattering wounds of our wartime enmity still raw, working together to prevent nuclear war.

> *"July 23. Moji Station"*
> At noon and still in Kitakyushu,
> half a hundred new marchers
> meet us at Moji Station.
> Among them is a man
> with white hair, thin and fine,
> down the back of his neck. Yet
> he looks young. He takes my hand.
> His name is Yojiro Taya.
> I tell him I am seventy-one.
> He says he is seventy-six
> and again takes my hand.
> "Haiku," he says. He explains
> through our interpreter,
> "For fifty-five years
> I have been walking around Japan
> writing haiku."
> "What kind?" I ask him.
> "All kinds. Country scenes,
> nature, the seasons, but mainly
> in the last twenty years
> haiku against war."
> "And now you're marching with us."
> "Every year I've marched
> in demonstrations against war.
> I march and write.
> I've written thousands of haiku."
> Seventeen syllables
> each a breath
> against death.
> (Millen Brand)

There is much more to be discovered in surveying poetry on nuclear war and waging peace in the nuclear age. At the beginning of the '80s, these poems were like Biblical cries in the wilderness. By the end of the decade, they had deftly foreshadowed the dramatic power of an international movement for waging peace that, unexpectedly, crumbled the military barriers of the Cold War.

Refusing to be silenced by the roaring, sleepless shadow show cast by the movies, TV and rock music, or to remain silent as hermits in the face of impending oblivion, these poets proclaimed that the end of poetry has not yet arrived. They reclaimed the cultural tradition that the power of poetry—the very best "end of art"—is to sustain and recharge the human spirit, when the future looks most bleak.

Notes

[1]Barry, Jan, ed. *Peace Is Our Profession: Poems and Passages of War Protest*. Montclair, NJ: East River Anthology, 1981. The title was taken from the official motto of the U.S. Air Force's Strategic Air Command and its nuclear-armed B-52 bombers.

[2]"In Celebration of Peace." *Time* 9 April 1979: 33.

[3]Sheppard, R.Z. "The Tape-Recorder War." Rev. of *Peace Is Our Profession*, et. al. *Time* 20 April 1981: 88.

[4]Pumpyansky, Alexander. "No Longer Unconcerned." *New Times* [Moscow] 32 (1987): 27.

Works Cited

Berrigan, Daniel. "Neither you nor I." *Peace Is Our Profession*. 254.

Berry, Wendell. "To a Siberian Woodsman." *Collected Poems*. Berkeley, CA: North Point Press, 1985. 95-98.

Brand, Millen. "August 6, 1945." *Local Lives*. New York: Clarkson N. Potter, 1975. 61.

———— "July 23. Moji Station." *Peace March*. Woodstock, VT: The Countryman Press, 1980. 143.

Ehrhart, W.D. "The Last Day." *The Samisdat Poems of W.D. Ehrhart*. Brigham, Quebec: Samisdat Press, 1980. 21.

Ginsberg, Allen. "Plutonian Ode." *Collected Poems 1947-1980*. New York: Harper & Row, 1984. 702-705.

Hai Ha. "Invitations." *Of Quiet Courage: Poems from Viet Nam*. Ed. Jacqui Chagnon and Don Luce. Washington: Indochina Mobile Education Project, 1974. 150.

Hawkins, Tom. "Pax." *Peace Is Our Profession*. 216.

Horowitz, Shel. "Dead Wrong." *Peace Is Our Profession*. 252.

Knight, Walker. "The Peacemaker." *Home Missions* 43.12 (1972): 4-21.

Ogden, Don. "Enola Gay." *Peace Is Our Profession*. 31.

Rukeyser, Muriel. "Peace the great meaning." *The Collected Poems*. New York: McGraw-Hill, 1978. 389.

Shea, Joseph M. "After the Bomb." *Peace Is Our Profession*. 294.

Weber, R.B. "On a Bridge at Hiroshima." *Peace Is Our Profession*. 32.

Part II:
Specific Texts

News

Jim Schley

Anyone who cannot give an account to oneself of the past three thousand years remains
in darkness, without experience, living from day to day.

—Goethe

Here are four passages which a reader might come across in the same
day, each of which touches the question of nuclear weapons as a point
of contemplation, or point of location:

I

In the brief instant before an exploded nuclear device interacts substantially with
its surroundings, about half of the energy released is in the form of kinetic energy, or
energy of material motion. The other half is electromagnetic energy in the form of soft
x-rays radiated from the surface of the device, which is now at about 10 million degrees
K. Nuclear radiation, primarily neutrons and gamma rays, constitutes a few percent of
the energy. The precise apportionment of the energy from a specific device depends upon
the yield, weight, and details of construction.

The moving matter of the device and the soft x-rays can only travel through a small
amount of material, thus the environment in which a nuclear explosion takes place has
a critical bearing on the effects associated with the explosion. The general environmental
situations are: (1) high altitude (above 100,000 feet); (2) in the atmosphere (from the surface
of the earth to an altitude of 100,000 feet); (3) underground; and (4) underwater. The
four major effects associated with any nuclear explosion are: initial or prompt nuclear
reaction, thermal radiation, blast, and residual nuclear radiation or fallout.

II

Certainly the armies of the world are becoming more lethal. Third World inventories
of armored vehicles—the spearhead of land attack—have quadrupled in the last 20 years.
A dozen Third World countries have armies with more than 1,000 main battle tanks.
More than a dozen countries have ballistic missiles. Perhaps 20 have some form of chemical
weapons, and an additional 10 are researching biological and toxic weapons. By the end
of the next decade, it is not fanciful to expect that 10 countries may have tactical nuclear
weapons.

III

I will tell you that the Third World War has already started—a silent war, not for
that reason any less sinister. This war is tearing down Brazil, Latin America and practically
all the Third World. Instead of soldiers dying there are children, instead of millions of
wounded there are millions of unemployed; instead of destruction of bridges there is the

97

tearing down of factories, schools, hospitals and entire economies.... It is a war by the United States against the Latin American continent and the Third World. It is a war over the foreign debt, one which has as its main weapon interest, a weapon more deadly than the atom bomb, more shattering than a laser beam.

IV

Watching *Dark Circle*

'This *is* hell, nor am I out of it'
Marlowe, *Dr. Faustus*

Men are willing to observe
the writhing, the bubbling flesh and
swift and protracted charring of bone
while the subject pigs, placed in cages designed for this,
don't pass out but continue to scream as they turn to cinder.
The Pentagon wants to know
something a child could tell it:
it hurts to burn, and even a match
can make you scream, pigs or people,
even the smallest common flame can kill you.
This plutonic calefaction is redundant.

Men are willing
to call the roasting of live pigs
a simulation of certain conditions. It is
not a simulation. The pigs (with their highrated intelligence,
their uncanny precognition of disaster) are real,
their agony real agony, the smell
is not archetypal breakfast nor ancient feasting
but a foul miasma irremovable from the nostrils,
and the simulation of hell these men
have carefully set up
is hell itself,
and they in it, dead in their lives,
and what can redeem them? What can redeem them?

Four passages: each an articulation of mind and voice, broad-cast into print—with the intent of convincing readers that what is stated is true and indispensable information.

One of the conditions under which we live, because of the size and proximity of the world's nuclear arsenals, is that we constantly receive word of these weapons. Since the end of World War II, when the results of the Manhattan Project were first tested at Hiroshima and Nagasaki, public emotion over nuclear danger has crested and subsided like fever. In the 1980s, debate began to reach a pitch and prominence comparable to that surrounding the most fundamental questions of a society's identity, such as the continuing practice of slavery in the mid-19th century United States—forcing reexamination not only of policy but morality, relations between nations and relations between different aspects of the thinking, knowing self.

Probably no one was untouched by this questioning, whether the response was anguish, piety, licentiousness, philosophical fascination, despair, or fury.

Aside from differences in original setting, in style, rhetorical stance and attitude, the four texts given share a subject and a historical moment. All four carry news.

The question of medium is nevertheless critical. And leaving aside for the moment all discussion of ideology or ethics, I would scrutinize these texts to find commonalities and contrasts in their construction, as instruments of language. If it's true that "Poetry is news which stays news" (in Pound's irreducible formulation), we must ask how this is so, considering the ways in which we most often get our news in this age, and what means available to poetry in particular might give a good poem the immediacy of news and more—its resilient suddenness.

The assurance of the four passages is comparable—that is, none of them shows any hesitation in inhabiting and fulfilling its chosen form. What is the character of each form, and can it be said which is most memorable, most coherent, or most suggestive, acknowledging in advance that I have chosen these examples not at all arbitrarily, but because of their distinctive sounds, and their interactions as juxtaposed bulletins?

The authors of the passages above are (I.) John S. Foster, U.S. Department of State, in the "Nuclear Energy" entry of the *Encyclopedia Americana* (1980); (II.) John Barry and Evan Thomas in an article entitled "Getting Ready for the Next War" in *Newsweek* (Jan., 1990); (III.) Luis Inacio da Silva, Brazilian presidential candidate, quoted in *The Nation* (April, 1989); and (IV.) Denise Levertov (*Oblique Prayers*).

The first text is essentially concerned with that which is known from observation and experiment. Its territory is the confirmable. Consistent with its author's supposed obligation to defer judgment, the prose is expository, free of rhythmical or figurative inventions, assuming the tone and attitude of straightforward description.

Nevertheless, certain phrases vividly express their subject in action: "in the brief instant," or "soft x-rays radiated from the surface of the device, which is now at about 10 million degrees K...." There is also a peculiar, memorable beauty in other phrases, "an exploded nuclear device interacts substantially with its surroundings...," "precise apportionment of the energy," "moving matter," "soft x-rays can only travel through a small amount of material...," and "initial or prompt nuclear reaction," where precision is expressed in orderly, vigorous combinations. Perhaps it is because of a slightly arcane quality, an air of magic formulas, that the technical terms used, "nuclear device; kinetic energy; material motion; electromagnetic; neutrons and gamma rays; yield, weight and details," are arresting to the ear and to the mind as it seeks to follow this description's progression.

This voice's specificity and uninflected manner seem dramatically at odds with the cataclysmic heat, roar, and concussive force which we realize must result from a real detonation. Yet drama, in that sense, was surely not the writer's aim. This is drama which compounds out of the larger context of what we know, arguably including tensions between our desire to trust the calm certainty of the scientist and our terror when confronted with technological indifference.

The encyclopedia passage gives the synopsis of a physical process, while the second text summarizes a situation statistically, filling a different category of information. Again, the tone is expository and the approach matter-of-fact; while one can question details in a news account, in this case none are given, for an overall development is at issue, and its direction is impressively clear.

In this paragraph the primary building blocks are numbers, whose force is numerical—for example, armored vehicles have quadrupled in twenty years—weapons to years, a ratio in operation. The reader is told that "a dozen... countries" have "more than 1000 tanks," "more than a dozen countries have ballistic missiles," "perhaps 20 have some kind of chemical weapon" (by implication, the particular kind is not as significant as the trend in a summary such as this), and "an additional 10 are researching biological and toxic weapons." At the apex of that catalogue is the authors' statement that soon ten countries may have tactical-nuclear weapons.

There is only slightly greater rhetorical or figurative flourish in this passage than in the encyclopedia one. In terms of its syntax, and its recitation of data, the prose is nearly as skeletal as a list, a series of sentences in the repeating sequence of subject/verb/quantity/object.

Still, the authors' presence is noticeable at several junctures, for example in the initial "Certainly," which commences by assertion, a simulated vocalization of spoken argument. This is a stylistic device; magazine journalists adopt conversational phrasing as if to imitate everyday speech or "live" radio and television commentary. The second sentence is interrupted by apposition, "—the spearhead of land attack—", in which a rather ordinary metaphor reinforces both the commentators' naturalness (they might be speaking about a successful football team's offense) and also the "preparations for war" theme of the paragraph. Also striking is the placement of the word "lethal," which while no doubt self-evident in a discussion about heavyweight military hardware, nevertheless retains its sullen sound and abrupt power to unnerve. Moreover, there is that odd (considering the context) transitional phrase near the end, where the survey of military stockpiles culminates in the most "lethal" example of all, but only after an almost ornamental appositional maneuver and shift in diction: "it is not fanciful to expect...." This has a remarkable tonal effect, wherein the passage reaches its most disturbing observation, yet maintains a deferential, recitative manner by deliberate reassertion of understatement.

Whereas the encyclopedia definition briefly explicated "intermediate effects of nuclear explosion" without judgment, interpretation, or comparison, the *Newsweek* paragraph implicitly identifies (by use of rhetorical climax and placement in a series) nuclear proliferation as the most ominous of harbingers of "the next war," without ever speaking directly of the uses or effects of these weapons. Despite its "bare facts" manner and tone, ultimately the *Newsweek* passage appeals to emotion more than to intellect, addressing in the reader not exactly a desire for information so much as a generalized alarm. This passage presupposes both knowledge and interest on the part of its reader. Even a term as important as "tactical" is not defined—though what's meant is a shorter-range weapon, for battlefield or counter-insurgency use, conceivably more dangerous because it is more likely to be exploded than the gigantic intercontinental "strategic" weaponry possessed only by certain superpowers.

Although I have given only an excerpt from a longer article, preceding and succeeding paragraphs do not alter the impact of the passage given, an impact which is surely also a function of succinctness. One of the basic points of comparison between the four texts is their length: by what means does each speak of its subject within a similar number of sentences?

The third text is less strictly elucidative than the first, and less journalistic than the second. From the outset, this passage is first-personal, oratorical, and emotional. The writer assumes the role of public speaker, which makes the text dramatically and situationally more complex than the examples above; the relation between writer and reader is activated, and becomes part of the subject. While the author's posture is confiding, his tone is by turns pleading or chiding. Rhetorically more combative, he begins with a bolder and more dismaying assertion. Overlapping negations (war/silent/not/less) underpin the outright provocation of the first contention: "I will tell you that the Third World War has already started—a silent war, not for that reason any less sinister."

As before, the reader is presented with a series of sentences, here linked by word repetitions and syntactical parallels in the form of an extended analogy. The word "war" occurs five times over the course of five sentences, along with "soldiers," "dying," "wounded," "millions," "destruction," "tearing down," "deadly," "shattering," and finally "atom bomb" and "laser beam." Cohering in its echoes, "there is a war... it is a war," "Third World War... Third World...," the paragraph proceeds by successively more specific instance to its points: debt is destroying "factories, schools, hospitals and entire economies," and "It is a war by the United States against the Latin American continent and the Third World." As a serious contender for the Brazilian presidency, this writer has presumably elsewhere elaborated on the debt crisis with history, analysis, and proposals for solutions, but the purpose of the passage at hand (and of its inclusion in another writer's article in *The Nation*) was more caustic: to provoke thought, to enjoin debate, to rouse empathy and indignation, to predicate that the economic exploitation of countries in Latin America, Africa, and Asia is in actual practice more destructive than a nuclear war—challenging in one phrase the widely-held assumption (in the developed countries) that nuclear war is the worst we have to fear.

This passage's concluding reference to nuclear weapons is a climax, as in the *Newsweek* paragraph. The author is actually using nuclear war as a metaphor, the strongest he can summon, which speaks to his conviction and also his perception of how we respond to nuclear references. He demands that the reader consider how different might be the vantage point of someone starving, today, from that of someone whose greatest dread is being vaporized tomorrow.

Like the two texts already considered, this one delivers "news," describing a state which is observable and pressing. Unlike the other authors, this one acknowledges a personal need to deliver the message, and makes urgency his medium, calling upon simile, allusions to children dying, and an evocation of the "tearing down" of "entire" societies. He is using a mode of writing that is graphically and dynamically compelling, more than merely informative. While the rhythms of the encyclopedia and *Newsweek* texts were unobtrusive, indeed repetitive, as if to exemplify their authors' reasoning and discretion, even in printed form this third text communicates as heightened speech, employing parallel intensification suggestive of apocalyptic prophesy (c.f. Alter, *Biblical Poetry*.)

It is difficult to discuss the preceding quotation's compositional scheme without defending (or defending against) the anguish of its author, but in this way, concentrating on mechanisms and structures, we can approach the main question, the means by which poems in particular work with the material of the language.

The Levertov poem is made of seven sentences. It shares with the other three texts a reliance upon declarative sentences, and it even incorporates an expository rhythm like that of the *Newsweek* prose. One of the poet's intentions is to report. With its exacting pace and measured accumulation of clauses, the manner of the poem also shares some of the qualities of a scrupulous, detailed lab report or legal brief.

This ability to operate on several contradictory or intersecting verbal planes at once rapidly distinguishes Levertov's piece from the other three passages. The poem is a kind of sonata of manipulated tones. It is as though, despite the poem's brevity, all the available resources of discourse had been sifted through, and drawn upon—anecdotic, delineative, juridical, didactic....

The first and fourth sentences begin with the same phrase, "Men are willing...." A number of other phrases are repeated twice, in some cases three times, repetitions which link each part and grant the whole an insistent sonic and rhetorical unity: pigs, scream, simulation, real, agony, hell, live, and the entire final interrogative clause. Even the epigraph participates in a pattern of repetitions; Levertov's inversion of Marlowe's "nor out of it" by means of her own "in it" connects as if by humming wire the poem's beginning and end, intensifies the echo-chamber effect, and encompasses one very specific incident in a wilder, blacker context of magic, sin, and blasphemy.

An acutely-visual "setting" is established at once. Quickly the scene becomes physically engulfing—heard and smelled and felt: "writhing," "bubbling," "charring," "continue to scream as they turn to cinder," "a foul miasma irremovable from the nostrils...." What is described is graphic in its savagery, and repulsive, yet the reader is carried into sensory experience as if by unopposable undertow. This is accomplished by cadence as well as by imagery, for the poem's phrases enter like measures in music. Notice also the elaboration on sensations of burning—"swift but protracted charring of bone," "turn to cinder," "it hurts to burn," "even a match," "the smallest common flame," and strangest of all, "calefaction," a chemical-alchemical-etymological melding.

That third sentence stands out as the only one in the poem which corresponds exactly to its line, "This plutonic calefaction is redundant." Taut, unenjambed, combining in its braided diction the mythic proportions of a Hell invoked throughout (by name, by Faustian epigraph, and by heat) with the strict, clinical clarity of the Latinate, "calefaction," this line culminates in a grammarian's term, a lawyer's distinction. An abject horror is abruptly deemed intolerable on grounds not only of its callousness and gruesomeness but its "redundancy." One might be reminded of wry Zbigniew Herbert's conclusion that totalitarian brutality is an offense "fundamentally" against good taste ("Yes taste/ in which there are fibers of the soul the cartilage of conscience...."). Levertov layers irony upon understatement upon incongruity upon metrical inversion upon an interruption in the anticipated rhythm and syntax, and this short third sentence of the poem serves as hinge or pivot for the reiterations and echoes which follow.

Stanza two recapitulates the first, but repeatedly regenerates its linguistic impulse (even, in one startling turn, grazing the comic, "archetypal breakfast or ancient feasting,"), and restates the offense against "the subject pigs" in what sound like a scientist's own terms, noting "their highrated intelligence,/ their uncanny precognition of disaster." The latter phrase likewise doubles back into cognition of the present tense disaster-at-hand, and once more emphasizes the consciousness of those being burned, alive and "real," "pigs or people." The end of the poem is again compacted, furiously superimposing human and bestial; while the screaming, suffering "animal" is equated indelibly with human innocence, "something a child could tell it"—the supposedly living blur with those "dead in their lives." The reader may remember suddenly that the lab technicians are researching the response of living beings to "the intermediate effects of nuclear explosion" so straightforwardly outlined in the encyclopedia entry, conditions deliberately produced by detonation of a device intended to incinerate people and places. All that is implicit; political context suffuses these scientists'

circumstantial equation, their obfuscations with "simulation," and darts
through explicitly only by insertion of a single word, "Pentagon."

Finally it is a question of damnation and redemption, literally a question,
aimed straight into the brain of the reader, a question (like so many of
this poem's impacts) which is doubled in intensity by repetition.

The catalyzing occasion of the poem must also be considered, for in
relating an episode from a documentary film the poet poses complicated
questions about mediated and direct experience. What is the relation between
viewer/reader and citizen, exposed to horror as to a dose of radiation?

Levertov herself was not present during the experiment described; as
is true for many Americans, her encounter with such raw but refined violence
comes slantwise through the filters of a camera. Yet ultimately her reader's
vision and grasp of the scene is probably less instead of more hampered
by being framed at one greater remove. The poet so fully accounts for the
intimate shock of viewing this film, and does so with such visceral fluency
(and personal unobtrusiveness), that an event in her own memory is translated
then conveyed "irremovably" to another person—who is thereby made a
witness, with all the obligations to somehow respond which that entails.

Here we return to the question of news, and the comparison of this
text with the other three. Levertov's poem utilizes the resources apparent
in each of the others, and then some; what is extraordinary is how the poem
combines the elucidative functions of an encyclopedia definition, the timely
observations of a piece of analytical journalism, the rhetorical appeal of
a political tract, as well as literary allusion; linguistic, phonetic and metrical
music; the psychology of sensual apprehension; personification; extended
metaphor; temporal compression; dramatic narrative; and searing imagery.
The filmmaker Tarkovsky has said that "the image stretches into infinity
and leads to the absolute . . . many-dimensioned and with many meanings . . ."
(104). The greatest asset of poetry (whether in the form of poems, or as
a force in other arts) may be its ability to carry the witnessing consciousness
into an experience which is not actual but imagined, where one nonetheless
undergoes a physical, mental, and emotional exchange with someone or
something which is not one's "self."

Levertov has written movingly of the difficulty of finding a medium
for multiple and conflicting desires: "Out of those conflicts, sometimes, poetry
itself re-emerges. For example, the impulse to reconcile what one believes
to be necessary to one's human integrity, such as forms of political action,
with the necessities of one's inner life, including its formal, aesthetic dynamic,
motivates the attempt to write engaged or 'political' poetry that is truly
poetry, magnetic and sensuous,—the synthesis Neruda said is the most
difficult to attain (but which our strange and difficult times cry out for)."
(Couzyn 79).

Levertov's poem enacts crucial relationships between the dissertation,
the editorial, and the song, having found a way of being all of these,
simultaneously.

Like a report from a correspondent in an exceedingly dangerous location, the poem tells us something we need to know about what is actually occurring, about others we live among, and about the society we have made. It requires us to use every one of our faculties and senses to fully comprehend. If we were all to die tonight, a poem such as this one would at the very least prove that some of us were thinking and feeling, right to the end.

One cannot sign the poem as legislators sign a piece of paper into law. One cannot initial the page where the poem appears as an international arms control agreement. The poem offers no program or set of steps, but an instance of keen alertness, a model of access to the real.

We are not necessarily in less danger, now, because Levertov wrote "Watching *Dark Circle*," yet we would be in greater danger still if no one were capable of writing, or no one bothered to read, poems such as this.

The Hungarian novelist George Konrad has written, "I belong to a generation of murderers. . . who in order to avoid being killed became killers themselves."

Unless people can face the weirdness and hugeness of our predicament and our own circuitous part in its genesis and sustenance—no treaty, no visionary leader, no technological breakthrough can possibly save us.

—for Robert Nichols

Works Cited

Alter, Robert. *The Art of Biblical Poetry.* NY: Basic Books, 1985.

Barry, John and Evan Thomas, "Getting Ready for Future Wars." *Newsweek* 22 January 1990: 30.

Couzyn, Jeni, editor. *The Bloodaxe Book of Contemporary Women Poets: Eleven British Writers.* Newcastle upon Tyne: Bloodaxe Books, 1985.

Da Silva, Luis Inacio. qtd. by Alexander Cockburn. "Scenes from the Inferno." *The Nation* 17 April 1989: 510.

Foster, John S. "Immediate Effects of Explosion," in "Nuclear Energy." *The Encyclopedia Americana International Edition.* 1980.

Herbert, Zbigniew. *Report from the Besieged City.* Trans. John and Bogdana Carpenter. NY: The Ecco Press, 1985.

Konrad, George. *The City Builder.* Trans. Ivan Sanders. NY: Viking Penguin, 1987.

Levertov, Denise. *Oblique Prayers.* NY: New Directions, 1984.

Tarkovsky, Andrey. *Sculpting in Time: Reflections on the Cinema.* Trans. Kitty Hunter-Blair. London: The Bodley Head, 1986.

Knowledge and Understanding in
Riddley Walker

Jack Branscomb

"O what we ben! And what we come to!" (100), whispers Riddley Walker, the narrator of Russell Hoban's 1980 novel of the same name, as he looks at the ruins of an ancient nuclear power plant whose aura of force he can feel, but whose secrets are lost to him. This vision of a present wasteland and a past that seems more powerful and more authentic is one that haunts Hoban's fiction, and nowhere more pervasively than in the post-apocalyptic *Riddley Walker*. In this, his finest novel to date, Hoban creates a remarkably vivid image of a world plunged back into the dark ages by nuclear destruction and uses this world as a setting to explore man's hunger for knowledge and the power knowledge brings. Caught up in a struggle among political, religious, and technological seekers for knowledge, Riddley comes to understand that "what we ben" means much more than the technological achievements of the twentieth century and that "what we come to" implies the need for him to search for his own personal reintegration.

Like so many alienated characters in twentieth-century fiction, particularly science fiction and fantasy, most of Hoban's characters find themselves cut off from a meaningful past. Whether placed like the protagonist of his *Pilgerman* (1983) in the twelfth century, or *Kleinzeit* (1974) in the twentieth, or Riddley Walker two thousand years hence, they are displaced persons. Their experiences in the novels serve to reconnect them, though usually not in ways that they might expect. Time exists for them in three modes: a present marked by sad decay; a past which the characters feel to be more authentic and heroic; and a recurring mythic or ritualistic time the significance of which only gradually is revealed to them. They may, like Riddley, learn something of the historical past, but the changes in their lives take place because of their absorption into a larger pattern. Riddley, in particular, is a riddler and a traveler who finds truth to be paradoxical and experiential: "Walker is my name and I am the same. Riddley Walker. Walking my riddels where ever theyve took me and walking them now on this paper the same" (8); he learns by going where he has to go.

The true subject of *Riddley Walker* is, as one reviewer has observed, "the human mind" (Lively 58). Nevertheless, Hoban does a remarkable job of creating a powerfully oppressive physical and cultural setting, England as future wasteland. Riddley, the twelve-year-old narrator, is a member of a small group of foragers in the southeast of England who eke out a subsistence by hunting and by digging up scraps of ruined machinery which they barter. They use bows and arrows to defend themselves from packs of vicious, uncannily intelligent dogs—representatives of outraged and alienated Nature—which wait, just out of bowshot, for stragglers. There is a pervasive sense of a ruined, legendary civilization beneath the surface of this wasteland, but only gradually does Hoban reveal that the civilization is our own and that the time of the novel is over two thousand years after a late-twentieth-century nuclear holocaust.

The effectiveness of the setting is due partly to Riddley's impressionistically vivid depiction of his squalid environment, but much more to the most remarkable feature of the novel, the language which Hoban has invented for his characters. In an incident early in the novel, for example, Riddley says:

On my naming day when I come 12 I gone front spear and kilt a wyld boar he parbly ben the las wyld pig on the Bundel Downs any how there hadnt ben none for a long time befor him nor I aint looking to see none agen. He dint make the groun shake nor nothing like that when he come on to my spear he wernt all that big plus he lookit poorly. He done the reqwyrt he ternt and clattert his teef and made his rush and there we wer then. Him on 1 end of the spear kicking his life out and me on the other end watching him dy. I said, 'Your tern now my tern later. . . .'
The woal thing felt jus that littl bit stupid. Us running that boar thru that las littl scrump of woodling with the forms al roun. Cows mooing sheep baaing cocks crowing and us foraging our las boar in a thin grey girzel on the day I come a man. (1)

Passages like this one are typical in suggesting, by means of unconventional spelling and punctuation and an occasional metathesis, twentieth-century English transmitted orally. It is a terse, direct language well adapted to expressing the pervasive fatalism of the culture—"Your tern now my tern later"—in which the best one can hope for is to do "the reqwyrt." The grim, understated humor is characteristic both of Riddley and of most of the other characters of the novel.

More immediately striking than the linguistic texture illustrated in the passage cited is the imaginatively distorted vocabulary, consisting usually of corruptions of twentieth-century words, especially the language of science, computers, and politics. In addition to the sheer pleasure provided by its wit and exuberance, this richly crafted vocabulary serves important thematic purposes. Most obviously, it shows the relationship of Riddley's culture to that of the distant past. As Hoban has commented, "the language we speak is a whole palimpsest of human effort and history" (Dowling 201). The terms derived from the jargon of computers, science, and politics are all-pervasive, and the changes they have undergone reflect the inner nature of the things named. For example, the government, or "Mincery," chops as much as it administers; and the Pry Mincer spends much of his time prying into the affairs of the folk. The seat of the Mincery is the "Ram," shortened from present-day Ramsgate, but suggesting also a computer's

Random Access Memory (RAM) and thus the linkage of political and technological power. More humorously, a foreign secretary becomes a "farring seakert tryer" (201) trying to get his secrets from one place to another; and "scatter my datter" (48) becomes a mild curse. The elite technocrats who controlled the computers at Canterbury are remembered as the "puter leat," and the title of their present leader, "Ardship of Cambry," reflects both man's tendency to make a religion of his own accomplishments and the bitter hardship that his technology has produced.

If the vocabulary of the novel provides capsule histories of complex relationships, the many stories told by Riddley and others provide far richer veins of (mis)understanding to be mined. The idea of the story is a central one for Hoban. In *Pilgermann*, the novel which follows and in some sense completes *Riddley Walker*,[1] the narrator says, "a story is what remains when you leave out most of the action; a story is a coherent sequence of picture cards" (38), minus the spirit which animates the pattern. For Hoban, "story" in this sense is an icon, an image like the mural *The Legend of St. Eustace* or the various puppet figures which play important parts in *Riddley Walker*. They embody enduring patterns in human life, patterns which are interpreted or played out with almost infinite variations, but whose essence persists.

The principal example of the importance of story in *Riddley Walker* is the Eusa Story, the central myth of the culture. The story tells of the legendary Eusa's pursuit and division of the "Littl Shynin Man the Addom" (30) and the power and destruction, or Bad Time, which followed. Under the influence of Mr. Clevver, the devil figure of the story, Eusa seeks ultimate power over his enemies by trying to harness the "1 big 1" (30), nuclear energy. Like the Biblical account of the Fall, the story explains the miserable state of man as being due to the excessive pursuit of knowledge. In the Eusa version, however, Eusa's search is less a violation of a divine prohibition than an assault on the very nature of things, man's nature included. The Fall is shown as a descent into abstraction, represented primarily by mathematics, "counting which wer clevverness and making mor the same" (19), and dualism—the "Littl Shynin Man" is literally torn apart. Eusa splits the "Addom" only to discover that he has split himself and cut himself off from the natural world. Having discovered the secrets, the "Master Chaynjis" (35) of nature, he is now condemned to go through all the Chaynjis "Reqwyrd by the idear" (36) of himself. Ultimately he is cast out, blinded, mutilated, and killed, before emerging as the cult scapegoat figure of the Eusa story. Riddley, like the rest of his society, sees himself as going "Down that road with Eusa" (44) in the hope of some ultimate liberation.

The Eusa story's status as an icon is suggested by the fact that it is written out and only an elite group—Mincery men, Eusa folk, and "connexion" men, or interpreters like Riddley—are allowed to have copies. It is disseminated to the people through a two-fold process of interpretation. Eusa showmen like the Pry Mincer Abel Goodparley travel around the country performing puppet Eusa shows reminiscent of Punch and Judy shows, especially in the figure of Mr. Clevver, the Devil of the older tradition. The showmen may try to manipulate the story for political purposes. Goodparley, for example, shows Eusa building a mechanical head, a computer, to help him with his thinking, only to discover that his human head has been emptied. Mr. Clevver steals the mechanical head, and he, not Eusa, starts Bad Time. Goodparley's message is that technological progress is all right if it is kept in the right hands. The second stage of the presentation is carried out by a representative of the people, a connexion man like Riddley whose interpretation of the performance may undercut the Mincery position, as does a connexion made by Riddley's father (56-60). Interpretation and reinterpretation may thus essentially cancel one another out, as they do in this instance.

From the welter of interpretations of names, texts, and events found in *Riddley Walker* emerges a sense, not of the indeterminacy of meaning, but rather of meaning inherent in things, meaning which may be expressed in many ways. As the wisewoman Lorna Elswint says, "You hear diffrent things in all them way back storys but it dont make no diffrents.... What they are is diffrent ways of telling what happent" (20). Riddley relates, for example, a story told to account for a place name. The original teller of the story admits, though, that the place really got its name in a more prosaic manner. Where did the false etymology come from? The storyteller says, "that story come in to my head. That story cudnt come out of no where cud it so it musve come out of some where. Parbly it ben in that place from time back way back or may be in a nother place only the idear of it come to me there" (93-94). But although meaning is inherent in the place or the icon, Hoban suggests that interpretations can vary in worth, and what distinguishes helpful interpretations from destructive ones is the motivation of the teller. Stories which come to the storyteller of themselves are likely to contain at least some of the essence of true meaning. Interpreters like Goodparley, greedy to make use of the instrumental power of words, are apt to go wrong. "Words!" he says to Riddley, "Theywl move things you know theywl do things. Theywl fetch" (122). But what they fetch for power-seekers is violence and death.

Riddley suspects from the beginning that this preoccupation with power and the resulting self-division are unnatural. His goal is to find out "what the idear of us myt be" (7). As Lorna Elswint has told him, there is "1 girt thing bigger nor the worl and lorn and loan and oansome" which "thinks us but...don't think *like* us." This universal being is always in process, always "in the woom of things," never completed. "Our woal life," says Riddley, "is a idear we dint think of nor we dont know what it is. What a way to live" (7-8).

Riddley's quest to discover "the idear of us" begins as he finds himself increasingly cut off from his group and their patterns of thought. Very little of Riddley's development is planned; his changes are experiential. Upon becoming connexion man after his father's death at the first of the novel, he plans to develop his connexions carefully, point by point. But when his first opportunity comes, he goes into a trance and does not speak; he only imagines his "reveal" (62). In spite of himself he is moving away from conventional patterns of thought. The process continues after he leaves his tribe and discovers that he is "dog frendy" (85), taken up and protected by one of the packs of wild dogs which represent alienated Nature. Although at the beginning of civilization they let man see the night reflected in their eyes and thus gave him his "1st knowing" of the primal female principle which gives birth to everything (18), after the holocaust they have refused to show their eyes. Having been allowed to look into their eyes, Riddley senses that he has come into contact with "1st knowing," though he does not yet understand its significance.

The process of his development is marked by his incessant movement, his "roading," like that of the Eusa showmen and of Eusa himself after his fall. In the course of his travels he comes under the influence of representatives of four different approaches to knowledge: an intuitive theoretical scientist, Lissener; a progressive politician, the Pry Mincer Goodparley; his dour conservative opponent, the "Shadder Mincer" Ernie Orfing; and a practical technician, Granser. The first two have considerable appeal for Riddley, though ultimately he abandons all of them except Orfing and follows his own way.

The first of the four for whom Riddley feels sympathy is Lissener, the current Ardship of Cambry, whom Riddley rescues from the ritual questioning and execution which are the fate of each Ardship when he reaches manhood. Lissener is Riddley's "moon brother" (79), exactly his age, and also his Jungian Shadow: whereas Riddley is a walker, Lissener listens; he seeks power through the storing up of theoretical knowledge. He is the present leader of the Eusa folk, the deformed descendents of Eusa and the puter leat who controlled nuclear energy and brought on the holocaust. Both he and his people are fragmented; only when they gather together to "do some poasyum" (107), a form of computer networking using only liveware, can they put together scraps of their hereditary memory of theoretical science. Lissener's concerns are elitist and abstract, and his "some poasyum" ultimately results in violence. Riddley learns from him how to listen better, but eventually rejects his path.

Lissener's opponent, the Pry Mincer, sees knowledge pragmatically as a means of getting Inland moving "frontways" (41) and uses whatever means come to hand: "Spare the mending and tryl narrer" (119). His men direct excavations for old bits of machinery, hoping to discover "Eusa's head," the storehouse of knowledge. Every twelve years he conducts the ritual questionings of the Ardship to try to recapture knowledge of the "1 Big 1," a process which ends always in failure and the ritual murder of the Ardship. His most elaborate attempt to probe the past for the knowledge he seeks is his interpretation of a museum guide description of the fifteenth-century mural *The Legend of St. Eustace* which inspired Hoban to write the novel (*Riddley Walker*, "Acknowledgments" n.p.). From the description the reader sees that the images of the painting are the same as those described in the Eusa story. Eusa is thus more than just an allegory for the U.S.A.;

he looks back to a fifteenth-century representation of a second-century saint's realization of an even more fundamental pattern of human life, a pattern which involves a glimpse of spiritual truth but which ends in separation from family and in death. Goodparley's interpretation of the description, on the other hand, is ingenious but thoroughly pragmatic: he sees the figures as alchemical symbols for the process which will produce the "1 Big 1." He is only partly wrong: his pursuit of power will lead him unknowingly to follow Eusa's road to blinding, ostracism, and death.

Less immediately sympathetic are the Shadder Mincer Orfing and Goodparley's old teacher, Ganser. Orfing appears to be pure negation, denying even the possibility of human improvement. Ganser is simply a technician. Nuclear weapons are beyond him, but he knows the formula for the "1 Littl 1" (181), gunpowder. When in the course of the novel the last ingredient, sulfur, becomes available to him, he makes up a batch without any thought for larger consequences and accidentally blows up both himself and Goodparley.

All four of these characters search for knowledge as a form of control, whether theoretical, political, or physical, and all bring on violence and destruction. For a time Riddley, too, is caught up in a similar wonder at human understanding and control of Nature. As he and Lissener look at the ruined machinery of a nuclear power plant, Riddley says,

> Tears begun streaming down my face and my froat akit.
> Lissener hispert, 'Whats the matter?'
> I hispert back, 'O what we ben! And what we come to!'
>
> * * *
>
> How cud any 1 not want to get that shyning Power back from time back way back? How cud any 1 not want to be like them what had boats in the air and picters on the wind? (100)

Up until this point he has opposed Goodparley and his dream of putting the Littl Shynin Man back together, but now he understands Goodparley's vision. Later in the novel Riddley's sense of the awesome power in Nature becomes even stronger, yet he comes finally to reject the drive to control power. He becomes, not passive, but increasingly spontaneous and open to experience.

The defining event in Riddley's growing understanding of "what the idear of us myt be" comes to him as he makes his way to the ruins of Canterbury Cathedral. He has known, of course, that Cambry, or Canterbury, was the center of power, the location of Eusa's great Power Ring before the coming of Bad Time. But he learns only now of the spiritual power that the place possessed long before Eusa's time. His experience is both mystical and sexual. Feeling first the remnants of the physical power of the place, he experiences it as masculine, a "Big Old Father" (159) which takes him sexually; and he feels, for the last time, the desire to possess power himself. But the fundamental spirit of the place is feminine, and Riddley passes beyond the desire to know and to master. He goes through a period of revulsion against all power but discovers finally that he can

Feal the goast of old Power circeling hy over me. Only this time I fealt a Power in me what circelt with it. Membering when that thot come to me: THE ONLYES POWER IS NO POWER. Wel now I sust that wernt qwite it. It aint that its *no* Power. Its the not sturgling for Power thats where the Power is. Its in jus letting your self be where it is. Its tuning in to the worl its leaving your self behynt and letting your self be.... (197)

Yet even at this stage of understanding, Riddley is incomplete, for he still feels a spiritual restlessness which grows out of two things: his inability to accept death and his fear that the very vitality of the world that he loves is amoral. He must continue his roadings and riddlings.

   The form that Riddley's quest takes at the end of the novel is that of art—an improvised puppet show like the Eusa shows he has known. But Eusa is the property of the establishment, so Riddley turns to two more ancient puppets he has discovered in his diggings: Punch and a figure he names Greenvine. Greenvine, the head of a man with vines growing out of its mouth, embodies both Riddley's sense of the unity of man and Nature and his revulsion against death. Greenvine is Everyman,

dying back in to the earf and the vines growing up thru his arse hoal up thru his gullit and out of his mouf.... A man myt get 100s of childer but the onlyes new life growing out of him wil be that dead mans vine at the end of his run. (168)

On the other hand, literally, is the irrepressible Punch of the traditional Punch and Judy show, a figure of enormous, completely amoral vitality. Punch's wife in this show has become Pooty, a pig, and their baby is a piglet, but the other puppets are traditional, including the Devil and Drop John, a ghost. The show as Riddley performs it is full of sex and violence, with Punch murdering everyone in sight, doing his best to eat the baby and feeling the weight of Drop John on his back.

   Riddley's itinerant Punch show expresses his understanding of the human search for truth. He has abandoned the quest for dualistic knowledge and power in favor of "1st knowing" and the sense of unity between himself and Nature. Still his awareness of a mysterious perversity in the human heart remains. At Canterbury he has learned that

   Them as made Canterbury musve put ther selfs right. Only it dint stay right did it. Somers in be twean them stoan trees and the Power Ring they musve put ther selfs wrong....
   May be all there ever ben wer jus only 1 minim when anything cud be right and that minim all ways gone befor you seen it. May be soons that 1st stoan tree stood up the wrongness hung there in the branches of it the wrongness ben the 1st frute of the tree. (162)

He has had a glimpse of "what we ben," but his understanding of "what we come to" is necessarily incomplete because the "idear of us" is always in the process of becoming. Riddley finds that he can continue his explorations best through the spontaneous interpretation of the icons of the old puppet show. At the end of the novel he asks,

Why is Punch crookit? Why wil he all ways kil the babby if he can? parbly I wont never know its jus on me to think on it. (220)

Riddley Walker presents Hoban's vision of a world radically flawed by the human desire for knowledge and power. His solution to its problems lies not in technological knowledge but in Riddley's continual exploration of the meaning of fundamental patterns of human life. It is a hard path, but Riddley says, "Stil I wunt have no other track" (220).

Note

[1]For a fuller account of the relationship, see my article, "The Quest for Wholeness" pages 33-38.

Works Cited

Branscomb, Jack. "The Quest for Wholeness in the Fiction of Russell Hoban." *Critique* 28.1 (Fall 1986): 29-38.
Dowling, David. Fictions of *Nuclear Disaster*. Iowa City: U. of Iowa, 1987.
Hoban, Russell. *Pilgermann*. NY: Washington Square, 1984.
—. *Riddley Walker*. NY: Summit Books, 1980.
Lively, Penelope. Review of *Riddley Walker*. *Encounter* 56:1 (Jan. 1981): 58-59.

Reinventing a World:
Myth in Denis Johnson's *Fiskadoro*

Millicent Lenz

When Riddley Walker cries out, "O what we ben! And what we come to!"—lamenting the irremediable loss of an entire civilization, much of his regret is for the death of "the idear of us," the idea of what it means to be human (Hoban 100, 7). In traditional societies with fully functioning mythologies, "the idear of us" is valorized through heroic myths. The four functions of myth as identified by Joseph Campbell are pertinent to the search for identity and coherent meaning in life. A functioning mythology, according to Campbell, (1) awakens and maintains a "sense of awe and gratitude" in the face of the mysteries of the universe; (2) provides a cosmology, an image of the universe in accord with contemporary scientific thought; (3) validates and supports the norms of the contemporary moral order; and lastly, (4) guides the person through the stages of life, from childhood, through puberty, to competent adulthood, and ultimately through death, in "health, strength, and harmony of spirit..." (*Myths to Live By* 221-222).

The post-cataclysmic world can supply none of these cultural comforts, and the very mention of them in connection with the realities of life in a nuclear wasteland may seem ludicrous. Nuclear holocaust shatters everything, including cultures, ideas, myths, and languages, leaving the human spirit shorn of all but an intense longing for what anthropologist Gregory Bateson called "a pattern that connects" (Capra 71-89). The myths of a society, which Campbell described as an "exterior 'second womb,' " protecting the psyche as it grows to its full potential in a given cultural setting ("Bios and Mythos" 53), disintegrate in the wake of atomic cataclysm. It is equally true to remark that the inner absence of meaning and coherence— the lack of a living mythology—makes the proliferation of the weapons of destruction possible: the void within allows the rule of "Dr. Strangegod," in Ira Chernus's astute phrase. *Fiskadoro* explores the spiritual lack that leads human beings to use force upon one another, and the reader is allowed a glimpse into the abyss, the inner emptiness at the root of all war. It is, thus, a cautionary tale that can help to illuminate the inadequacy of the contemporary myths by which we live and die.

The mythic elements of Denis Johnson's *Fiskadoro* highlight the protagonist's coming-of-age and also show why the Campbellian monomyth provides an inadequate paradigm for a nuclear age. Russell Hoban's *Riddley*

Walker supplies some parallels and contrasts. Though these two novels are markedly different, they have in common protagonists who seek wholeness in a fragmented society and endeavor to reconstruct meaningful myth in their efforts to reinvent a world. The youthful protagonists' experiences simultaneously reflect and diverge from the tripartite pattern of the mythological hero's journey as described by Joseph Campbell. My chief concern will be Johnson's story, viewed as a tale about coming-of-age in a world deprived of myth.

In a post-cataclysmic world, the mythology of the shattered culture is bound to be lacking as a guide in the process of growing to maturity. The traditional heroic rhetoric fails when the culture disintegrates. To supply a perspective on a post-cataclysmic world where all has been turned topsy-turvy, I have sought a mythic model in a seemingly unlikely place: the mock-heroic tradition of comedy (as incongruous it may appear to mention comedy in the same breath as nuclear cataclysm) as elaborated in Joseph W. Meeker's study, *The Comedy of Survival: In Search of an Environmental Ethic.*

At the outset of *Fiskadoro*, a mysterious narrator who invokes the compassion and mercy of Allah introduces the three central figures of the narrative: A.T. Cheung, Grandmother Wright, and the boy Fiskadoro, who is cryptically called "the only one who was ready when we came" (12).

Fiskadoro is a bright, restless, black thirteen-year-old, who bears a name redolent with mythic connotations, derived from *pescador*, fisherman, and *fisgador*, harpooner, terms endowing him with a link to Christ, fisher for the souls of humankind. In their miserable shanties, his tribe of fisherfolk turn for entertainment to the garbled news and old rock music on Cubaradio, and try to find meaning for their lives and cures for their ills from practitioners of voodoo. Sometimes they join in the orgiastic, rock music soundshows of the Israelites, a tribe of pseudo-Islamic blacks who live in dismantled boats along the seashore. Fiskadoro's fascination with music, shown in his devotion to the clarinet, suggests an affinity with Pan, albeit an ironic one, for music, like all else in his world, has suffered a tragic devolution. He shares the love of music with A.T. Cheung, a sensitive middle-aged man, director of the pathetic, grandiosely-named "Miami Symphony Orchestra," who yearns to keep history and classical music alive in the midst of barbarism, and agrees to tutor Fiskadoro on the clarinet without charge. The third major character, Grandmother Wright, half Chinese, half British, and now over 100 years old, is the only person alive who remembers the pre-holocaust civilization. Her muteness symbolically represents the silencing of historical memory.

The three major characters are embodiments of different modes of consciousness. As central character, Fiskadoro is the growing, developing one, though in a real sense his growth comes about through the peeling away of his separate identity. He passes through the three stages of Campbell's monomyth of heroic adventure: separation, initiation, and return, but in the ironic mode of the book, his ability to deliver the traditional "boon" to his people, to transform the wasteland into a fertile, life-giving garden, is gravely in doubt, and he must virtually invent his own mythology. His life is fraught with more than ordinary coming-of-age traumas as he endures initiation into the realities of death and sexuality—his father drowns at sea, his mother is afflicted with "killme," radiation-induced cancer, and the lad himself undergoes a traumatic, drug-involved initiation rite of ritual subincision conducted by the Quraysh, a tribe of quasi-Islamic swampdwellers who capture him to replace one of their own youths who drowned in a wild orgy by the sea. The initiation is conducted by Abu-Lab, whose name means "Father of the Flames"; a shamanic figure, he hypnotically creates in Fiskadoro a religious frenzy to be "like" other men (175, 177). Ironically, Fiskadoro's need to become like the Quraysh men results in his loss of memory, and his self-inflicted sexual wound leaves him unlike the men of his own culture. This "likeness-difference" endows him nonetheless, like the legendary blind prophet Tiresias, with peculiar shamanic powers and vision. In a mythic sense, he achieves a mystical marriage with the feminine, intuitive side of his own nature, becoming a conduit of the racial memory, the collective unconscious, which is without gender, or rather androgynous, encompassing both masculine and feminine principles.

Fiskadoro's transformation of consciousness and myth-making powers are bought at the price of his individual identity. In the post-cataclysmic world where misinformation, ignorance and pseudomyth prevail, human beings seek meaning in personal myths forged out of a triumph over their own sorrows. Spiritually impoverished, they must create new myths or resign themselves to the half-lives of the depressed masses. In a remarkably powerful flashback, Fiskadoro relives this initiation rite and the narrative relates how, at one point in it, he remembered his own birth, his awakening in the world.

In contrast to Fiskadoro, Cheung exhibits an historical/mystical consciousness. He seeks meaning and coherence in the attempt to recover historical knowledge. When he listens to the reading of a factual account of the bombing of Hiroshima, he reacts so vividly that he believes he has actually experienced the event but comes to realize how the bomb has destroyed history, causing the now universal amnesia. Mysteriously, he and the other listeners suffer headache, nausea, and other stereotypical symptoms of radiation sickness. Cheung's suggestibility combines with his susceptibility to attacks of something like epilepsy, during which he experiences mystical visions of a White Dot he believes to be the Nucleus of the Atomic Bomb. His world has mythologized its defective memory of the bomb, as evidenced by the legendary status of atomic bomb pilot Colonel Major Overdoze, whose memory is invoked by a practitioner of voodoo in her unsuccessful effort to cure Fiskadoro's mother of "killme," radiation-induced cancer. An archetypal conservative, who does not care for rock music, Cheung views the cataclysm of nature and time as "the rocknroll of destruction." He realizes he is "aligned" only with the past, not with "anything real." "I am against everything," he declares, in a lucid moment. He feels the spiritual energy of the Israelites' soundshow but resists being caught up because he cannot identify with "forces" for which he has no empathy. Provoked by a melon vendor's commercialism, Cheung calls him a "decayed person" and mocks the man's ignorance of the historical fact that once money was managed by electronic machines (124, 117, 118).

Books, most of them half-decayed, function in the novel as icons of the simultaneous drive for meaning and fear of knowing; the people who gather at the library are both keenly desiring knowledge of Nagasaki and terrified of possessing it. Cheung has memorized as great a quantity of historical fact as he can, as for instance the names of the American states and the Declaration of Independence. Yet these modes of knowing—through books or through rote memory—are not valorized in the novel. Rather, it is *direct*, unmediated experiences of reality, the shamanic mode exemplified by Fiskadoro and the mystical mode seen in both Cheung and his Grandmother Wright, that are finally prized. Cheung's presence in the book accents the tragedy of having to sever oneself from the nightmare of history; he comes to believe that the memory of the lost past, so dear to him, must be extinguished in order to retain sanity. This explains why Fiskadoro, innocent of memory, is admirably fitted for survival.

Cheung's historical-mystical and Fiskadoro's shamanic modes of consciousness show both similarities and differences with Grandmother Wright's mode of interior monologue/dream vision. Virtually mute, she is a mythic figure, incarnating the silenced muse of history, a living reminder of the paradise-now-lost—the world before the End of the previous civilization. Simultaneously, nonetheless, she embodies the mystery of survival by gratuitous accident. As Cheung's ancient grandmother, her life has spanned the Vietnam War, the "End of the World" (the nuclear holocaust), and the present desolation. She expresses the mystery of life's persistence, the sheer wonder of survival through mere rescue. Her presence reinforces the antiwar theme: by being rescued from the madness of Vietnam, she exemplifies the need for the help of a spiritual resource transcending the individual ego. Physically slight, she looms over the narrative as a chthonic figure, memorializing the atomized past civilization at the same time as she expresses the primal life force. Her insights into the nature of reality and time are imaged through fire, as when she beholds the flame she sees through the window of the big kitchen stove as "the filament of time...never tangled...a deep red event" that confirms her intuitive sense of what *is*:

It catches, then burns, then blazes; it rages and sings, it wanes, it shifts and flares, it burns a little longer and then weakens, whatever it is, and goes out. But if you lay the small wood across it in the morning, it all begins again.... Whatever it was, it was happening now, today, all of it, this very moment. This very moment—*now*, changing and staying the same—was the fire. (125)

(Those familiar with Richard Rolle and other medieval mystics will recognize the tradition of fire imagery). This is the essence of life, to change yet stay the same, and though Grandmother Wright finds a certain peace in her vision, she also plumbs a sorrow that goes beyond tears. The simple joys of her girlhood in Saigon contrast with her present "drowning" in "the wet cement of old age," hardly able to move her limbs, not even able to cry, for "the holes for tears were pinched shut, and her eyes were always as dry as two corks." (125) Her mute suffering and Fiskadoro's inability to remember, much less articulate what he undergoes, show Johnson's fascination with characters who cannot voice their own tragedies (Wojahn 38).

Like Fiskadoro, Grandmother Wright is twice-born, for her rescue from the China Sea is a scene of transformation: alone in the water, she drifts with the sense of "a perfect and invaluable presence, a rubble of treasure growing up from the bottom of the world...until it touched and lifted her...." With a shock, she finds herself at "the bottom of everything..." (215, 216). At the novel's close, she relives the experience of a floating spiritual presence, as she sees the "white vessel" on the horizon, and speculates that it may be a ghostship floating both in the air, and "in the heart of Allah, the Compassionate, the Merciful" (220). Her waking up, as narrated in the last statement of the book, may signify her death, mythically treated as a birth into another dimension: "And in her state of waking, she jerked awake. And from that waking, she woke up" (221).

In this closing beach scene, redolent with memories of other beaches in nuclear literature, all owing something to Matthew Arnold's "Dover Beach," Grandmother Wright's mode of consciousness provides a counterpoint to the modes displayed by Fiskadoro and Cheung, and the difference between the latter two is made vivid through interplay. Cheung and Fiskadoro have agreed to play for an Israelite festival. With his expanded consciousness, Fiskadoro can now play the clarinet beautifully, like a musical idiot savant, tapping the melodies buried in the collective unconscious of the race. The ancient Grandmother, brought along to witness, indulges in a reverie of her past, as related above. Cheung, who has experienced an unnameable terror from witnessing the fact that Fiskadoro's memory could be abolished, meditates on the cyclic nature of time and the "quiet knife" in the mind that constitutes the awareness of personal mortality (216). He sees himself and Fiskadoro "standing between two civilizations"—that of the people and that of the seagulls, whose eyes were "too tiny to hold any questions" (219). On another level, the "two civilizations" refer to the one lost and the yet-unknown impending civilization-to-come. Fiskadoro sees the seagulls, in their presumption of knowledge—their "flat assumption like small professors"—as resembling Cheung, and he communicates this perception to Cheung in a meaningful glance. This insight provides the clue to Fiskadoro's mode of consciousness: intuitively, he sees into the analogies between nature and human nature. His insight reveals the dilemma of the human condition: for to "hold questions" is the role of our human "eyes" and *humility* the fruit of knowing we do not know the answers. Fiskadoro's last interchange with Cheung, his last speech in the novel, is a confession of ignorance: indicating with a gesture the arc of the heavens, he says simply, "I don't know what es." Cheung assures him he does not know either, "but we're here." Possibly, Grandmother Cheung, he tells Fiskadoro, alone among all humankind, may remember "what is" (217). She is, of course, not telling.

It is when Cheung perceives how Fiskadoro sees him—as like the seagulls in his arrogance—that he is able to accept the cycle of time, the "pattern-that-connects," as one of eternal recurrence. Cheung's prophecy that Fiskadoro will be a great leader harmonizes with the prophecy of Flying Man, an Israelite friend of Cheung, who explains the occasion for the celebration: "Bobbylon allover now. Time nex' planet now—planet Israh-el!" (207). The Israelites are followers of Allah, who proclaim the coming ascendancy of their deity, Jah. A new beginning is clearly at hand, but the reader may well wonder, with William Butler Yeats in his poem "The Second Coming," "what rough beast. . ./Slouches towards Bethlehem to be born?"

In ways both similar and different, the twelve-year-old Riddley Walker of Hoban's novel lives out the separation and initiation stages of Campbell's monomyth, with the "return" stage again aborted by the absence of a social construct capable of receiving his message of spiritual insight. Nonetheless, Riddley's movement from fascination with power as "control" (the technological mode of consciousness) to the realization of the internal, spiritual powers of his creative gifts (his story-weaving, "connexion man" consciousness), and his assimilation of the "1st knowing" (the feminine, intuitive knowledge gleaned through Lorna Elswint and her telling of the myth of "Why the Dog Wont show its Eyes") points to the emergence of a primordial, biologically based mythic model. This ecologically-based mythic model may be able to bring *bios* and *ethos* into balance and succeed in transforming the mentality of the nuclear wasteland into the consciousness that prizes and nurtures life.

Hoban's novel is set some two thousand years in the future, and mythology in the twelve-year-old Riddley's world is (though crude) more highly developed than in Fiskadoro's. I shall, in this limited space, paint only some broad-brush contrasts and comparisons, and a number of richly elaborated tales, central to the novel's full mythic meaning, must remain unexplored. Riddley, like Fiskadoro, suffers the loss of his father very early in the narrative. His mother "dyd of the coffing sickness" when he was five (15). His father is killed when a "girt old black machine" being lifted by a crew of men and boys falls down into the "muck" with his dad under it. The machine is a relic of the precataclysmic civilization, and Riddley's ignorance of its name throws him into a temporary state of hysteria: " 'My dad ben kilt by some thing I dont even know the name of aint that a larf.' I begun larfing then I cudnt stop" (11). Riddley takes his father's place as the "connexion man," the one responsible for performing the "Eusa" story, the major myth of his culture, which attempts to explain the origin of the atomic bomb (the "1 Big 1") in the ruthless pursuit of power through technology, and the "Fall" that resulted.

Like Fiskadoro, Riddley undergoes an initiation with sexual and mystical dimensions; for Riddley, this occurs at the site of the ruins of Cambry (Canterbury), also the site of a ruined nuclear power plant. Spellbound by the primal feminine life force he feels concentrated there, the power of "her what has her woom in Cambry" (161), he meditates among the "stoan trees" that once buttressed the cathedral. These stone trees are associated with imagery of the "appel" (an allusion to Adam) and of the "hanging man" (Christ) (161). Riddley thinks the people who made Canterbury must have been "bettern us," for they must have known how to "put ther selfs with the Power of the wood be come stoan" and mastered "the idear in the hart of every thing." In other words, they were mystically literate, in harmony with the Riddle of Being. The imagery blends the musical with the mystical, for he imagines how these gifted forebears must have been able to move in harmony with "the girt dants [dance] of the every thing the 1 Big 1 the Master Chaynjis" (162).

The intuitive Riddley senses, however, that between the magnificent "stoan trees" of the once glorious cathedral and the Power Rings of the nuclear plant nearby, something went profoundly wrong. "Them as made Cambry" somehow "put ther selfs wrong." Rightness with the transcendent cannot be long sustained; there may be, he thinks, "only 1 minim when any thing cud be right and that minim all ways gone befor you seen it." Wrongness may be the "1st frute of the tree" (162). When he beholds the "stoan man" figure, with green leaves and vines growing out of the orifices, he sees it as the face of Everyman.[1] Riddley calls this stoan man "Greanvine," and it is Greanvine's countenance that leads Riddley to a moment of epiphany in which he proclaims, " 'THE ONLYES POWER IS NO POWER' " (167). Thus he rejects "power as control," the power of technology, misused by those who brought on the Bad Time.

It is in his realization of the limits on human "seeing" that Riddley most resembles the picaresque figure of mock-heroic comedy described by Meeker as the most life-affirming paradigm for our imperilled times. Meeker writes out of his concern with "the widely spread cultural ideology which has contributed to our contemporary ecological crisis," rooted, he argues, in the outmoded view that ascribes nobility to the "tragic hero," an alienated and prideful figure whose ascendancy as a cultural ideal has "led to cultural and biological disaster" (xv, 17). The tragic view leads inevitably to war, whereas the comic view requires accommodation to limits—one's own and those of nature, and encourages reconciliation as the ideal—values peace above principle. "The comic point of view is that man's high moral ideals and glorified heroic poses," based on illusions, lead to misery or death. The lesson of comedy, "humility and endurance," agrees with "ecological wisdom" and provides a model for human behavior in our era (40, 41, 49). Dante's "comedy of salvation," he adds, "translates in our time into the comedy of survival." Hell, in Dante's scheme, equals imprisonment in one's private vision, in the pollution of self-absorption; purgatory equals the awareness of others and their claims as equal to our own; and paradise is a mode of consciousness expanded to celebrate the complex unity of Being (49, 137).

Humility, so valued in Meeker's paradigm, is an ancient virtue; it is the "pearl" of medieval Christian theology. Campbell's recounting of the tale of the Vedic-Aryan deity, Indra, who discovers he is but one of innumerable, perishing Indras, demonstrates a yet more ancient view of the wisdom of the humble. In Campbell's thought, as in Meeker's, humility has its roots in a larger perspective, what Campbell calls the "cosmic view" (*Inner Reaches of Outer Space* 50). What is missing in Campbell's monomyth, however, is an ecological dimension. This lack constitutes its failure as a model for the kind of self-transcendence required for coming-to-age in a nuclear wasteland.

Fiskadoro shows Johnson's valuing of what Meeker calls the "picaresque" mode of action—which uses the intellect to study immediate realities, and the imagination to create strategies for survival. The pastoral mode, rejected by Meeker along with the tragic, seeks what we *ought* to be, and criticizes present inadequacies by romanticizing of a simpler, more innocent way of life. The tragic view is egocentric, prizing the human personality as supreme, and placing morality ahead of "natural limitations," thus subverting, Meeker argues, the "natural world" (104). The comic view of life has preeminent survival value, for its essential message is humility before life and its processes.

Fiskadoro, having lost all connections with the past and hence with all traditions of morality, must draw upon the collective unconscious to create a new myth of origin for his world. Like Riddley, he must reinvent a personal mythology out of fragments of the old; they share the qualities of the shaman, endowed with intuitive and mystical modes of knowledge. Both have artistic natures, but Fiskadoro's medium is music, Riddley's is words. Riddley's calling is to articulate myth for others. Only Riddley, however, possesses metaphorical insights: he sees the world as a "great dance." In the Greanvine sequence he comes close to grasping an ecologically-based mythic model for a world of complex interdependencies. Only such a mythology, which incorporates an "ecology of mind," a view of the "survival unit" as resting upon the health of the total system (Bateson's "cybernetic epistemology"),[2] can answer our coming-of-nuclear-age needs.

Notes

[1]Riddley reflects on the face of the "Ardship"—a corruption of "Archbishop"—as different in kind, for he no longer shares the universally human countenance, being sadly deformed by genetic mutation and centuries of inbreeding among the "Eusa" folk, both revered and despised for their psychic powers. The implications for the state of religion in Riddley's world are clear.

²For Bateson's views, which harmonize well with Meeker's, see "Form, Substance, and Difference," in *Steps to an Ecology of Mind* (New York: Ballantine Books, 1972), 460 ff.

Works Cited

Campbell, Joseph. "Bios and Mythos." *The Flight of the Wild Gander: Explorations in the Mythological Dimension*. New York: Viking, 1969.

———. *The Inner Reaches of Outer Space*. New York: Alfred Van Der Marck Editions, 1985.

———. *Myths to Live By*. Foreword by Johnson E. Fairchild. New York: Bantam Books, 1973.

Capra, Fritjof. "The Pattern Which Connects: Gregory Bateson," in *Uncommon Wisdom: Conversations with Remarkable People*. New York: Bantam, 1988, 71-89.

Chernus, Ira. *Dr. Strangegod: On the Symbolic Meaning of Nuclear Weapons*. Columbia: University of South Carolina Press, 1986.

Hoban, Russell. *Riddley Walker*. New York: Summit Books, 1980.

Johnson, Denis. *Fiskadoro*. New York: Vintage, 1986.

Meeker, Joseph W. *The Comedy of Survival: In Search of an Environmental Ethic*. Foreword by Konrad Lorenz. Introduction by Paul Shepard. Illustrated by William Berry. Los Angeles: International College Guild of Tutors Press, 1980.

Wojan, David and Linda Hull. "The Kind of Light I'm Seeing: An Interview with Denis Johnson." *Ironwood*, No. 25 (1985): 31-44.

Haiku and Hiroshima:
Hara Tamiki

Richard H. Minear

Poets have reacted to the atomic holocaust at Hiroshima with poetry of various forms. These include free verse, running in some poems to 100 lines or more; tanka, the traditional form with lines of 5, 7, 5, 7, and 7 syllables; and haiku. All poetry—indeed, all writing—faces an immense challenge in dealing with holocaust, be it atomic holocaust or any other. But at least at first glance haiku seems the form least suited to the event, for the epiphanies haiku normally celebrates seem wholly out of proportion to the subject. Yet haiku poets have not been deterred from attempting to deal with Hiroshima. In 1983, a Tokyo press published a 15-volume compendium of "the atomic bomb literature of Japan." Volume XIII, devoted to poetry, includes almost 800 haiku about Hiroshima drawn from anthologies published in 1955 and 1969, and these haiku constitute only a fraction of all the haiku written about Hiroshima.

The most distinguished literary figure to deal with Hiroshima in haiku was Hara Tamiki (1905-1951). Forty years old in August 1945, he survived the bomb to write the classic literary account of the experience, *Summer Flowers* (*Natsu no hana*, 1949). *Summer Flowers* includes a single free-verse poem, and Hara also published a collection of free-verse poems about Hiroshima (a total of nine poems). Nearly 300 of Hara's haiku survive, haiku he composed between 1935 and 1945. A few of the poems of 1945 treat the conventional bombing of Tokyo, which Hara also experienced; 23 treat the atomic bombing of Hiroshima and its aftermath. Except for the 23, Hara composed no haiku after August 6. In form, Hara's haiku are quite traditional. In them he specifies the time of year and the setting and records something that had an impact on his emotions.

More than most poetic forms haiku defies translation. In the following English-language renditions of Hara's 23 atomic-bomb haiku, I have leaned to the literal side, sometimes at the expense of the poetic. Where possible, I offer commentary based on Hara's other writings.

The Poems
Summer fields:
fragments of nightmare

Modern Haiku Volume 19:1 pp. 11-17 (Winter-Spring 1988).

flash before my eyes.

After August 6 Hara took refuge in a village west of Hiroshima. There apparently he wrote most if not all of these haiku. In *Summer Flowers* he writes of the late-summer fields (p. 28): "It was a scene too beautiful to be real. No longer was there fear of air raid; now the great sky wore an air of deep tranquility. I felt like a person newly fallen to earth with that one clap of the atomic bomb. Still, what of the people who had died desperate deaths that day on the riverbed near Nigitsu and on the riverbank by the Asano Villa? In contrast with this quiet scene, what has become of those charred ruins?" These are presumably the specters that Hara refers to here and in the 20th haiku.

> Summer night:
> ruined mountains, rivers
> cry out with one voice.

> Flaming trees
> dance up
> into the angry autumn sky.

These two haiku hark back to August 6 and 7 in Hiroshima. Hara began taking notes for *Summer Flowers* on August 7, less than 36 hours after the bomb; but he does not mention attempts at haiku. The line "summer night" is "brief night" in the original, the brevity a function of the season. In *Summer Flowers* Hara gives another account of flaming trees (p. 10): "...I noticed, in the sky downstream above the middle of the river, an absolutely translucent layer of air trembling and moving toward us. A tornado, I thought; and at that very moment violent winds were already blowing overhead. The trees and plants all around me trembled; suddenly, I saw many trees above my head sucked up by the wind, just like that, and carried off into the sky. Dancing crazily in the air, the trees fell with the force of arrows into the midst of the maelstrom." The line I have translated "into the angry autumn sky" reads literally "into the thunderstorm." I have translated it this way for these reasons: there was no thunderstorm on August 6; Hara may have used that term to set the season rather than to be taken literally; in Japan as elsewhere, thunder and lightning are often thought of as the anger of the gods.

> The heat of the sun:
> crape myrtle full
> of the stench of death.

Crape myrtles, red, presumably remind Hara of blood. The scene is likely Hiroshima weeks after August 6, when flowers blossomed in profusion. Hara did return to the city a number of times before leaving permanently for Tokyo.

The spring water
victims come and drink:
warm.

Corpses
even on a ladder:
high clouds.

Girls drinking,
dying:
the cicada's cry.

Fingernails into the next person's shoulder,
dead:
the summer moon.

These four poems speak to the immediate aftermath of August 6. Normally chilly, spring water in August is warm. The corpses on a ladder Hara mentions in *Summer Flowers* (p. 25). The standard advice for burn victims was not to drink anything; the cicada's short life presumably underlines the short lives of the girls. In *Summer Flowers* (p. 25) Hara tells of a scene someone reported to him: "In a line waiting for the bus, corpses were standing just as they had been; they had died with their fingernails sticking into the shoulder of the person ahead of them in the line." Reference to the moon underlines the fact that the corpses had not been disposed of by nightfall; indeed, it was weeks before all corpses were tended to.

Dullheaded,
I stoop over the river:
evening primrose.

Evening primroses are yellow; the literal meaning of their Japanese name is 'moon-viewing grass.' Presumably the scene is Hara's place of refuge in the hills.

Coming into view
once we pass the ruins:
a swarm of dragonflies.

Hara describes this scene in *Summer Flowers* (p. 23). It occurs as he departs Hiroshima on a horse-drawn cart: "The wagon proceeded along the road through the endless destruction. Even when we got to the suburbs, there were rows of flattened houses; when we passed Kusatsu, things finally were green, liberated from the color of calamity. The sight of a swarm of butterflies flying lightly and swiftly above green fields engraved itself on my eyes."

Autumn water:

> I walk
> the burned-out riverbank.

To attend the funeral of his brother-in-law some time after August 6, Hara walked along one of Hiroshima's many rivers. Here is the description from *Summer Flowers* (p. 42): "The destruction to left and right still called to mind some of the feelings I had had as I fled on the day of the bomb. When I came to Kyobashi Bridge, the burned-out embankment stretched as far as the eye could see, and distances were far more compressed than they had been. Come to think of it, I had noticed some time before that beyond the endless heaps of ruins the mountains were clearly visible. No matter how far one went, there were the same ashes...."

> Thinking how long I've been hungry,
> I walk in verdant paddy:
> a breeze stirs.

> Thinking how long I've been hungry,
> I walk in verdant paddy:
> the sound of the breeze.

> Sitting
> in someone else's bath:
> the cry of a new insect.

> Autumn rain:
> growing weaker,
> I nod off.

> Fleecy clouds:
> the sun grows faint
> on village persimmons.

> Indian summer:
> I walk,
> hungry as ever.

> November:
> across harvested paddy—
> Itsukushima.

These haiku relate to Hara's time in the village west of Hiroshima. Hunger was a fact of life, as Hara recounts in *Summer Flowers* (p. 29): "We lived every day in dire need of food. No one in this town extended a helping hand to the victims. Day after day we had to live on a bit of rice gruel, so increasingly exhausted, I became absurdly sleepy after eating. When I looked out from the second floor, I saw rice paddies stretching all the way to the foot of the low mountain range. Tall green rice plants quivered under the hot sun. Was this rice the fruit of the land? Or was it there in order to make people hungry? Sky, mountains, green fields: in the eyes of hungry people they might as well not have been there.'' Itsukushima, also known as Miyajima, is the famous shrine in Hiroshima Bay with its first torii—a huge one—out beyond the low-tide mark. The rice stalks block the view; once the harvest is in, the distant view reappears.

> Blizzard:
> in my mind's eye,
> specters.

> Daybreak,
> long-awaited:
> high clouds.

The implication here is of pain, either real or psychological, such that daybreak brings with it relief at having survived the night.

> Onion field:
> in someone's house
> the clock strikes.

Although only by implication, this poem suggests that Hara was in the onion patch to steal onions. There is nothing in *Summer Flowers* corresponding to this poem.

> Mountains right there:
> the sky does not fall—
> mountains right there.

The repetition of the first line is for emphasis. "The sky does not fall"—literally, the sky does not break open—refers either to autumn typhoons or to the atomic bomb. The sense is of relief and peacefulness, of the tranquility that elsewhere is jarred by specters of August 6. Here the emphasis is on the absence of disaster.

To this reader Hara's haiku dealing with Hiroshima are less effective than either his prose or his free verse on the same subject. Let me give an example of each. The single most moving passage in *Summer Flowers* tells of the chance discovery of the corpse of Hara's nephew. The passage constitutes an entire brief "chapter" of the work.

Loaded with my brother's household and Yasuko and me, the cart left Toshogu and went in the direction of Nigitsu. It happened as the cart set off from Hakushima toward the entrance of the Asano Villa. In an open area over toward the West Parade Ground my brother happened to spot a corpse clothed in yellow shorts he recognized. He got off the cart and went over. My sister-in-law and then I also left the cart and converged on the spot. In addition to the familiar shorts, the corpse wore an unmistakable belt. The body was that of my nephew Fumihiko. He had no jacket; there was a fist-sized swelling on his chest, and fluid was flowing from it. His face had turned pitch-black, and the white gleam of teeth could barely be seen. Though his arms were flung out, the fingers of both hands were clenched tightly, the nails biting into the palms. Next to his body was the corpse of a junior high school student and, farther off, the corpse of a young girl, all rigid just as they had died. My brother pulled off Fumihiko's fingernails, took his belt as a memento, attached a name tag, and left. It was an encounter beyond tears.

Two pages later comes the encounter with the swarm of butterflies. It is perhaps significant that Hara treated the latter in haiku but not the former.

Hara wrote only a handful of free verse dealing with the atomic bomb. One of the most moving is entitled "Water, Please!"

> Water, please!
> Ah, water, please!
> Give me a drink!
> Better to have died!
> Died
> Ah
> Help! Help!
> Water
> Water
> Somehow
> Someone
> > Ohhhhh
> > Ohhhhh
>
> The sky was ripped open
> The city, destroyed
> The river
> flows
> > Ohhhhh
> > Ohhhhh
>
> Night is falling
> Night is falling
> In dried up eyes
> In inflamed lips
> In faces
> burned and smarting
> dizzy
> hideous
> the moans of humanity
> the moans

Hara Tamiki's haiku about the atomic bomb are less impressive than either his prose or his free verse. But they do mark the serious attempt by the most distinguished writer-survivor of Hiroshima to express aspects of that experience in the form of haiku. As such, they constitute a significant chapter in the history of haiku.

Waging Nuclear War Rationally: Strategic 'Thought' in Arthur Kopit's *End of the World*

Daniel L. Zins

Endeavoring to fathom the positive appeal of nuclear weapons, Ira Chernus concludes that they have helped us to face the ever-mounting absurdity of technological rationality gone wild

by suggesting that a world so deeply steeped in madness might not be real at all. Ill and evils that are unreal do not need to be confronted or coped with; a world that is unreal is actually easier to accept. More specifically...the Bomb has eased our way by urging us to see itself, ourselves, and all of life as part of one great "play," both in the sense of theatrical spectacle and in the sense of a game to be played. (74)

Reminding us that the concepts of "scenario" and "nuclear theater" are frequently employed by strategic analysts, Chernus proposes that such metaphors "indicate that nuclear war can—perhaps must—be seen as a play in which the 'actors' play out their roles in the scenario" (74).

If Chernus is correct, then perhaps we might look to our playwrights to most successfully dramatize this phenomenon for us. One outstanding American dramatist who has accepted the challenge is Arthur Kopit. In the spring of 1981 Kopit was approached by insurance millionaire Leonard Davis, who wished to commission him to write a play about nuclear proliferation, based on a brief scenario Davis had written. Working on the project for more than two years, Kopit did manage to complete a "scenario," but one which turned out to be very different from his benefactor's.

In the "Author's Note" to *End of the World*, Kopit informs us that "the events that unfold in my play mirror, almost exactly, the experiences I had when I embarked on the commission" (ix). Dramatizing not only his own concerns but also presenting fairly perspectives that he clearly does not share, Kopit has based his play on both personal interviews and the written work of a number of champions of the nuclear national security state (Herman Kahn, Colin Gray, Keith Payne, Richard Pipes, Edward Teller), and some of its critics (Freeman Dyson, Jack Geiger, Jonathan Schell, George Kennan, Robert Scheer). The resulting play of ideas is a testimony of Kopit's sense of the dramaturgist's mission.

According to critic John Lahr,

129

Arthur has a gift for intuiting the ideas and moods of American culture and discovering metaphors that somehow clarify them. That, to some extent, is what a playwright's job is, finding a way of expressing to the culture the anxiety it can't quite comprehend. People don't want to know; they pay for escape, not disenchantment. Arthur has found a way, which is the trick of really good playwrights, to essentially corrupt an audience with pleasure. (Shewey 105)

As Kopit himself has put it, the playwright who asks an audience to pay money and sit in a theater has a responsibility "to do more than just delight them. Television can do that. Movies and musicals can get by just with glitz, dancing, entertainment, sheer technical excellence. In the theater, you must feel and think also. It has to do with why theater has always existed in civilization. Theater *matters*" (Shewey 105). And Trent, Kopit's alter ego in *End of the World*, asseverates: "...you have a kind of pact with yourself. And it says you don't screw around with what matters or else it's gone" (Kopit 11).

The suggestion, of course, is that what is at stake transcends artistic integrity and responsibility; at issue is not merely dramaturgy, but the survival of the planet. Detective Trent opens Act One, "The Commission," warning that he has "now, at most, two hours left to solve a mystery which so far seems to yield no solution. If I fail, it is highly possible that I and all of you will die sooner than we'd hoped. Do I exaggerate? Of course. That is my method. I am a playwright" (3). For Trent's wealthy patron, Philip Stone, it is *not* an exaggeration. Feeling a sense of great urgency, Stone wants his play produced, and quickly. Believing that the earth is doomed, Stone informs Audrey, Trent's agent, that a production of his play could perhaps prevent this doom.[1]

Trent, however, is convinced that Stone's scenario cannot *be* dramatized. Finding Stone's idea "terrible" but also "a definitional sweetheart deal,...the deal of a lifetime," Trent requests Audrey's help in resolving his dilemma. But when he is told to take the deal, Trent demurs: "Audrey, you don't understand. You haven't read this man's scenario. There is no way anyone, ANYONE! can write a play based on this. Do you know why? Because the characters are completely cardboard, and the plot preposterous" (9). Audrey herself later cautions agent Paul Cowan, "My client feels it is unethical to accept a deal knowing from the outset that there's no way it can be done" (21).

After immersing himself in the arcana of nuclear war literature and strategic thought, Trent becomes even more certain that will not be able to bring Stone's idea to fruition. "I cannot write a play from this material," he tells Audrey. "NO one can write a play from this material! This stuff is *INDESCRIBABLE!*" (41). Insisting that even *this* subject, however, is surely less daunting than Trent imagines, Audrey rejoins, "Dear, that is the silliest thing you've ever said—*anything* can make a play. You just have to figure out how to *handle* it" (41). And Kopit himself concluded that the best way to "handle it" was by focusing on the perplexities of a playwright who tries to write a play about nuclear war.

What Trent, Kopit's playwright, seems to find particularly bewildering is trying to make some sense of his own nation's nuclear war plans and strategies. Beginning his quest by arranging (through Stone) to meet with a number of nuclear strategists, Trent especially desires to talk with those who hold opinions that seem to him "to go against all common sense" (42). The first individual he talks to is General Wilmer, who has a Ph.D. in physics and is one of the president's chief advisors on nuclear policy. Learning of Trent's dramaturgical ambitions, Wilmer inquires if he is planning to write "some kind of Strangelove thing." When Trent indicates that this is not the case, Wilmer responds, "Good. Because the Strangelove scenario only works if you postulate a Doomsday weapon, and no one contemplates that. To save ourselves by threatening to annihilate ourselves is surely the height of preposterousness!" (43). Because, as we know, this is precisely what the superpowers are *doing*, Kopit urges his audience to consider the possibility that "deterrence" itself is "a Doomsday weapon," and that U.S. nuclear weapons policies themselves may be nothing less than preposterous. But until this possibility is much more widely contemplated, Kopit seems to be suggesting, major changes in these policies remain unlikely.

Why is General Wilmer unable to recognize the fundamental absurdity of the policies he champions? While interviewing nuclear strategists in Washington, Trent noticed that on their walls were not posters of Bo Derek, but rather prints of M.C. Escher. In his essay on Kopit's play, Thomas P. Adler points out that

... Escher's comment about his own drawings has an uncanny applicability to the arguments of the nuclear strategists: "If you want to draw attention to something impossible, you must try to deceive first yourself and then your audience, by presenting your work in such a way that the impossible element is veiled and a superficial observer would not even notice it." Deterrence theory is apparently based on logic, and yet is illogical, plunging us into a morass akin to what Douglas Hofstadter characterizes as Escher's "extremely weird worlds." (113)

Hoping to obtain additional insights into the "extremely weird worlds" of nuclear strategists, Trent decides to check out some "war-gamers," i.e., those who *play* with war scenarios, and interviews Jim and Pete, who are connected with the Harley corporation, a government think tank in nearby Virginia. "There's a curious paradox built into deterrence strategy," one of the war-gamers concedes,

and no one has a *clue* how to get around it. The paradox is this: Deterrence is dependent upon strength—well, that's obvious; the stronger your nuclear arsenal, the more the other side's deterred. *However*, should deterrence *fail* for any reason, your strength *instantly* becomes your greatest liability, *inviting* attack *instead* of preventing it.... And *that* is where all these crazy scenarios come in in which war breaks out PRECISELY because *no one* WANTS it to! Really! I'm not kidding. This business is *filled* with paradox! (58)

The fact that "deterrence" has been defined in myriad ways, and is used to legitimate multifarious policies and weapons systems, does not help to render the paradoxes of the doctrine any less mystifying. The enigma becomes at least a little less inscrutable, however, if we remain mindful that U.S. *declatory* policies have not infrequently been at odds with the *real* purposes of maintaining and continually modernizing such a colossal and ever more sophisticated nuclear arsenal. Writing in the early years of the Reagan presidency, Christopher Paine elucidated why protecting American *lives* is not necessarily the *summum bonum* of "maintaining deterrence":

Eliminating constraints on U.S. freedom of action in the global arena while imposing such constraints on the Soviet Union is what most American policymakers mean when they speak of "maintaining deterrence." For Eugene Rostow, recently fired as chief of the Arms Control and Disarmament Agency, this means confronting Soviet expansion...with the prospect of unacceptable risk, to which they have always responded with prudence. In effect, maintaining deterrence has become a quest for nuclear weapons and doctrines that will somehow convince Moscow that in moments of extreme crisis U.S. leaders might not be daunted by the prospect of unacceptable risk. Maintaining an ability to sow such doubts in the minds of Soviet leaders, we are told, is the essence of deterrence. When U.S. "vital interests" are at stake, these must somehow be made to appear more vital than even the immunity of American and allied citizens to nuclear attack; that is, the unacceptable risk of nuclear war must be manipulated in such a way as to make it appear less unacceptable to us than it is to the Russians. (427)

Another critic of this kind of "thinking," Michael McGwire, points out in his essay, "The Dilemmas and Delusions of Deterrence," that the policy

tends to encourage exaggerated rhetoric, to favor intransigence (as a demonstration of resolve), to discourage serious negotiation and the search for compromise, and to value a bellicose posture. Moreover, while creating the conditions that make war more likely, it fosters the delusion that war itself is not the danger. And in that delusion lies the *real* danger of deterrence.[2] (Prins 96)

Conceding that the United States has both overt and *covert* nuclear weapons policies, General Wilmer tells Trent that

for every level of engagement, we must possess a credible response, even if this response is quite incredible on its surface. This is one of the reasons it's important for our President, whoever he is, to every so often say something that sounds a bit insane. (Pause) Fear, you see. That's the great deterrent...Don't want to do too much to reduce the fear. By the way, that's the problem with a nuclear freeze: to the extent that it makes people feel safer, it raises the chances of war. (48)

What Wilmer fails to realize, however, is that there may be two very different kinds of fear, and that it may not be in a nation's best interests to attempt to induce *both* of these in an adversary. In his important discussion of "dissuasion versus appeasement," Dietrich Fischer writes: "It is often said about potential opponents that the only language they understand is military strength. This may be true in some cases, but there must be a clear distinction as to *when* that strength should be applied. A potential aggressor should feel afraid if he attacks a country, but *only then*" (38).

But what is important to keep in mind is that deterrence as it appears to be understood by most Americans—that the leaders of the Soviet Union would be unlikely to initiate a nuclear attack against the United States because sufficient second-strike capability would remain to annihilate the aggressor—has long been only one purpose of our immense nuclear arsenal. For that purpose merely, far fewer nuclear weapons would surely suffice, even if the Soviets were to retain their own absurdly redundant arsenal. Why, then, the obsession not only with the chimerical pursuit of "superiority" but also with parity or maintaining the "nuclear balance"? When he discovers that Trent is unable to comprehend why we need even *more* nuclear weapons, Wilmer informs him that he recently gave a talk at Princeton on this very topic.

And a number of the students started shouting, "Why don't we just *stop* this madness?" And I said, "You know, it's easy to avoid a nuclear war. All you have to do is surrender." (Grins) The problem is to find a way to *avoid* nuclear war while preserving the values that we cherish...Okay. Don't we have enough to accomplish this right now? Of course we do. Right *now*. But we don't need to deter the Russians now; why would they attack? They'd gain nothing...Deterrence comes into play during a *crisis*. During crisis, people tend to think in peculiar ways. A successful deterrent says to the Russians, "No matter what, your best case scenario is just no good." (44)

When Trent interjects that this is the situation that exists now, Wilmer exclaims:

Of course! But what makes you think we're going to stay where we are?...And things may turn better for us, or for them. Either way, it's dangerous. That's because any imbalance at all is dangerous, even if the imbalance is only *imagined*. In this business, it's how you're *perceived* that counts!...And all this comes about because of one simple, fundamental truth, and it governs everything we do: the guy who goes first goes best.[3] (45)

At the beginning of his explanation here, Wilmer has unwittingly acknowledged yet another serious flaw in "deterrence": it engenders a relentless search for more "usable" nuclear weapons. E.P. Thompson correctly points out that "There has never been a stationary state of mutual deterrence; instead there has been a ceaseless pursuit for advantage within that state" (5). But has either superpower ever actually *obtained* an advantage, one that has produced a foreign policy payoff? Former U.S. Defense Secretary Robert McNamara insists that because of the quantum leap in destructive power made possible by the splitting of the atom, even imbalances of major proportions may mean very little in actual practice. While visiting the Soviet Union in the mid-nineteen eighties, McNamara was asked by several Russian political and scientific leaders for a definition of nuclear parity. Parity exists, he explained,

when each side is deterred from initiating a strategic strike by the recognition that such an attack would be followed by a retaliatory strike that would inflict unacceptable damage on the attacker. I went on to say: 'I will surprise you by stating that I believe parity existed in October 1962, at the time of the Cuban Missile Crisis. The United States then had approximately 5,000 strategic warheads, compared to the Soviets' 300. Despite an advantage of seventeen to one in our favor, President Kennedy and I were deterred from even considering a nuclear attack on the USSR by the knowledge that, although such a strike would destroy the Soviet Union, tens of their weapons would survive to be launched against the United States. These would kill millions of Americans. No responsible political leader would expose his nation to such a catastrophe.' (44)

Many U.S. policymakers, however, view the matter very differently. Zbigniew Brzezinski, Jimmy Carter's national security adviser, argued in a 1986 essay that the current U.S. nuclear arsenal would soon be inadequate:

To maintain MAD in the face of the likely and ongoing Soviet offensive and defensive strategic buildup we will have to be able to deploy vastly increased offensive forces, over those that we now have, in order to cope with the anticipated problems of the future. In order to secure deterrence we will have to deploy much larger strategic offensive forces than we now have, given the Soviet strategic and defensive buildup. (448)[4]

More than a few strategists who *claim* to be primarily concerned with maintaining MAD (Mutual Assured Destruction) actually seem to be considerably more interested in something very different, and far more ominous: nuclear *war-fighting*. According to General Wilmer, "In order to *prevent* a nuclear war, you have to be able to *fight* a nuclear war at *all levels*, even though they're probably unwinnable and unfightable" (47). Trent finds a similar argument advanced by Stanley Berent, a Georgetown University Russian scholar and "a real hard-liner, particularly where the Soviet Union was concerned." "To be secure," Berent tells Trent, "the United States must possess a credible nuclear-war fighting policy" (55). Earlier in their conversation, however, Berent conceded the paradox of this pivotal pillar of his strategy: "Now. Do I *really* know how to fight a limited nuclear war? Not at all. No one does. No one's *fought* one. And yet if we're not prepared, we're in the soup" (51).

What Wilmer and Berent fail to consider is that perhaps *preparing* for nuclear war is itself the supreme danger, ineluctably fostering the illusion that the controlled use of "weapons" of such inconceivable destructive power is possible. Again, there is a vast disparity between declaratory and actual policies. Discussing the 1982 Defense Guidance Statement and its concept of "prevailing" in a protracted nuclear war, Robert W. Tucker points out that the document did not really break new ground, its principal points adding up

to little more than a refinement of the Carter Administration's 1980 Presidential Directive 59, which in turn built on strategic concepts that may be traced back a generation. From Kennedy to Reagan, no administration has been able to disavow the prospect, however skeptically it may have viewed that prospect, of the controlled use of nuclear weapons. Equally, no administration has been able to disavow the prospect of emerging from a nuclear conflict with some kind of meaningful victory. Unable to disavow these prospects, no administration has been able to disavow the force structure that might make possible fighting a limited nuclear war. (9)

And maintaining the force structure, in turn, helps to maintain the illusion that nothing fundamental has changed in the nuclear age. This lack of frank public debate about our detailed warfighting plans has engendered enormous confusion, and not only on the part of ordinary citizens. Accentuating that even members of Congress seem not to know what their nation's actual nuclear war policies are, Jeremy Stone reminds us that

When Secretary of Defense James Schlesinger threatened nuclear first use in Korea, more than one hundred members of the House of Representatives co-signed a no-first use resolution of Congressman Richard Ottinger. Within a few days, when the administration explained to them that we had been threatening first use for years in Europe and that it was indeed a mainstay of our policy, most of these members of Congress withdrew their names from the resolution. They did not know the policy because the United States had never been eager to emphasize in public what was well known to all students of the subject. (O'Heffernan 126)

Even today, most Americans still seem not to know that U.S. policies call for possible first use in Europe. What we have seen throughout the nuclear age, then, is a failure of policymakers ("the nuclear priesthood"), the mass media, educators, and others to adequately inform the American public about profoundly important national security issues which, at least in some ways, do affect all of us. Most citizens, of course, in their apathy, silence and deferential obeisance to the "experts," have colluded in their own exclusion from the debate. What is particularly ironic is that American elites, apparently lacking sufficient confidence in the judgment of their own citizenry to communicate these issues *to them*, ostensibly believe that nuclear missiles themselves can, during an actual nuclear war, effectively communicate with *an adversary!* "Limited war in the nuclear age," writes Desmond Ball, "is not so much concerned with military objectives as with being a means of communication, but nuclear weapons may not be very useful media. They are not suited to signaling any precise and unambiguous message but, on the contrary, are supremely capable of degrading the whole environment of communications" (30).

That the arguments of strategists who continue to act as if nuclear warfighting could possibly be a sane policy have not been much more summarily dismissed from national security debates might be in no small measure due to the fact that "the whole environment of communications," or virtually the entire realm of private and public discourse on nuclear issues, has been thoroughly debased since Hiroshima. There is still too little evidence of the "new thinking" called for by Einstein and others. Agreeing with Trent that our present nuclear policy makes no sense, Berent proffers a "very simple" solution: "we must stop regarding nuclear war as some kind of goddamn inevitable holocaust...and start looking at it as a goddamn WAR!" (50). When Berent realizes that Trent's concerns have not been entirely allayed by this assertion, he adds that "We have to learn how to wage nuclear war *rationally*"[5] (50). Berent continues his exposition with comments on limited nuclear war, controlled counterforce strikes with restraint, an adequate civil defense system, and the defensive nature of "*pre*-pre-preemptive strikes," or anticipatory retaliation.

Trent, in fact, discovers that *all* U.S. policies and weapons systems are viewed as genuinely defensive. Berent explains to Trent that we need weapons systems such as the MX, Pershing II, Trident 2, and cruise missiles to enable us to "surgically remove" hardened targets. If we get into a major crisis, Berent underscores the importance of being able to disarm the Soviets to the greatest extent possible. Told that what he is advocating is a first strike policy, Berent emphatically disagrees, "Because the connotation is *aggressive*. This is a *defensive* act" (52). Preferring to call his strategy "anticipatory retaliation" rather than the more "cumbersome" term "preemptive strike," Berent exclaims that his designation "simply covers everything!" (53). After Trent informs Audrey of what he has learned from his interviews, she correctly concludes, "Dear, by this scheme, nobody ever does anything *offensive*." "Exactly," Trent replies. "Every act of aggression is defensive here. It's a completely moral system!" (88-89).

If all nations tend to see their own actions as defensive and those of their adversaries as aggressive, Americans are hardly exempt from this proclivity. In his perceptive study of this phenomenon, William H. Blanchard contends that "...U.S. officials have shown a remarkable capacity to remain unaware of the aggressive *implications* of their behavior" (29). In the era of the preemptive strike, observes Blanchard, building a weapon can itself be an act of provocation if there will be no defense against it. Thus we live in "the era of 'inadvertent' aggression—a form of aggression that takes place, not from a desire for conquest, but from an effort to increase the security of one's people." This form of national self-deception "is a process of thinking in bad faith by admitting the reality of the acts, but denying their significance" (2).

At the heart of this problem is an inability or refusal to achieve realistic empathy, i.e., to see how the world looks from the Soviets' point of view.[6] Because of this complacent, self-righteous mindset, observes Raymond Gartoff in his essay "Worst-case Assumptions: Uses, Abuses, and Consequences," "...the West does not concede that the Soviet Union and the Warsaw Pact need *any* deterrent or defense, because we pose no threat. Beyond that, the United States and NATO have *never* estimated Soviet deterrence or defense requirements, or even what the *Soviet* military and political leaders might see as their force requirements for those missions" (Prins 103).

Because it is the peculiar nature of the U.S.-Soviet conflict which drives the arms race, a *sine qua non* for ending it is a thorough rethinking of the "Soviet threat." Most nuclear strategists, unfortunately, have tended to view the Soviet Union as immutably implacable, and calls not merely for arms control but for *dis*armament as hopelessly naive. After listening to Berent's theories on nuclear warfighting, Trent suggests that it might be a good idea to immediately enter into serious negotiations with the Soviets. The following exchange ensues:

Berent: Of course! That would be *wonderful*! And yet, if history shows anything, it shows that the Soviet Union cannot be trusted to keep the terms of a treaty!
Trent: Hold it! Hold it, hold it! Are you trying to tell me we shouldn't enter into treaties with these guys till we're convinced that they can be TRUSTED?
Berent: That's correct.
Trent: If we knew they could be trusted, why would we need TREATIES? (56)

It is at this point that an exasperated but ebullient Trent calls Stone to inform him that he has solved his mystery, and has discovered why we are doomed: "We're in the hands of assholes!" (56) But Trent has been chosen by Stone to dramatize his scenario precisely because he believes that *this* playwright knows very well that the nuclear predicament cannot be blamed solely on the deranged ruminations of nuclear strategists. A particular incident years earlier *convinced* Stone that Trent had a thorough understanding of "evil." At the end of his play Kopit has Trent recall that a number of people, including Stone, came over to the playwright's apartment shortly after his son was born. Alone with his son for the first time, Trent picked him up and began walking around the living room, and realized that for the first time he had never had anyone completely in his power before.

And I'd never known what that *meant*! Never felt anything remotely like that before! And I saw I was standing near a window. And it was open. It was but a few feet away. And I thought: I could...*drop him out*! And I went *toward* the window, because I couldn't believe that this thought had come into my head—*where had it come from*? Not one part of me felt anything for this boy but love, not one part! (94)

Contemplating throwing him twenty stories down to his death, Trent felt a thrill. Although he was, without difficulty, able to resist his "temptation," he did not stay by the window, and he closed it. Although there was absolutely no chance that he would have harmed his infant son, he "couldn't *take* a chance, it was very, very...seductive. If doom comes...it will come in *that* way" (95).

Stone, a former weapons designer, concurs. Recalling a nuclear test he once witnessed in the Pacific, Stone discusses the "glitter" and irresistible appeal of the awesome power of nuclear weapons, and the *thrill* of the idea of nuclear apocalypse (92-93). More than a few thinkers, of course, have argued that humanity might indeed harbor a death-wish, that at least subconsciously nuclear cataclysm exerts an intense attraction.[7] If there is more than a modicum of truth in such suggestions, they are hardly the entire explanation for our current crisis, and they need not paralyze us with despair. The stunning recent events in the Soviet Union and in Eastern Europe demonstrate that extraordinary changes in geopolitical realities are indeed possible. And perhaps human beings everywhere will soon realize that only when we decide to finally liberate ourselves from our idolatrous thralldom to the nuclear deity is genuine human freedom really possible anywhere.

Notes

[1]To those who might be inclined to be amused at Stone's seeming megalomania here, I would suggest that the pervasive, diametrically opposed attitude—that individual citizens are utterly powerless to do anything to prevent the planet's destruction—is surely no less extreme. The only thing more corrupting than absolute power, it has been said, is absolute powerless*ness*.

[2]For incisive discussions of why so much nuclear deterrence theory is intellectually dishonest, see chapter six of Jeff Smith's *Unthinking the Unthinkable: Nuclear Weapons and Western Culture* (Bloomington: Indiana University Press, 1989), and James Stegenga, "Nuclear Deterrence: Bankrupt Ideology," *Policy Sciences* 16:2 (November, 1983), 127-145.

[3]For an interesting study, based on extensive and revealing interviews with high-level American nuclear strategists, on whether it actually *matters* who is ahead in the arms race, and what purposes nuclear weapons really serve, see Steven Kull, *Minds at War: Nuclear Reality and the Inner Conflicts of Defense Policymakers* (New York: Basic Books, 1988). On possible limitations of Kull's analysis, see Erik Yesson, "Strategic Make-believe and Strategic Reality: Psychology and the Implications of the Nuclear Revolution," *International Security* 14:3 (Winter, 1989-90), 182-193.

[4]Richard Falk suggests what is going on here: "Each side observes the other acting *as if* superiority was important and is encouraged thereby to embrace the fiction." Falk and Robert Jay Lifton, *Indefensible Weapons* (New York: Basic Books, 1982), p. 150. Americans who have dared to point out that in a nuclear age the pursuit of superiority is indeed a *fiction*, and an extremely costly one, have generally been dismissed as irresponsible, naive, or pro-Soviet. If, as many of its critics maintain, the arms race, among other things, is a form of madness, then the kind of thinking which remains obsessed with real or imagined numerical "advantages"—particularly when superpower nuclear arsenals have long passed the point of grotesque redundancy—would also seem to be pathological. (One is reminded of "body counts" during the Vietnam War.) Psychotherapist James Hillman asks, "Can we deconstruct the positivism and literalism—epitomized by the ridiculous *counting* of warheads—that informs current policies before those policies literally and positively deconstruct our life, our history and our world?" "Wars, Rams, Arms, Wars: On the Love of War," in Richard Grossinger and Lindy Hough, eds., *Nuclear Strategy and the Code of the Warrior: Faces of Mars and the Shiva in the Crisis of Human Survival* (Berkeley: North Atlantic Books, 1984), p. 264. This is not to suggest that numbers

never matter, merely that they are generally much less significant than we have been led to believe.

[5]Kopit's source here is clearly a frequently cited 1980 article by Colin S. Gray and Keith B. Payne, "Victory is Possible." According to Gray and Payne, "Recognition that war at any level can be won or lost, and that the distinction between winning and losing would not be trivial, is essential for intelligent defense planning." *Foreign Policy* 39 (Summer, 1980), 14. This would seem to be precisely the kind of deranged "rationality" or "crackpot realism" that sociologist C. Wright Mills warned against more than two decades earlier in his *The Causes of World War III.*

[6]For an important discussion of the difference between "sympathy" and "realistic empathy" here, see Ralph K. White, *Fearful Warriors: A Psychological Profile of U.S.-Soviet Relations* (NY: Free Press, 1984), especially pages 160-167.

[7]See especially Chernus.

Works Cited

Adler, Thomas P. "Public Faces, Private Graces: Apocalypse Postponed in Arthur Kopit's *End of the World. Studies in the Literary Imagination* 21:2 (Fall, 1988): 107-118.

Ball, Desmond, and Jeffrey Richelson, eds. *Strategic Nuclear Targeting.* Ithaca: Cornell University Press, 1986.

Blanchard, William H. *Aggression American Style.* Santa Monica: Goodyear Publishing Co., 1978.

Brzezinski, Zbigniew. "The Strategic Implications of Thou Shalt Not Kill." *America* 31 May 1986: 445-449.

Chernus, Ira. *Dr. Strangegod: On the Symbolic Meaning of Nuclear Weapons.* Columbia: University of South Carolina Press, 1986.

Fischer, Dietrich. *Preventing War in the Nuclear Age.* Totawa, N.J.: Rowman and Allanheld, 1984.

Kopit, Arthur. *End of the World.* New York: Hill and Wang, 1984.

McNamara, Robert. *Blundering Into Disaster: Surviving the First Century of the Nuclear Age.* New York: Pantheon, 1986.

O'Heffernan, Patrick, eds. *Defense Sense: The Search for a Rational Military Policy.* Cambridge: Ballinger, 1983.

Paine, Christopher. "Reagatomics, or How to 'Prevail'." *The Nation* 9 April 1983: 423-433.

Prins, Gwyn, ed. *The Nuclear Crisis Reader.* New York: Vintage, 1984.

Shewey, Don. "Arthur Kopit: A Life on Broadway." *New York Times Magazine* 29 April 1984: 87-91, 104-105.

Thompson, E.P. *Beyond the Cold War: A New Approach to the Arms Race and Nuclear Annihilation.* New York: Pantheon, 1982.

Tucker, Robert W. "The Nuclear Debate." *Foreign Affairs* Fall 1984: 1-32.

"Under the Wheat":
An Analysis of Options and Ethical Components

Nancy Anisfield

The images of nuclear war that are available derive from the fixed experiential information on the bombings of Hiroshima and Nagasaki. However, now that the world's nuclear arsenal is capable of thousands of times that destruction, a substantial imaginative projection is demanded of any fiction writer wishing to comment on nuclear war. Although an infinite number of locations, characters and events appears on a writer's palette, there are only three basic temporal options—past, present, and future. Each of these color the nuclear war narrative in a distinctive way.

To write about Hiroshima or Nagasaki, or perhaps select one of the atomic bomb tests as a narrative focus, is to work with the facts of nuclear destruction as they have been experienced and documented. Temporally, this sets the narrative in the past and it is inherently limited by the nature of historicity. The second temporal option is to work within the framework of a less fantastic narrative, placing it in current time, relying on imagery and symbolism to illustrate the physical and moral implications of nuclear war. Keeping the narrative within mimetic boundaries does not restrict the text's ability to effectively represent the ecological, sociological and ethical hazards of the nuclear age, though it does require a more intricate system of figurative images.

The third choice would be to work with a future projection of nuclear war and its aftermath, as is found mostly in science fiction narratives ranging from *Riddley Walker* and *Warday* to shorter works such as "Lucifer" and "Lot's Daughter." This option frees the fiction writer to explore all plot, setting, and linguistic possibilities, released somewhat from archetypal patterns inappropriate to a nuclear scenario. Unfortunately, though, our culture's subtle disregard of most science fiction as marginal or escapist literature jeopardizes the seriousness with which such fiction should be received. Hence, if a writer's primary motivation is political, choosing to write science fiction risks alienating some of the potential audience.

This is not to say that all non-science fiction writers are automatically taken seriously or that their works are always probed for significant political statements. In fact, one general criticism of contemporary nuclear war fiction is that it lacks political perspective. The reason for this absence is endemic in the subject matter. After a nuclear war, what caused it or who won or the topical politics so often analyzed in non-fiction texts would most likely be irrelevant. As "the enemy" in Mordecai Roshwald's *Level 7* ironically points out:

> This morning we picked up a radio message from the enemy suggesting that we should conclude a peace treaty. It also informed us that the entire civilian population over there, including the government and its various officials, is gone.... As a reason for making peace they pointed out that there was no longer anything to dispute: no territory, no strategic positions, no wealth, no markets, no uncommitted areas—nothing. "And," they added, "peaceful relations may add some fun to life underground, which is not very interesting." (168)

As a result, instead of considering arms negotiations, verifiable treaties and strategic targets, the politics that are explored in many contemporary nuclear war fictions are those of a broader, more humanistic dimension.

Each of the temporal options dictates a different use of non-literal language. The first option, focusing on actual past incidents of nuclear destruction, carries the immediate resonance of authenticity, but the core of the nuclear experience—annihilation—cannot be expressed. As a result, even though the fiction writer can draw on actual accounts and witnesses' testimony, these accounts are solely those of the survivors. Only the survivor's tale can exist, not that of those who perished in the firestorm or were vaporized at ground zero. Furthermore, describing the 1945 atomic bombings can only hint at the devastation now possible from just one B-52, which carries the equivalent of three thousand Hiroshima-size bombs (Franklin 167). There is a limit, then, to the experiential advantage of setting the narrative in the past; and, if the writer wishes to express the total nuclear experience, figurative images are required though they may risk being confused with authentic detail.

A futuristic or science fiction approach might use symbols and metaphors to suggest the nature of nuclear war, but because they operate within a self-reflexive framework, their meaning may be relevant only in a futuristic scenario. Transference of the symbols so they are relevant in the present time is difficult. This does not invalidate their use; it simply distances them. For example, in Edward Bryant's "Jody After the War", there are several references to war-survivor Jody's job as a free-lance hologram photographer (117-123). Her occupation, capturing other peoples' images, sharpens (by way of contrast) the story's focus on her inability to have children, create people herself. However, references to the Concord II, soybeef sandwiches and other futuristic artifacts detract from the symbolic impact of the holograms. They appear just another descriptive item, adding detail to the futuristic landscape.

In "current time" nuclear fiction, figurative language is essential because nuclear war has not occurred and futuristic projections would conflict with textual mimesis. Writers must convey the implications of nuclear war through non-literal modes of expression. The great hole that William Cowling digs in Tim O'Brien's *The Nuclear Age*, for example, literally is intended as a bomb shelter, and literally ends up with the potential to be an imploding, suffocating grave. This danger hidden in something supposedly rendered for defensive purposes suggests the escalating danger in nuclear deterrence policies. Furthermore, the hole figuratively connects nuclear war to other wars through the concept of a foxhole, and it brings the substance of nuclear destruction back to basics—the earth and soil. Finally, the fact that a hole is a negation, an absence of something, casts a nihilistic shadow over the state of William's existence and obsession with nuclear war. Works such as *The Nuclear Age* never literally depict a nuclear conflict or explosion, but manage to explore them not only through characters' thoughts and direct narrative discussion, but through a rich pattern of images, symbols and metaphors as well.

Along with studying a narrative's temporal options, figurative demands and the assumptions underlying their use, readers can roam the range of literary criticism to determine the methods and meanings of various nuclear fictions. However, the fact that for the first time our global civilization has devised the means for exterminating itself (the eschatological status of the nuclear age) demands a more culturally integrated analysis of this literature. As Jacqueline Smetak explains in her argument against approaching nuclear literature traditionally, as texts without contexts:

There is no automatic connection between exposure to an idea and a belief in that idea; no guarantee that belief will lead to action, effective or otherwise. If we wish to use Nuclear texts to increase awareness of impending doom in order to avoid that doom, falling back on familiar methods will not do.... We need to believe, as Ohmann puts it, that "literature doesn't happen in an autonomous realm of culture, but responds and participates in the *whole* of history." Literature is, finally, about *something*, something other than itself. (58)

H. Bruce Franklin, author of *War Stars: The Superweapon and the American Imagination*, also insists on the need to view nuclear literature as vitally connected to the actions and attitudes of the nuclear age, noting: "American weapons and American culture cannot be understood in isolation from each other. Just as the weapons have emerged from the culture, so too have the weapons caused profound metamorphoses in the culture. Comprehending this process may show us how we got into our current predicament. It might even help us find our way out" (6).

One way to connect the critical study of a nuclear fiction with its reflection of and relevance to the current state of nuclear consciousness would be to approach the text through an ethical analysis. Robert Mielke points out in the introduction to his "Ethical Taxonomy"[1] of nuclear fictions that, "...fictional representations conceal their ethical biases regarding nuclear weaponry with greater facility than the counterforce strategists, but they cannot maintain ethical neutrality" (165). In *Nuclear Ethics*, Joseph S. Nye Jr. takes this awareness further when he stresses the need for a careful ethical examination of nuclear issues stating:"...citizens in a democracy can carry on a moral discourse on a subject that sometimes seems to pose an intractable challenge to our most basic values" (xi).

Although Nye then proceeds to use traditional standards of reasoning to develop a rather shortsighted defense of the morality of nuclear deterrence, the system of judgement he employs is applicable to an evaluation of a fictional text dealing with nuclear war. At the heart of Nye's examination are three criteria for judging morality: motives, means, and consequences. By extension, just how carefully an author has considered the implications of nuclear war becomes apparent when these ethical criteria are used to analyze a short story or novel.

Rick DeMarinis' short story, "Under the Wheat," bears the accessibility of a mimetic text (as opposed to science fiction), is temporally located in the present, and, by employing effective metaphoric and symbolic detail, manages to depict not only the threat of nuclear war, but the brutality of the moment of nuclear explosion and its aftermath.

Motives for nuclear war are suggested in this story through Lloyd's greed and restless apathy. He never seems to ponder the implications of his job checking the sump pumps at the bottom of empty North Dakota missile silos. He only reflects on how good the pay is, good enough to justify relocating from friends and family in California. In regard to the expectant silos he points out that it is, "Just a hole with a sump in it. Of course you can fall into it and get yourself killed. That's about the only danger. But there are no regulations that can save you from your own stupidity" (12). Unintentionally offering an ironic comment on the danger of nuclear capability, Lloyd just sees his small segment of the nuclear scenario. His ambivalence is offset only when the silos can give him a rush or a thrill to break the boredom of his job and banality of his life. For example, he dangles the small child Piper over the hole to scare her and her mother; he plays secrecy games with local children he lets in to see the silos; and he pretends to launch the missiles, working the switches in D-flight control center. In the control room Lloyd reflects, "I feel it too, craziness...It's good down here—no rules" (17). Though possible motives such as territory, politics, religion, racism, or world-wide economy are never mentioned, the basic drives of greed, power, and excitement[2] are pervasive in Lloyd's acceptance of a nuclear possibility.

The 'means' of nuclear war are presented through the fact of the empty silos awaiting their missiles. An even greater image of the means, however, grows through constant references to tornados. The shape of the tornado easily symbolizes the nuclear mushroom cloud, getting "bigger fast," often "curdled underneath." The tornados rarely touch down in this area, but are "close enough to make you want to find a hole" when one "splits the sky." At one point the storm is described as a "big white fire...blazing in the sky," at another point as a "giant hammerhead," which also summons the visual image of the flat-topped nuclear cloud. The idea of mass destruction from the sky is clearly expressed when Lloyd reflects on the farmlands wasted by hail, thinking, "Head-on with the sky and the sky never loses" (7). The oppressive threat of such horror causes Lloyd's wife Karen to have a "dream of being uprooted and...sees her broken body caught in a tree, magpies picking at it" (6). Thus, even though this story is set in the present, metaphor and allusion offer an insightful view of a possible future event.

Associated with this future event are its future consequences. DeMarinis depicts these in several ways. First, there are the wasted, unproductive farmlands. Second are the empty missile silos, which look as they would after launch. Third is the 'ghost town' across the lake, once built for the men who worked on the dam. Piper is fourth, conjuring up images of the post-nuclear genetically damaged child. She screams and whines, never speaks, and is described in animal-like terms. Fifth is the relationship between Lloyd and Myrna, a local widow of Russian descent. Like Lloyd, Myrna feels the exhilaration of the ultimate and becomes mischievous down in the control room. Because he is American and she is Russian their union (underground and in the ghost town) is comparable to the post-nuclear peace between the enemies in *Level 7*. Karen's disappearance, without clothes or money, represents the instant victim dead, notable also because it is Karen who, unlike ambivalent Lloyd, yearned for a more populated area and greater contact with life. Finally, the consequences of nuclear war are projected through the language and random images of the story. Two catalogs are listed: one naming objects drifting by the top of the silo, one naming movements in the ghost town. Both of them significantly include as an item, "nothing." In addition, there are many death images, including the rotted fish heads Karen leaves for Lloyd to eat, the fat farmer he thinks he sees drowned with the submerged farmhouse in the lake, tales of chain saw murders, and a description of Lloyd and Karen in bed as, "The world could have been filled with dead bodies" (7).

"Under the Wheat" can be read as a compressed allegory of nuclear war. DeMarinis considers motives, means and consequences. The ease with which Lloyd and Myrna toy with the idea of nuclear attack and the vehemence of nuclear war's symbolic depiction suggest the frightening paradox of nuclear capability. Rather than offering any plot resolution, however, the story closes with Lloyd in the ghost town, a tornado closing in, and Myrna's abortion story murmuring in the background. Abortion clearly serves as a metaphor for the loss of future generations, denied life by the direct human intervention of nuclear war. Lloyd seems to be moving towards a greater ethical or moral awareness when he keeps "watch on the sky, because there is a first time for everything" (19), an idea which is quickly reinforced when a long board is described as "spinning like a slow propeller" evoking the image of Enola Gay. The closing lines strengthen this sense of awareness:

Myrna is standing behind me, running a knuckle up and down my back. 'Hi, darling,' she says. 'Want to know what I did while you were out working on the dam today?' The dark tube has begun to move out from behind the bluff, but I'm not sure which way. 'Tell me,' I say. 'Tell me.' (19)

Literally, Lloyd seems to want to be distracted from his thoughts. Figuratively, he implies the desire to know whether or not nuclear destruction (the tornado) is impending. Symbolically, the dam suggests the ability to hold back, in this case, perhaps, nuclear disaster, but this ability is undercut by the fact that Lloyd and Myrna are simply pretending to be part of the dam workers and the workers are ghosts—long gone.

As a result, "Under the Wheat" joins longer writings like *Level 7* and *On the Beach* in Mielke's highest ethical ranking, "cautionary discourse." DeMarinis uses several strategies common to such works: an emphasis upon loss, the use of symbolic detail to expose the consequences of nuclear war, and stress upon a fate shared with the enemy (175). In addition, he presents metaphors that are clear and images that are distressing yet accessed through a contemporary scenario. Sixteen years after Rick DeMarinis wrote this story of the missile silos of North Dakota, the nuclear arsenal housed there is still so large that if the state were to secede and form its own country, it would be the world's third largest nuclear power ("In" 3). Accordingly, this "text" can enter "context," and as a fictional nuclear narrative, it is able to issue a clear, still relevant warning.

Notes

[1]Mielke evaluates nuclear fictions on a six level scale, ranging from hard survivalism to cautionary discourse. His taxonomy takes into consideration social structures, awareness, and attitudes.

[2]For an excellent contemplation of power and excitement as a motivating factor in nuclear war, see Arthur Kopit's play, *End of the World.*

Works Cited

Bryant, Edward. "Jody After the War." *Beyond Armageddon: Twenty-One Sermons to the Dead.* Eds. Walter M. Miller and Martin H. Greenberg. New York: Donald I. Fine, 1985.

DeMarinis, Rick. "Under the Wheat." *Under the Wheat.* Pittsburgh: University of Pittsburgh, 1986. 3-19.

Franklin, H. Bruce. *War Stars: The Superweapon and the American Imagination.* New York: Oxford University, 1988.

"In the ICBM belt, a foe of the bomb." *The Boston Globe.* 14 March 1990: 3.

Kopit, Arthur. *End of the World.* NY: Hill & Wang, 1984.

Mielke, Robert. "Imagining Nuclear Weaponry: An Ethical Taxonomy on Nuclear Representation." "WARNINGS: An Anthology on the Nuclear Peril." *Northwest Review* 21 (1984): 164-180.

Nye, Joseph S. Jr. *Nuclear Ethics.* New York: Macmillan, 1986.

O'Brien, Tim. *The Nuclear Age.* New York: Dell, 1985.

Roshwald, Mordecai. *Level 7.* London: Heinemann, 1959. Chicago: Lawrence Hill, 1989.

Smetak, Jacqueline. "'So Long, Mom': The Politics of Nuclear Holocaust Fiction." *Papers in Language and Literature.* 26:1 (Winter 1990): 41-59.

Testament:
To Deserve the Children

H. Wayne Schuth

In 1983, two films were released dealing with the effects of thermonuclear bomb explosions over the United States: *Testament* and *The Day After*. I suspect that the reason these films both appeared at the same time had to do with concerns over the NATO deployment of medium range nuclear missiles in Western Europe, and the possible responses from the other side. Although both films deal with the same subject, their approaches are very different. This analysis compares and contrasts the two, but concentrates on *Testament*, for it possesses qualities of universality and profundity which indicate that it is a major artistic accomplishment of the nuclear film genre. *Testament* is also more watchable than *The Day After*, not only because it is less graphic in its presentation of physical horrors, but because it presents a much more hopeful statement about the human condition.

Testament was directed by Lynne Littman, a former documentary film-maker who had won four Emmy awards for her work and an Academy Award for her short subject *Number Our Days* (not about nuclear war, as the title suggests, but about elderly Jewish people in Venice, California). Littman made *Testament* originally for public television, but when finished, the film created such interest in the industry that it was distributed by Paramount theatrically before its television release. *The Day After* was made for ABC Television and directed by theatrical film director Nicholas Meyer (*Time After Time, Volunteers*). It was shown on the network on Sunday night, November 20, with considerable debate and fanfare (for example, the cover story of *Newsweek* [November 21] was devoted to the film).

Testament's budget was very small; *The Day After*'s was very large. And it shows. *Testament*, although well made, lacks the enormous crane shots, the innovative special effects, the hundreds of dying extras, and the other indications of expense and spectacle readily found in *The Day After*. But a large budget was not necessary for *Testament*. Littman tells a quiet story of one family and what goes on around them. *The Day After* is about many families, and in fact, resembles other exciting "disaster" films as *Airport, Earthquake, The Towering Inferno* and *Roller Coaster*, where people are suddenly confronted with major emergencies. Both *Testament* and *The Day After* deal with the bomb exploding and its effects, but these are handled in different ways. In *Testament*, the television set in the living room is

146

interrupted by a civil defense warning, and then there is a great flash. After that, the family and neighbors come together to try to make sense of what happened (the bombs went off over San Francisco, miles away) and everything looks pretty normal. When the film follows the family and its attempt to cope with life after the blast, there is little reliance on gross makeup or vivid imagery. In *The Day After*, there are several nuclear explosions over Kansas City, Missouri, and the images are shown very graphically. People and animals turn into skeletons and vaporize before our eyes. Fire breaks out everywhere. The scenes are brutal and difficult to watch. There are survivors (amazingly enough) in and around Lawrence, Kansas, and when the film follows their various stories after the blasts, there are numerous images of injured people and destroyed property. In *The Day After*, all that expensively filmed gore may unintentionally cause some viewers to tune the film out, either psychologically or physically. Research on fear arousing communications indicates that when the level of fear becomes extremely high, a person may respond defensively to a message, which interferes with message reception[1]. And both films, I think, have the same message. Like Scrooge awakening on Christmas morning, the viewers are reminded that, although too late for some, it is not too late for them. Something can (and must) be done about the potential for total destruction.

Testament is based on a story by Carol Amen with the screenplay by John Sacret Young. It is about a family living in Hamelin, the name of the town in the poem by Robert Browning, "The Pied Piper of Hamelin." In fact, the mother, Carol Weatherly (Jane Alexander), is directing the school play based on the Pied Piper story. She has three children: Scottie (Lukas Haas), the youngest; Brad (Ross Harris), the middle one; and Mary Elizabeth (Roxanna Zol), the eldest. Her husband is Tom (William Devane), who competes with Brad on morning bike rides, and who, being an adult, can race to the top of a hill when his son can't. (This competition subtlety may allude to the nuclear arms race itself). The family seems to love each other, although there are petty conflicts and arguments. Tom goes on a business trip to San Francisco, and later the bomb goes off. The rest of the film is how Carol and her family deal with the after effects in Hamelin.

Although struggling to maintain order and carry on, things go from bad to worse for Carol and her family. Tom was killed in San Francisco. Mary Elizabeth and Scottie eventually die. The one means of communication with the outside world, the short wave radio, reaches fewer and fewer people. Community services come to a halt. It becomes more and more difficult to find food and water. Carol finally decides to commit suicide and take her remaining son and his friend with her, but cannot carry it out. In a moving finale, Carol lights birthday candles on crackers covered with peanut butter, and before they are blown out, makes this moving speech:

(her wish is) "that we remember it all—the good and the awful. The way we finally lived. That we never gave up. That we will last, to be here, to deserve the children."

This is an ending that comments eloquently on the human spirit.

In *The Day After*, many of the characters are also helpless and dying. Although a baby is born and the President comes on the radio and says things will get better, there is, both in words and images, a feeling of hopelessness and doom. Unlike the ending of *The Day After*, where a dying heart surgeon kneels crying in the ruins of his house comforted by a stranger who is holding him, the mother in *Testament* does not give up. Although her persistence may seem to some so (existentially, perhaps) futile set in the scene of a town nearly dead and world/community so vanquished, nevertheless, she makes the decision for life over death, no matter what the future holds for her or her children.

Testament is a well structured film, and the Pied Piper story is brilliantly used as a frame of reference. In the poem, the Piper is hired for one thousand guilders to rid Hamelin of rats. He does so, by leading them with the music of his pipe into the river. When he asks for his money, the mayor and the corporation refuse. The piper then spirits the children away into a mountainside, except for one who was lame and could not dance the whole way.

Why this story? One, Scottie plays a rat and later a child in the school play. His rat costume has big ears, and Scottie is shown holding his hands to his ears during family arguments and whenever he does not want to hear anything unpleasant. This plays off Carol's earlier remarks to her husband, "We have to talk," to which he responds, "Some other time," and she says, "There is no other time." This symbolic ear holding is like a warning to the viewer to listen well, to analyze both pleasant and unpleasant messages, and to make sure we know who our pipers are. Will we, like the children in the poem, be led into the mountainside (fallout shelter), to someday rise

> Out of some subterraneous prison
> Into which they were trepanned
> Long time ago in a mighty band
> Out of Hamelin town in Brunswick land,
> But how or why, they don't understand. (Browning 271)

Two, the idea of deserving the children is found in the Pied Piper story. At the end of the poem, which was written for a real child he knew, Browning writes:

> So Willy, let me and you be wipers
> Of scores out with all men—especially Pipers!
> And, whether they pipe us free from rats or
>   from mice,
> If we promised them aught, let us keep our
>   promise! (Browning 271)

In a sense, we are capable of letting the children down, not keeping our promise to them of a future. A testament is a will that relates to the disposal of personal property. The film *Testament* makes the point that in order to deserve the children, we must not destroy their world. There is a native American expression which goes, "We do not inherit the land from our ancestors, we only borrow it from our children" (Wellemeyer 40). As in *The Day After*, *Testament* does not blame one side or the other for starting the war. The bomb just explodes. The promise is not kept.

Testament is filled with quiet, emotional moments that make their points effectively without the use of graphic violence or brutal images. For example, Scottie buries his toy dinosaurs near a graveyard (creating the chilling idea that humans could become extinct like the dinosaurs if they are not careful). Carol combs her hair while looking in the mirror at the beginning of the film, and she is attractive and sexy. The same set-up is used at the conclusion of the film, but now her hair is falling out and she looks old and very tired. Brad finally rides his bike to the top of the hill to take over the short wave radio, but the absence of his pal, the older radio operator, is painfully clear.

Lynne Littman has said,

> In *Testament*, I have people disappear. I don't care about the symptoms of their disease, the radiation poisoning. I care about their disappearance. This film is about loss and grief. I want you to come out of it and say: 'I have seen my worst nightmare and it hasn't really happened yet. Thank God, there's still time.' (Chase C8)

Both *Testament* and *The Day After* provoked much thought and discussion in 1983. And today, the films are still relevant, even though there is less tension between the super powers as historic changes take place in the Soviet Union and between East and West Germany. But in the future, I predict that *Testament* is the film which will last for two reasons. One, it has a universality which is directly related to human experiences. Most viewers have not been involved in nuclear explosions in all their gore and devastation. But they have been involved with family, home, and loss, and they can better identify with *Testament*'s less graphic suburban landscape and the domestic focus. Two, the film has a profound meaning. Although it questions whether or not we deserve the children, or will deserve them, it suggests that we can. By not committing suicide and not killing her children as well, she proves that she deserves the children. And by not committing suicide and not killing our children with nuclear weapons, we can prove that we deserve the children. Carol chooses life. She will do what she can, just as we have time to do what we can. *Testament* ends on a note of nobility.

Note

[1] Many variables are involved. For a good discussion of appeals to fear, see Stewart Tubbs and Sylvia Moss, *Human Communication*, pages 324-325.

Works Cited

Browning, Robert. "The Pied Piper of Hamelin." *The Complete Poetical Works of Browning.* Ed. Horace E. Scudder. Boston: Houghton Mifflin, 1895.

Chase, Chris. "Lynne Littman Explains Why She Made *Testament.*" *New York Times* 4 Nov. 1983: C8.

Tubbs, Stewart, and Sylvia Moss. *Human Communication.* New York: Random House, 1987.

Wellemeyer, Marilyn. "Investing in Planet Earth." *Investment Vision.* Nov./Dec. 1989: 40.

Nuclear Family/Nuclear War

Paul Brians

There exist in English over a thousand depictions of nuclear war and its aftermath. Despite the overwhelming importance of the subject, few are moving or memorable.[1] The coming nuclear holocaust has been trivialized in a variety of ways: as the creator of a mutated super-race, as a background for horror fiction, as an excuse for the ever-popular last-man-and-woman theme, and—more and more often during the past decade—as the setting for scenes of violent combat which make the mushroom clouds looming in the background seem relatively insignificant.[2] Among the handful of exceptions which approach the theme more thoughtfully and memorably, three seem to cluster together, as a small, but powerful humanistic counter-tradition to the dominant trends in novels and films about nuclear war: Judith Merril's *Shadow on the Hearth* (1950), Helen Clarkson's *The Last Day* (1959), and the film *Testament* (1983), directed by Lynne Littman, and based on "The Last Testament" (1981) by Carol Amen.[3] The most obvious link between them is that they are all self-consciously and explicitly intended as women's views of women's experiences.[4] All concern housewives suffering after a devastating nuclear attack from the impact of radioactive fallout, trying to preserve their families from a menace they are powerless to defeat. The bare fact that they are by women makes them exceptional; only about five percent of all nuclear war fiction is by female authors. A few of these are as belligerent, sadistic, and ignorant as the worst such fiction by men, but women generally depict nuclear war with more sensitivity and intelligence than most male authors. However, these three works are united by more than gender.

In all three, the setting is a small community more or less removed from the urban centers where the bombs are dropped. No blast damage is depicted in them.

In all three, loving relationships between husband and wife are severed by the war.

In all three, the fate of children is the major focus of the plot.

In all three, separation from distant family members by the war is a source of anxiety.

"Nuclear Family/Nuclear War" appeared in *Papers on Language and Literature*, volume 26, number 1. Reprinted by permission of the journal.

In all three members of the community risk their lives to aid each other, and great importance is placed on cooperation.

All three depict the course of radiation disease in far more detail and far more accurately than the vast majority of other works, using the best scientific knowledge available to their creators.

All three use the death of birds as a striking image of the impact of radiation on nature.

In all three, the authorities are depicted as ineffectual, and civil defense is revealed to be a fraud.

These similarities would not be so striking were it not that most nuclear war fiction is very different: children are usually absent or presented only as mutilated corpses, grief for the loss of loved ones is less common than the excitement of forming new relationships, extreme individualism and the destruction of community ties are routine, blast effects are far more often depicted than radiation disease, the effect of radiation most commonly depicted is the creation of superhuman mutants, and attention is rarely paid to the impact of atomic weapons on nature (except recently, in climatological terms). In their doubts about the effectiveness of civil defense, however, they are in the mainstream. Few authors think much can be done to mitigate the effects of nuclear war.

Strikingly, although these works seem to form a tightly linked tradition, no one of the later works is indebted to its predecessors. Although dozens of authors had treated the subject before her, Judith Merril was a pioneer in depicting nuclear war in a realistic fashion, focusing on its impact in a domestic setting. Helen Clarkson wrote her book in direct reaction to the sensation surrounding Nevil Shute's *On the Beach*, but had never read or heard of Merril's book.[5] Carol Amen had not read either novel, or even considered treating the subject, until she had a vision of nuclear war and sat down to write it out in the form of a fictional journal. Lynne Littman was as little interested in the subject as Amen until she encountered "The Last Testament" in *Ms.* and determined to make it the basis of a feature film. Littman used Amen as her sole fictional source, as ignorant of her predecessors as was Amen.[6] Yet it almost seems as if these four women were collaborating to create a collective interpretation of nuclear war from a special and powerful point of view.

Other parallels can be drawn, especially between Clarkson's novel and Littman's film. For instance, in both the community gathers in a church and hears the local doctor describe the symptoms of radiation disease. One coincidence is especially astonishing. In *The Last Day*, Clarkson compares the willingness of modern adults to expose their children to a kind of war which victimizes children above all to the foolishness of the citizens in the story of the Pied Piper of Hamlin (119). Littman, quite independently, used the same motif in her film, which features a powerful scene where the parents of Hamelin, California, weep as they hear a kindergartener in the school play—*The Pied Piper of Hamlin*—solemnly pronounce that the children will return when the adults deserve them. Strangest of all, when Littman arrived to shoot her film in the town of Sierra Madre, she discovered that the local school was preparing—again, independently—to stage a play: *The Pied Piper of Hamlin*. The school children were able to use the stage set designed for the film.

Striking as such coincidences are, it is more useful to compare these works with each other in such a way as to bring out their unique qualities.

Shadow on the Hearth is least effective in "bringing home" the horrors of nuclear war. Its title hints at its understated treatment of the theme. The family comes off relatively unscathed: the youngest daughter suffers from a moderate case of radiation disease which is treated and halted, and the father of the family goes into shock temporarily and is grazed by a bullet. Would-be intruders are fought off with a frying pan. Instead of focusing on the real dangers posed by nuclear war, our attention is distracted by family squabbles, an overly-attentive civil defense worker who lusts after the mother, and other, overly complicated plot threads. The protagonist is a panicky, ignorant housewife whose continual refusal to face facts is no doubt meant to teach the reader the importance of informing oneself about nuclear issues; but she is such an irritating character that it is difficult to care about her fate. Unsurprisingly, the book has a moderately happy ending as the family is reunited and seems likely to survive. And although the U.S. has been badly battered, Russia has surrendered, so that the war is not depicted as entirely futile.

What makes *Shadow on the Hearth* worth discussing is, first, its depiction of the development of the teenaged daughter, who rejects her mother's willful ignorance and carefully arms herself with the technical knowledge needed to deal with the emergency. This is more than a routine coming-of-age story; it is a warning that women can no longer afford to leave technical matters to men, that in the atomic age science is everybody's business. Second, Merril speaks out against the anticommunist hysteria building in 1950 by depicting the search for subversives as foolish and destructive. The high school math teacher who must hide from the police because he is considered a security risk proves to be the hero who protects the family at the risk of his own life. He is clearly modelled on real-life cases such as that of the Rosenbergs and Klaus Fuchs, and anticipates strikingly the case of Robert Oppenheimer. It is true that Merril rather muddles the issue by stating that the Russian missiles were guided to their targets by fifth columnists, so that the subversive-chasers are not behaving in an entirely irrational manner; but nevertheless, given the date and the mood of the country, defending an Oppenheimer-like character took courage and insight.

The virtues of Helen Clarkson's *The Last Day* are much more evident. It was the most carefully researched nuclear novel before Whitley Strieber and James Kunetka's 1984 best-seller, *Warday*. It is also one of the most effective, because of its believable and sympathetic characters, its well-crafted prose, its eloquent and consistent articulation of a credible political point of view, and its striking use of symbolism.

At the beginning of the novel Clarkson subtly creates a mood of impending disaster by depicting a number of ominous incidents hinting at death and destruction: a cat gives birth to a dead kitten (9), the protagonist kills an ant (10), a child is beaten (11), the protagonist cuts her finger and wonders whether she will ever get to Athens "before I die" (13), a looming wave seems poised to destroy her and her husband (16), he explains that birds sing to express territoriality and warn other birds off (19), then he says, remarking on the wind, "Hurricanes can kill and a mistral can drive some people to suicide" (20), and a fisherman knifes an inflated puffer fish, remarking, "That's the way we all bluff our enemies.... If we can" (23). Listed together like this, these portents might seem heavy-handed, but in fact their effect in the novel is subtly to undercut the prevailing good feeling as a happy, loving couple prepare to spend a vacation at their cottage near the beach.

Clarkson is highly unusual in expressing a consistent and well-informed political view. She creates a belligerent Secretary of State clearly based on John Foster Dulles, a scientist who becomes—like Oppenheimer—a security risk because of his qualms about working on nuclear weapons, his eloquent pacifist wife who argues passionately against the policies which have led to war, and a doctor who does the same. The substantial political speeches are well integrated into the plot and do not seem extraneous or overbearing. They are also almost unique in nuclear war fiction, which is generally notable for its lack of political analysis.

The neighbor who is the scientist, like the teacher in *Shadow on the Hearth*, has quit his job in atomic research because of his objections to nuclear weapons and has become the target of security investigations. In both cases these scientists risk their lives trying to save the victims of the very weapons they had helped to develop.

Clarkson's political ideas often have a strikingly contemporary quality which makes her sound like the activists who in recent times have combined feminism with opposition to nuclear reactors and weapons. She speaks, for instance, of a *Life* magazine editorial which said that "the only people who wanted to end nuclear testing were 'scared mothers, fuzzy liberals and weary taxpayers.' In other words: mothers are a lunatic fringe, a minority group..." (42). Indeed, it was women who reacted most strongly to the threat of test-generated fallout which first penetrated public consciousness when the 1954 Bravo test in the Pacific went awry and contaminated the crew of a Japanese fishing boat, an event to which Clarkson alludes specifically (34).

The concern for the welfare of children which was associated with the ensuing movement for a test-ban treaty permeates *The Last Day*. Even though the protagonist's only daughter is grown and studying in Europe, she thinks and talks constantly about the threat nuclear weapons pose to children. And her concern is shared by most of the other characters in the novel. Almost the first thing her husband says after the bomb goes off near them is, "Listen!...Do you hear a child crying?" (45).

Clarkson tries not to sentimentalize parental concern. One of her main characters is an immature, irresponsible woman who alternately abuses, insults, and neglects her little girl. But Clarkson also reacts to the vogue for blaming society's ills on domineering mothers inaugurated by Philip Wylie's attack on "momism" in *A Generation of Vipers* (1942), by asserting that what America suffered from was not too much nurturing love, but too little (95). Although she avoids simplistically depicting women as natural peacemakers, she does articulate an implicitly feminist ideology of opposition to nuclear weapons.

Clarkson determined to treat the subject of nuclear war in a scientifically accurate manner, consciously reacting to the criticism aimed at the credibility of *On the Beach*. She consulted with the editors of the *Bulletin of Atomic Scientists*, and created the first really technically well-informed novel on the subject. Like Clarkson, Lynne Littman was also unusual in carefully researching fallout effects for her film *Testament*, mainly through consultation with members of Physicians for Social Responsibility. Although the apocalyptic attitude of both works—which envisions the death of all humanity in a nuclear war—is not supported by most scientific estimates of the results of conflicts producing anything less than a nuclear winter, the treatment of radiation disease in both of these works is extremely rare in works depicting future nuclear wars.[7] In one respect, Clarkson was ahead of her successor, in noting the effects of atomic explosions on broadcasting. She comes very close to anticipating the concept of electromagnetic pulse radiation (EMP), which many now believe would eliminate most communication in the wake of an attack. The concept is dealt with in passing in *Testament*, through a reference to transistors having been blown, but a good deal of the film depicts the continuing functioning of short-wave radio equipment, presumably old-fashioned sets using tubes.

Despite the general scientific accuracy of *Testament*, one wonders why no one in this prosperous and well-educated community seems to understand the importance of staying indoors, in as much shelter as possible. True, in *The Last Day*, the characters roam about a good deal; but they are consciously exposing themselves to known risks to aid others, particularly children. One of the more striking scenes in *Testament* depicts parents rushing about the streets immediately after the blast searching for their children. This seems most natural, but no one makes the slightest effort after that point to minimize their exposure to fallout, except by drinking bottled water and eating canned food. Littman states that the people of the town of Hamelin don't understand what they are dealing with, but in fact the scene in the church makes it clear that they have accurate information available to them. The main reason the people do not seek shelter seems to have been that they did not do so in Amen's story, and Littman was trying to follow that story as closely as possible. Artistically, it was undoubtedly a wise decision, since the film concentrates above all on people interacting with each other in a community and not as isolated individuals. This would hardly have been possible had each family been cowering in its house.

Littman is remarkably faithful in following the main outlines and even most minor details of "The Last Testament." The vast majority of lines of dialogue written by Amen are incorporated verbatim into the script. Littman was struck powerfully by Amen's story, and gives its author the entire credit for inspiring her work on the film. Both Amen and her husband died shortly after the release of the film, but she left behind a legacy which will endure in the shape of Littman's film.

However, though Amen's story provided the inspiration and the framework for Littman, it is in fact little more than a sketch, and it was Littman herself who fleshed out the characters and contributed many of the most striking scenes in *Testament*. The long prologue introducing us to the members of the family, especially the father, and preparing us to grieve their deaths, is entirely new. Other new scenes include the teenaged daughter's piano lessons, which give an artistic dimension to the determination not to surrender to annihilation; the very moving scene in which the mother speaks lovingly of marital love, and her daughter replies, "But not for me"; the home movies which contrast the losses of the present with the joys of the past; the scene of the son dancing with his mother to the Beatles' "All My Loving," whose lyrics refer insistently and ironically to a blissful future; and the scene in which the mother, salvaging batteries from the answering machine, discovers a last, poignant message from her husband.

The children's deaths, which are related in an artlessly direct fashion in Amen's story, are made simultaneously unsentimental and even more powerful by the indirect way in which we are informed of them. When the youngest boy dies, we are introduced to that fact by the mother's wordless, frantic search for his favorite stuffed bear to bury with him. A really remarkable shot shows the mother tearing a sheet and beginning to sew, as the camera pulls back to reveal that she is making the shroud for her daughter.

Littman made other important changes, making the population of Hamelin more ethnically varied than in the original, greatly expanding the older son's role, so that he takes on his father's duties, and then those of their ham radio operator friend. There is a fight over feeding a stray cat in a time of short rations (a similar scene occurs in *The Last Day*). One wonders whether Amen approved of the passionate kiss between the protagonist of *Testament* and the local preacher, which symbolizes a turning toward merely human love when divine mercy seems to have failed.

Another fine contribution of Littman is the last scene, in which the mother, a mentally handicapped boy they have taken in, and her son, celebrate the latter's last birthday in a pathetic ceremony consisting of lighting three birthday candles on as many squares of graham cracker. It strikingly anticipates the similarly pathetic celebration of the last Christmas in the recent Soviet nuclear war film, *Letters from a Dead Man*. In both cases the ceremony implies a will to live on, not to surrender meekly, although the entire human race is almost certainly doomed to extinction.

One other alteration was not Littman's doing. The Catholic editors of the *St. Anthony Messenger* who first published Amen's story, requested that she not have the mother commit suicide with the children. Amen, who was not a Catholic, agreed to change the ending. The result is one of the most memorable scenes in the movie, in which the mother's inability deliberately to take their lives and her own seems far more in character.

None of these works has been greatly influential. Merril's novel is unknown except to students of science fiction, the field in which she did most of her work. Although a version of her story was broadcast on television, it has been out of print for many years. Clarkson, well-known as a detective novelist under her married name of "Helen McCloy," undertook the writing and publication of *The Last Day* as a labor of love. It was totally obscured by the much greater success of two inferior novels: *On the Beach*, and Pat Frank's *Alas, Babylon*, which remained the only fictional treatments of nuclear war read by a large number of Americans for decades. Littman also undertook the filming of *Testament* in an idealistic spirit, creating it on a low budget ($750,000) for PBS's "American Playhouse" and recruiting actors who performed for much lower than normal salaries because of their belief in the importance of the film. Similarly, Littman's achievement was obscured by the near-simultaneous release of the sensational but banal and inaccurate television film, *The Day After*. One nuclear war story does not whet most people's appetites for more. Their interest in the subject is easily exhausted. Yet persons concerned with the dangers posed by nuclear weapons have much to be grateful for to these women—Merril, Clarkson, Amen, and Littman—for the intelligence, compassion, humanism, and artistry with which they have endowed a subject which is often thought to defy comprehension.[8]

Notes

[1]This and other generalizations about nuclear war fiction contained in this paper are based on the research done for my book, *Nuclear Holocausts: Atomic War in Fiction 1895-1984* and on continued work in the field since that time.

[2]See my article: "Red Holocaust: The Atomic Conquest of the West."

[3]To David Dowling goes the credit for first having noted in print the linkage between these works (221)...but although he considers them among the most powerful works of their kind, only Merril's novel is discussed further (59).

[4]Martha A. Bartter's "The Hand that Rocks the Cradle" is an interesting survey of women's fiction depicting nuclear war; but although she discusses Judith Merril's other piece of nuclear war fiction "That Only a Mother," she does not mention *Shadow on the Hearth*. She does briefly mention Clarkson's novel and *Testament*, but mistakenly identifies the latter as "Carol Amen's film" (258).

[5]Source: personal conversation with the author. Other statements about Clarkson are based on the same conversation.

[6]These and other statements about Amen and Littman are based on a personal conversation with Littman.

[7]The subject is more common, of course, in novels depicting the attacks on Hiroshima and Nagasaki.

[8]A more recent novel which focuses on related themes, Gudrun Pausewang's *The Last Children of Schevenborn*, should also be mentioned (translated from the German [*Die letzten Kinder von Schwenborn*, Ravensburg: Otto Maier, 1983]) by Norman M. Watt, Saskatoon, Saskatchewan: Western Producer Prairie Books, 1988. Although it is told from the point of view of a young boy and does not focus on the mother's role the way the others discussed in this article do, it is the most accurately detailed depiction yet published of the impact of an all-out nuclear war on a family. Lacking the artfulness of either Clarkson's or Littman's works, it nevertheless produces a powerful impact through accumulating detail after nightmarish detail in a way that strives for scientific accuracy, avoids sensationalism, and directly addresses the issues of plague, starvation, nuclear winter, etc.

Works Cited

Amen, Carol. "The Last Testament." *St. Anthony's Messenger* Sept. 1980: n.p.

Bartter, Martha A. "The Hand that Rocks the Cradle." *Extrapolation* 30 (1989): 254-266.

Brians, Paul. *Nuclear Holocausts: Atomic War in Fiction 1895-1984*. Kent, Ohio: Kent State University Press, 1987.

———. "Red Holocaust: The Atomic Conquest of the West." *Extrapolation* 28 (1987): 319-29.

Clarkson, Helen. *The Last Day: A Novel of the Day After Tomorrow*. NY: Torquil, 1959.

Dowling, David. *Fictions of Atomic Disaster*. Iowa City: University of Iowa, 1987.

Merril, Judith. *Shadow on the Hearth*. Garden City: Doubleday, 1950.

Testament. Dir. Lynne Littman. PBS "American Playhouse." 1981.

Wylie, Philip. *A Generation of Vipers*. New York: Farrar and Rinehart, 1942.

Thinking Woman's Children
and the Bomb

Helen Jaskoski

Sometime in the pre-dawn hours of July 16, 1979, an earthen dam holding back wastes produced by United Nuclear Corporation's uranium mill parted in Church Rock, New Mexico. From the widening breach poured ninety-four million gallons of highly contaminated effluent and 1,100 tons of wet slurry sands.

The spill filled the nearby Pipeline Arroyo and flowed south into the Rio Puerco.... About one hundred and fifteen miles downstream, in Holbrook, Arizona, monitors registered chemical alteration at the junction of the Rio Puerco and the Little Colorado rivers.

This was the largest radioactive waste spill in U.S. history, releasing more contaminants into the atmosphere than the Three Mile Island accident. Flora Naylor, a Navajo shepherd, was one of the people affected by the Church Rock disaster. Not knowing about the contamination, she walked across the river that morning to get to some of her sheep. Her sister, Etta Lee, described what followed:

Not even a month later her feet started getting sores; open sores, with pus, in between her toes. She went to the Indian Health Service in Gallup.... They amputated below her ankle.... A month later they amputated again, above the ankle. Then a year later below the knee. (Hinchman 1)

American Indian people, the first inhabitants of the North American continent, have also been first and longest in their exposure to nuclear power and its effects on the continent and its inhabitants. As much as half of the uranium reserves in the United States are located on Indian-owned land in the west, mostly in the Grants Belt of northern New Mexico. Navajo, Jemez, Laguna, Zia and Zuñi own the land, though only the Navajos and the Laguna Pueblo have so far leased land for exploration and mining (Roxanne Ortiz 121). From mining and processing through testing and finally the nightmare of attempts at reclamation and coping with waste, the invention and development of the nuclear present and future has occurred in proximity with, and affected the lives of, people who have maintained with stubborn persistence the ancient cultures of North America.

"Thinking Woman's Children and the Bomb" is reprinted from *Explorations in Ethnic Studies*, journal of the National Association of Ethnic Studies.

This paradox has not been lost on writers dealing with American Indian themes. Authors like Wendy Rose and Linda Hogan in poems and journals, Paula Gunn Allen in fiction and Stephen Popkes in science fiction are among those who have addressed nuclear issues in relation to American Indian themes and values.[1]

The two authors who have presented the most extended examination of nuclear issues from the perspective of Native American people are Leslie Marmon Silko and Martin Cruz Smith. Silko's *Ceremony* and Cruz Smith's *Stallion Gate* provide extended critiques of the nuclear age.[2] Both authors identify themselves as Native American and both have made American Indian culture and characters central to much of their writing. In spite of fundamental differences in tone, plot and outcome, *Ceremony* and *Stallion Gate* are remarkably similar. In both, nuclear weapons and nuclear power (desire, invention, construction and use of nuclear power and its artifacts) are seen, not as a special case of weapons or power, or a new phenomenon, but as the logical and inevitable culmination of western empirical thought. In both novels this mode of thought is juxtaposed, and in conflict, with the philosophy of the peoples within whose lands the nuclear age is created.

The two books focus on central characters with very similar life experiences, though apparent differences in literary tone and mode could not be more extreme. *Ceremony* follows the design of romance and ritual comedy: a young hero undertakes a quest for a remedy to rescue his community from a plague or disaster (in *Ceremony* the plague is a drought); with the help of wise, powerful and sympathetic guides he reaches a resolution that sees the quester healed and matured while the drought is lifted and scapegoats are expelled. The protagonist of *Ceremony*, Tayo, is a young man lately come home from World War II and a Japanese prison camp. The novel follows his healing journey, centering on traditional Pueblo and Navajo beliefs and ceremonial practices through which he becomes cured of the maladies of psychological disintegration, guilt and despair contracted during the war.

Stallion Gate, by contrast, is a skeptical, pessimistic probing of intrigue, deceit, arrogance and greed. Its protagonist, Joe Peña, is a young sergeant from the fictional pueblo of Santiago who has escaped from the Philippines after the Japanese invasion and who is assigned to be chauffeur to J. Robert Oppenheimer at Los Alamos and to be "liaison" with the Indians in the area. Though it moves without deviation towards a tragic ending, the tone of *Stallion Gate* is cued to Joe Peña's wry, acerbic, often harsh wit. *Ceremony* by contrast, is lyrical in style and pervaded with the sense of reverence befitting a religious ceremony, which in fact its author suggests the book may be.

Ceremony and *Stallion Gate* contain remarkable similarities in their settings, in the backgrounds of their protagonists, and in the philosophical oppositions within the divided society the novels picture. Both novels are set in New Mexico at some time in the mid to late forties. In *Ceremony* Tayo has returned to Laguna some time after being released from a hospital where he was treated for illness apparently brought on by battle and prison camp. The sections of *Stallion Gate* are precisely dated, from November 1943 to the first atomic explosion, July 16, 1945; important events take place in the fictional pueblo of Santiago, as well as at the Los Alamos laboratories and the Trinity test site at a former ranch called Stallion Gate.

The protagonists in both *Ceremony* and *Stallion Gate* have taken on the traditional role of warrior in their stories: both are soldiers who have fought in the Pacific and experienced the Japanese occupation. Tayo has been a prisoner of war in an unnamed tropical country. Joe Peña has survived an incredible rescue in the Philippines when, after being wounded in the retreat from the Japanese invaders, he is sent adrift in a small boat and picked up by a United States naval vessel.

Warriors abroad, both men are outsiders in their birthplaces. While their mothers are Indian, the race or allegiance of their fathers is doubtful. Tayo's mother is Laguna but his father is unknown, a Mexican or possibly an Anglo, it is rumored. While Joe Peña's mother is a potter and so conservative that she still wears traditional dress, his father had been a bootlegger and silent partner in an Albuquerque nightclub.

Both Tayo and Joe Peña, furthermore, are rejected by the women who are or who act as their mothers, in favor of brothers whom the mothers consider more acceptable. Tayo's mother, seduced by men and alcohol alike, leaves her young son with her elder sister, always called simply Auntie. Throughout Tayo's childhood Auntie blames him for the embarrassment and shame she feels at her sister's behavior, as she blames him later for returning home alive without bringing with him her own son, Rocky, who has died in the prison camp.[3] Joe Peña's mother, Dolores, considers her younger son, Rudy, her "only real son" (*SG* 74), and tells Joe not to return home until he brings Rudy, also captured or dead in the Pacific war, home with him.

For all their similarities in background and in being cast in the classic Indian role of warrior, essential differences in temperament, outlook and goals mark the two men. Joe Peña is urbane, street-wise, witty and cynical. For him, traditional village life is oppressive and dull. A jazz pianist and prizefighter, he is loyal and principled but survives by his wits, "your usual scams" (*SG* 6) as his commanding officer, Captain Augustino, remarks. His goal in the plot is to get $50,000 to buy out his father's partner and own the Casa Mañana, an Albuquerque jazz club, and to further this end he steals and sells from the project stores, and then arranges a fight and the bets on it on the eve of the Trinity test. In between his legal and extra-legal jobs he finds time for a robust sex life.

Tayo, by contrast, is quiet, introspective and most at home in the open pastures, mesas and mountaintops. He acts out his quest for healing and for psychological as well as physical return to village life in the search for a small herd of spotted cattle that his uncle, Josiah, had purchased some years before in Mexico as a breed most suited to the high arid ranges of northern New Mexico. If Joe Peña in his expansive sex appeal and con-man skills calls to mind some traditional and contemporary urban tricksters of Native American lore, then Tayo exemplifies the pastoral figure of the shepherd, the exemplar of a materially simple life sought in harmony with nature.

Science and Prophecy

Both novels depict their protagonist's quests in a context of clashing cultures and opposing world views. In both, atomic power, its production and its effects, is seen to be a logical and inevitable product of Western—that is, European or Anglo-American—thought and values. This idea is made clear through the contrast between two ways of thinking: the philosophy of the civilization that opened the uranium mines and eventually produced the bomb, and the belief system of the older cultures that developed and persist on the land where the bomb is produced. In each book the differences in Indian and non-Indian thought are the differences between an epistemology that is essentially phenomenological and one that is basically empirical. Native American thought, as portrayed in these novels, seeks understanding that is holistic and integrating, and its mode of discourse is prophecy and story. The Western—European or Euroamerican—world view, by contrast, tends toward atomism and the dis-integration of dissection and calculation; its mode of discourse is mathematical model and reductive analysis.

In *Ceremony* the contrast between the two modes of thought occurs in Tayo's recollections of school days and science teaching:

He knew what white people thought about the stories. In school the science teacher had explained what superstition was, and then held the science textbook up for the class to see the true source of explanations. He had studied those books, and he had no reasons to believe the stories any more. The science books explained the causes and effects. (*C* 94).

Later in the novel another recollection of science class opposes two views of nature: the American Indian attitude, which requires reverent and careful treatment of a sentient, fragile world on the one hand, and on the other hand the analytic viewpoint that regards nature as merely functional and essentially dead. Tayo considers how his search for reintegration into his community through ceremony and myth might be

crazy, the kind of old-time superstition the teachers at Indian school used to warn him and Rocky about. Like the first time in science class, when the teacher brought in a tubful of dead frogs, bloated with formaldehyde, and the Navajos all left the room; the teacher said those old beliefs were stupid. The Jemez girl raised her hand and said the people always told the kids not to kill frogs, because the frogs would get angry and send so much rain there would be floods. The science teacher laughed loudly, for a long time; he even had to wipe tears from his eyes. "Look at these frogs," he said, pointing at the discolored rubbery bodies and clouded eyes. "Do you think they could do anything? Where are all the floods? We dissect them in this class every year." (*C* 195)

Empirical science, the way of thinking that belongs with analytical prose, textbooks and capitalist entrepreneurs, takes the view that the natural world is inert, a reactionless object from which formulas or laws may be abstracted through probing, dissection, and measurement.[4]

Stallion Gate emphasizes on every page invasive, objectifying Western empiricism. The apparatus of empirical science obtrudes everywhere: miles of cables, uncounted geiger counters, sensors, cameras, recorders and calculators litter a landscape that has been dug out, paved over and cleared of living things. The Trinity explosion is to be a gigantic exercise in testing and measurement, for the purpose of which the desert, the atmosphere, and the earth itself are seen as nothing more than a single giant laboratory.

In contrast to all this scientific testing and measuring is the epistemology of the elders and clown priests in the Pueblo village. Clowns have a special and complex role in Pueblo religious ritual. Among their duties are the testing of society's rules by showing the effects of breaking rules, and restoring community harmony and equilibrium with parodies of exaggeration and excess (Hieb 171-188). Whereas graphs, formulas and mathematical models are means of scientific discourse, the traditional discourse of the Pueblos is carried on in ritual, story and prophecy. In *Stallion Gate* the clown priests dance a story mocking the experimental bomb and its promoters, General Leslie Groves and J. Robert Oppenheimer; they go so far as to identify and involve Oppenheimer himself in finally setting off the firecracker that stands for the bomb. Captain Augustino, surely intended to represent the OSS, believes the clowns may be passing on secret information to some current or future enemy of the United States government. Oppenheimer, on the other hand, believes he has a deep empathy with the Indians—or rather, that they have a deep empathy with him and his project:

The Hill isn't a place; it's a time warp. We are the future surrounded by a land and a people that haven't changed in a thousand years. Around us is an invisible moat of time. Anyone from the present, any mere spy, can only reach us by crossing the past. We're protected by the fourth dimension. (SG 142)

Oppenheimer and Augustino are both wrong.

Late in *Stallion Gate*, as the bomb test date draws near, magic sticks painted like lightning appear planted in places that have suffered fire. Joe Peña knows the sticks are intended to draw lightning that will destroy the testing equipment and ruin the experiment. A soldier asks incredulously if the Indians "really think they can bring lightning?" Joe replies, "They think they make the world go round" (SG 202). Mere spying does not figure on the agenda of the Pueblo elders. Neither does expanding the limits of empirical science. Their allegiance is not to a nation state or an ideology, but to the earth itself.

Opposed to the empirical process of truth-seeking, with its probing, testing and measuring, is the prophetic mode of arriving at knowledge, exemplified in story and dream. Both *Stallion Gate* and *Ceremony* contain prophecies about the atomic bomb. Throughout the twentieth-century events of *Ceremony* Leslie Silko interweaves verse-pattern renditions of several Keresan myths. One of these is the ancient story of how Nau'ts'ity'i, mother of the Keresan people, punished her neglectful children when they abandoned their duties because they were fascinated with witchcraft; another is the legend of the hero called Tayo, who challenged the Gambler in his cave and won back the rain clouds.

She casts her account of the creation of Europeans in the form of one of these traditional legends. It all began with witchcraft, according to Silko's poem, when a society of witches convened at the beginning of the world. One of the witches, eschewing incantations and potions, offered his craft in the form of a story:

> Okay
> go ahead
> laugh if you want to
> but as I tell the story
> it will begin to happen.

A race of destroyers emerges. They are scientists. They look at the world objectively—that is, as an object, reductively:

> They see no life
> When they look
> they see only objects.
> The world is a dead thing for them
> the trees and rivers are not alive
> the mountains and stones are not alive.

Further characterizing this race of destroyers is a will to power fueled by greed and driven by fear:

> They fear
> They fear the world.
> They destroy what they fear.
> They fear themselves.

The work of the destroyers will culminate, according to Silko's prophecy, in destruction of the world:

> Up here
> in these hills
> they will find the rocks,
> rocks with veins of green and yellow and black.
> They will lay the final pattern with these rocks
> they will lay it across the world
> and explode everything. (*C* 132-138)

Later Tayo finds the myth confirmed as he begins to understand the events of the Second World War. Walking through the abandoned uranium mine on the Laguna reservation, he contemplates the ravaged landscape, his proximity to Los Alamos and the Trinity site, and the relationship of it all to the holocaust at Hiroshima and Nagasaki. The destroyers have created "a circle of death that devoured people in cities twelve thousand miles away, victims who had never known these mesas, who had never seen the delicate colors of the rocks which boiled up their slaughter" (*C* 246).

Stallion Gate also contains prophecies of the overwhelming devastation that will result from the careless release of nuclear energy. Two Pueblo elders, Joe Peña's uncle Ben Reyes and the blind old man called Roberto, advise Joe Peña early in the story that the business at Los Alamos should be stopped, even though according to Joe (and popular opinion) they do not know or understand what is going on (*SG* 98). Later, they explain to Joe that their information has come in dreams which predict in symbolic images the proximate events of the book—the preparation and detonation of the test bomb—as well as the long-term consequences which none of the scientists is taking into account. Four people—in Taos, Hopi and Acoma—have all had the same dream: "They were making a gourd filled with ashes.... They take the gourd to the top of a long ladder and break it open. The ashes fall and cover the earth.... The ashes will poison the clouds and the water and the ground and everything that lives on it" (*SG* 206-207). Joe Peña's scornful response ("Sounds like scientific proof" [*SG* 207]) betrays a careless obliviousness to the diseased and radioactive cattle that he himself has had to destroy.

Earth Mother/Thought Woman

The two ways of thought identified as Indian and European are associated in both *Ceremony* and *Stallion Gate* with opposing views of the natural world. In the Indian view, as presented in the two books, the earth is life-bearing, female and to be respected. This recognition stands in opposition to the western or capitalist notion that land is an inert commodity, an exploitable source of wealth that can be destroyed for the amusement of the destroyers. Both *Stallion Gate* and *Ceremony* associate the female character of the earth with life-giving and nurturant qualities as embodied in the ancient myths of the people.

Much has been written about landscape and the sense of place in *Ceremony*.[5] Paula Gunn Allen makes the connection of earth-life-female-myth most explicit in her discussion of "The Feminine Landscape of... *Ceremony*." She writes that

> There are two kinds of women and two kinds of men in Leslie Marmon Silko's *Ceremony*.... Those in the first category belong to the earth spirit and live in harmony with her, even though this attunement may lead to tragedy. Those in the second are not of the earth but of human mechanism; they live to destroy that spirit, to enclose and enwrap it in their machinations, condemning all to a living death. Ts'eh is the matrix,

the creative and life-restoring power, and those who cooperate with her designs serve her and, through her, serve life. They make manifest what she thinks. (*The Sacred Hoop* 118)

Allen places the alcoholic and sometimes sadistic veterans, the witches in the traditional stories, the destroyers in Silko's own prophetic myth, and Tayo's cousin, Rocky, in the category of those who follow "human mechanism." Rocky is not an evil person, but he is a "progressive Indian" who rejects the lifestories of the people in favor of the science books' teachings, and thus rejects the life-affirming view of the world in favor of sterile materialism. To these examples we may add the ranchers who have fenced off Mount Taylor and fenced in Josiah's cattle.

Ultimately, absent in person but present in their effects on the land, are the unnamed capitalists and government operatives who first expropriated the land and water rights and then exploited the area's mineral resources. Their development efforts have transformed the land at the Cebolleta uranium mine from a place of extraordinary beauty into a lifeless wasteland:

They were driving U.S. Government cars, and they paid the land-grant association five thousand dollars not to ask questions about the test holes they were drilling.... Ever since the New Mexico territorial government took the northeast half of the grant, there had not been enough land to feed the cattle anyway.... Rain eroded big arroyos in the gray clay, and the salt bush took hold. (*C* 243)

By the time of Tayo's story "they had enough of what they needed and the mine was closed.... They left behind only the barbed wire fences, the watchman's shack and the hole in the earth...the last bony cattle wandering the dry canyons had died in choking summer dust storms" (*C* 244).

The hole in the ground that is the mine forms a deadly counter-symbol to the Pueblo understanding of the earth as literally the mother of all life, including the people themselves. The creation story at Laguna Pueblo explains that Thought Woman is the genetrix of the universe: she originated all things by naming them (Boas 7-8). The process of creation also involves, as in all the creation myths of the southwest, the people's migration up through their earlier, underground world(s) and their final emergence into the present world (Boas 1, 9). The place of emergence is a sacred hole in the ground, and it is represented in the village by the sipapu of the kiva. The kiva is a special room where public dances and rituals originate and where esoteric ceremonies are carried out; the sipapu is a small hole near the center of the floor. Kivas now are sometimes square buildings, but the ancient ruins of abandoned cities show that they were round and often underground.

This origin place in the Pueblo world is not merely symbolic or representative, but understood as the actual opening through which the people emerged. A Pueblo scholar has called the Tewa center "earth mother earth navel middle place" (Alphonso Ortiz 37), though the term navel seems a euphemism, since the opening appears to function rather as a vagina.

In the traditional planting ceremony, "The medicine men are believed to be able to reach right through the ground and place the seeds of all cultigens in the navel, thereby reawakening all of nature for the new year" (Alphonso Ortiz 114). While details of kiva construction and arrangement of ceremonies differ from village to village, all the Pueblos share these concepts of a center in the earth that connects the village in this upper world to original world(s) beneath, and through which the life-sustaining water and plant and animal life emerge.

So, in *Ceremony*, the uranium mine shaft where the final horrifying scene of Tayo's drama plays out, and where the bewitched and drunken veterans turn on each other in a rage of fear and sadism, was created to exploit the mineral wealth of the earth's interior. It is more than a visual blight, it is a real rape: a confiscation of the earth's life-sustaining resources for the purposes of destruction. The mine is the work of capitalist enterprise in the service of violence:

The gray stone was streaked with powdery yellow uranium, bright and alive as pollen; veins of sooty black formed lines with the yellow, making mountain ranges and rivers across the stone. But they had taken these beautiful rocks from deep within the earth and they had laid them in a monstrous design, realizing destruction on a scale only *they* could have dreamed. (*C* 246)

There is more than aesthetic blight here; this is fundamental blasphemy. The concept belongs to religious thought and is in keeping with the premise of the sacredness of land and life. The discourse of history and public policy enlarges, in grim irony, the novel's religious conceptualization of the nuclear disaster: in 1972 the Nixon administration suggested designating the blighted Four Corners region (i.e., the Navajo reservation) as a "National Sacrifice Area"—that is, an area "rendered literally uninhabitable through the deliberate elimination of the water supplies...and the proliferating nuclear contamination" (LaDuke and Churchill 120).

Stallion Gate develops the same parallels between life/female/nature and earth, and death/male/the artificial and mechanical. Joe Peña's mother, Dolores, bequeaths to her son a token of her special relationship to the earth. Dolores is a potter. Besides being a shaper of earth (as is the blind elder, Roberto, who mixes adobe for his livelihood) she is related to some of the accounts of the making of people, in which the creatrix first forms people from mud (Boas 224). Some time after her death Joe finds one of his mother's pots, "a little black seed bowl, round as a ball with a small hole" (*SG* 100). This pot, "a dark moon with a seed-sized hole on top" (*SG* 105) is as Joe realizes "like a little, smooth earth" (*SG* 185), a miniature planet, container of potential life and complete with tiny navel/vagina emergence hole. The novel explicitly contrasts the seed pot against the mock-up of the bomb being constructed by soldiers and scientists: the bomb "was a sphere of steel plates bolted together at the edges. It looked like a large steel spore—or a steel seed pot with a jagged rim" (*SG* 169). Instead of life this pot carries destruction; it is, as in old Roberto's dream, a gourd of ashes.

Throughout *Stallion Gate* those who engage in wanton destruction also belong with the culture of the bomb, and are set in opposition to the people who belong to the land. On Joe's first visit to the test site, he meets two Mescalero Apaches and a Navajo who explain how the army has expropriated the land for itself: "Army bought the ranchers out," one tells him, "but they made it in one payment so the ranchers had to give it all back in taxes, and if the ranchers try to get back on the land, they bomb them" (*SG* 46). A few hours later Joe, Oppenheimer, Groves and Klaus Fuchs watch army bombers sighting horses with phosphorus bombs and then strafing them:

From the bomb came running shapes: horses, brilliant with lather and the glare of the bomb, racing under the wing. Mustangs out of the mountains for the night grazing and the mares the ranchers had left behind.... At a distance of a mile, he thought he could hear not only their hooves but their breath, although he knew they were drowned out by the sounds of piston hydraulics and .50-caliber rounds. (*SG* 54-55)

The scene is eerily prophetic of the book's ending, which finds Joe Peña himself running, crazed, away from a bomb in the same place.

Two other scenes in *Stallion Gate* of animals being shot serve to define the opposition between those who respect the earth, especially as genetrix, and those whom both authors characterize as the destroyers. Joe Peña is horrified when Captain Augustino shoots a gravid she-elk, and he almost shoots the captain in retaliation. As Alphonso Ortiz points out, the Tewa proscription against hunting animals in their mating season shows that the practical and the symbolic are inseparable aspects of the people's paramount project, survival and the continuance of life: "Most important, the Tewa do not want to kill the females with young because this would jeopardize the future availability of game" (113).

After the elk-shooting episode, in the course of destroying what he takes to be a radioactive steer, Joe Peña himself kills a cow that is about to calve. The sight brings back to him the earlier hunting incident:

Now he remembered why he was so upset with Augustino when they'd gone hunting.... Not shooting an animal that was carrying was an Indian stricture, a primitive taboo. Not against killing life, but against killing the *seed* of life. (*SG* 60)

This idea of the seed of life is contrary to Oppenheimer's fantasy that the pueblo is some sort of ancient, indulgent "time warp." What the traditionalists know, rather, is that it is the present that contains both past and future, and that must be protected. They see that the nuclear business is poisoning the land, which is immediate and present, and thereby destroying the cattle which are the people's subsistence and future. The explanation for the cow's radioactive condition lies in the volatile, fragile nature of the earth itself, which has been disturbed by aggressive mining undertaken on the pastureland: "Every canyon around Los Alamos had cows, and every canyon had sites where poisonous isotopes were vented or exploded, spewed and sown into the soil and water" (*SG* 60). The nuclear enterprise sows death.

In *Ceremony* Silko describes in a similar manner the destruction and devastation at the Cebolleta mine:

Early in the spring of 1943, the mine began to flood with water from subterranean springs. They hauled in big pumps and compressors on flat-bed trucks from Albuquerque.... But later in the summer the mine flooded again, and this time no pumps or compressors were sent. They had enough of what they needed, and the mine was closed. (*C* 243-244)

Both *Ceremony* and *Stallion Gate* depict the beginning of the spillage and contamination that continue today, poisoning Flora Naylor and her flocks and jeopardizing the future for all the people. In discussion of the Rio Puerco contamination among a group of Navajos

one man, seeing far into the future, said he felt guilty for handing down contaminated animals to his children and grandchildren. He said that the animals are part of the Navajo's religious and spiritual system and he was concerned that his descendants would reject their religious and spiritual heritage for fear that the animals would always be contaminated. (Hinchman 10)

For Leslie Silko and Martin Cruz Smith, as for the Navajo shepherds and their families, the fate of animals is both symbol for and prophecy of the fate of human children of Mother Earth. In fact, among the earliest victims of the nuclear industry were Indian mine workers, who besides being cheated in many cases out of ownership of early claims, suffered injuries from unsafe working conditions and equipment.[6] Some studies report the rate of death and incapacitation from cancer among Navajo mine workers as close to eighty percent (LaDuke and Churchill 114).

Pueblo myths personify the earth's creative potential as a woman, and both *Ceremony* and *Stallion Gate* refer to her by name as Thought-Woman or Thinking Woman. Thinking Woman created the world in the beginning, bringing all things into being by thinking of them and naming them, and so she is the originator of language as well as of material things (Boas 9).

In *Ceremony* Thought-Woman is the originator and muse of the story: at the very beginning Leslie Silko presents her authorial self as Thought-Woman's amanuensis:

Ts'its'tsi'nako, Thought-Woman
is sitting in her room
and whatever she thinks about
appears.
* * *
She is sitting in her room

> thinking of a story now
>
> I'm telling you the story
> she is thinking. (*C* 1)

Thought-Woman comprehends the whole of *Ceremony*, witchcraft and evil as well as nurturance and healing. This comprehensiveness stands in sharp contrast to the manner in which she enters *Stallion Gate*, and it is related to the difference in the moral universes of the two novels.

For Joe Peña, Thinking Woman is a mythical figure from a culture he has intellectually rejected (though he adheres to its ethical precepts of respect, loyalty and competence). Her avatar is Anna Weiss, a Jewish refugee from Germany working for Oppenheimer on the bomb project. Anna Weiss's job is to produce simulations, mathematical formulas that will predict the nature and extent of the bomb's damage. She is the only person on the project who considers the future, and like old Roberto and the other Indian dreamers she prophesies to Joe about the bomb:

No one looks ahead to after the bomb is used. Or asks whether the bomb *should* be used, or, at least, demonstrated to the Japanese first...they don't think of the consequences. I have. On the punch cards are not only the fireball, the shock wave, the radiation, but also an imaginary city—so many structures of steel, of wood, of concrete. Houses shatter under shocks of one-tenth to one-fifth of an atmosphere. For steel buildings the duration of the shock is important. If the pulse lasts several vibration seconds, peak pressure is the important quantity. (*SG* 184)

With knowledge comes responsibility, and Anna Weiss in her prophecy is the only person who truly realizes and accepts the terrible responsibility which the bomb creates:

Nobody else sees it, as if they can't imagine a shadow until the sun is up. I see it every day. Every day, I kill these thousands and thousands of imaginary people. The only way to do it is to be positive that they are purely imaginary, simply numbers. Unfortunately, this reinforces a new fantasy of mine. There are times when I feel as if I am one of those numbers in one of the columns on one of the punch cards flying through the machine. I feel myself fading away. (*SG* 184)

Both Anna Weiss in *Stallion Gate* and Tayo in *Ceremony* feel responsible for the destruction they witness, and both find that they are themselves subject to being eroded away by the destructive forces they encounter. What Anna Weiss describes as "fading away" is precisely Tayo's condition when he first returns to the U.S. after the war. For a long time he is invisible, a vapor, lacking even an outline and fading into the white walls of the institution where he spends some time before returning to the village. Like Tayo, Anna seeks healing in a renunciation of her connection with the project of destruction. But although she allies herself with the Pueblo traditionalists and their perception of the destructiveness of the bomb, her powers for healing are limited or nonexistent. *Stallion Gate* is a naturalistic work, and insofar as Anna Weiss embodies a prophetic voice, she is Thinking Woman as Cassandra, not as Demeter.

Good and Evil

The continued presence of Indian people on the North American continent and the existence of the atomic bomb have a parallel function with relation to the prevailing national mythology: both require that the American people confront their fallacy of collective innocence and their obsession with freedom from guilt. R.W.B. Lewis has documented how the formation of the country in the first half of the nineteenth century included the invention of an American national character endowed with prelapsarian innocence: America as the New Eden, and (descendents of European immigrant) Americans as the New Adam. Reginald Horsman details the simultaneous and concomitant creation of doctrines of Anglo-Saxon racial superiority, which served to justify the continental takeover.

Both fictions were necessary to justify aggressive expansionism and capitalist exploitation of the continent's resources, and the removal or domination of peoples who did not belong to the privileged group. The ideal of a New Eden required a garden. Thus was born the fantasy of a wilderness—pristine, voluptuous, and above all, empty—the romantic vision most poetically evoked in Nick Carraway's farewell to Jay Gatsby:

> ...a fresh, green breast of the new world. Its vanished trees, the trees that had made way for Gatsby's house, had once pandered in whispers to the last and greatest of all human dreams; for a transitory enchanted moment man must have held his breath in the presence of this continent, compelled into an aesthetic contemplation he neither understood nor desired, face to face for the last time in history with something commensurate to his capacity for wonder. (Fitzgerald 123)

But, contrary to Nick Carraway's fantasy, and the dreams and desires of millions of immigrants and their children—the New World Garden of Eden was not empty.

This pervasive American myth of innocent beginnings in a new, unpopulated, Eden cannot be sustained in the face of Indian testimony, and especially in the presence of surviving Indians. "Man" had not just recently arrived from Europe, the land was not empty, not wilderness, not unsettled, not—according to the people already living in it—undeveloped. It was not an unpopulated garden of Eden created expressly for a new race of men, but a continent with a population placed at the mercy of invaders with a superior technology in the service of an insatiable greed.

Likewise, the development and especially the use of nuclear weapons cannot have been the work of a people with no capacity for evil. Acute defensiveness even now permeates the attitude of apologists for the bomb: there is a compulsion to prove that the destruction of Hiroshima and Nagasaki was not merely militarily effective but morally defensible as well. *Stallion Gate* contains an extended example of this moral defensiveness in a debate carried on between J. Robert Oppenheimer and another physicist, Harvey

Pillsbury, on the relative ethics of using the bomb on various targets. The simple admission that it will be used because it will mean conquest is not enough: the bombing of cities must be justified as saving lives, so that the act will seem guilt-free as well as successful.

In both *Stallion Gate* and *Ceremony* evil manifests itself as the atomistic and dis-integrating forces of greed and racism. Yet the books' visions of the moral universe are radically different. Silko presents good and evil as metaphysical entities, mysteries beyond rational thought. *Stallion Gate* has no gods: evil emerges in the actions of the novel's fallible, flawed characters.

Silko identifies fear and greed as propellants of racist destruction, which she sees as having its birth in European thought. According to the prophetic myth she constructs for *Ceremony*, the Destroyers, coming from far across the ocean, indiscriminately "kill what they fear." Their self-destructive rage to consume and to destroy will turn against them, however, and "stolen rivers and mountains/ the stolen land will eat their hearts/ and jerk their mouths from the Mother" (*C* 136).

Tayo recognizes race hatred as the work of the destroyers when he understands why he had persistently identified Japanese soldiers with his uncle and cousin:

From the jungles of his dreaming he recognized why the Japanese voices had merged with Laguna voices, with Josiah's voice and Rocky's voice; the lines of cultures and worlds were drawn in flat dark lines on fine light sand, converging in the middle of witchery's final ceremonial sand painting. From that time on, human beings were one clan again, united by the fate the destroyers planned for all of them, for all living things. (*C* 246)

Silko also links dis-integration associated with racism to dis-placement that removes people from the sustaining land to which they belong. Displaced by war from the arid United States southwest to the humid south Pacific jungle, Tayo lacks the proper resources for dealing with constant rainfall, and he acts inappropriately: he curses the rain and thus, in his mind, at least, brings on the drought that besets his village when he comes home. The nature of his illness, and therefore the first step towards his cure, become defined in the Los Angeles railroad station when he collapses in the midst of a group of Japanese-Americans returning from the concentration camps in the desert and midwest to their forcibly abandoned homes and farms on the west coast. The first step toward healing must be a step towards home, a return to one's own place.

In *Stallion Gate* individual characters exemplify the same greed and paranoid hatred that Silko personifies in the mythical race of destroyers. The pottery broker, Mrs. Quist, embodies capitalist lust for profit in her relationship with Dolores, buying pots for a dollar and selling them for fifty times as much. Joe Peña explains to the avaricious woman that his mother was not driven by market and profit, but by traditional Pueblo reserve, decorum and respect: "You always made that kind of money off Dolores. She always knew. I used to tell her, but she was too embarrassed for you to say anything. She was embarrassed for your greed" (*SG* 101).

If the venal Mrs. Quist personifies the demeaning greed of the capitalist mentality, mendacious and vindictive Captain Augustino provides the counterpart in paranoid fear. In charge of security at the project, Augustino bears an eerie resemblance to Oliver North: he is a man who says, "I don't need orders from anyone" (*SG* 31). Further, he pursues a fanatical vendetta against Oppenheimer, "the Third Great Jew...intent on developing an atomic weapon here only so that he can deliver the finished plans to his Soviet friends" (*SG* 31-32).

But Augustino is only the fullest efflorescence of the racism that flourishes everywhere in the America of *Stallion Gate*: from the crude and explicit bigotry of Indian Service agents, to the whining nastiness of Klaus Fuchs, who makes known from the first his contempt for Joe and all Indians. Even Oppenheimer betrays the thinness of his fantasied empathy with the people he has been living among; when advised of Indian objections to the project he asks if Joe "really think[s] I'm going to let the effort of all these good men be endangered by a...tribe" (*SG* 309; ellipses in original).

Augustino's worst crime, however, is not against any person or group, but an attack on thought itself. He orders Joe to help him plant a piece of evidence in Oppenheimer's clothes to link the physicist to Gold, the spy working with Fuchs. Augustino's plot against Oppenheimer parallels Santa's work on propaganda. Santa is the project psychiatrist. Ostensibly present to study the effects of the bomb project on the mental condition of the men involved with it, he actually concocts propaganda stories intended to deceive the public:

If the bomb makes a big bang, then we'll report that an ammunition dump exploded without loss of life. If we blow up the desert and everyone in it, then we'll have to come up with a different story....an alternative, assimilable emergency. 'Epidemic,' 'tainted water,' 'chemical warfare.'...The Freudians want 'tainted water,' naturally. (*SG* 219).

Like the witches in *Ceremony*, who create a counter-myth of destruction against the traditional myth of creation, both Santa and Augustino create stories. Their stories, too, are counter-myths, corruptions of the European mythology of empirical science. Falsifying evidence and distorting results, they act out in Martin Cruz Smith's novel the self-destructive tendencies Leslie Silko personifies as witches.

Both Leslie Silko and Martin Cruz Smith meditate in their novels on the paradox of the creation of the nuclear world in such close proximity to ancient Pueblo culture. In an interview Silko has acknowledged that

The Pueblo people have always concentrated upon making things grow, and appreciating things that are alive and natural, because life is so precious in the desert. The irony is that so close to us, in Los Alamos, New Mexico, scientists began the scientific and technological activity which created the potential end to our whole planet, the whole human race. The first atomic bomb was exploded in New Mexico, very close by us. To me it is very striking that this happened so close to the Pueblo people. (Seyerstad 26-27)

Stallion Gate and *Ceremony* can be read as extended meditations on that paradox. Both books present the perspective of the Pueblos as being a long-tested philosophy of human survival, and a critique of Western faith in technology.

The two novels differ radically in the possibilities they present for coping with the nuclear menace they describe. Silko's novel allows for redemptive healing in a world that can accept and give priority to a simple, pastoral life. It is a profoundly religious vision, affirming the possibility of spiritual transcendence and the creation of a nurturing community separate from the dominant culture, so long as the necessary connection with the land can be sustained. *Stallion Gate* offers only a secular world, where even—as Captain Augustino says—the laws of science are no longer dependable, and where each person lives out individual values in unsupported isolation.

Their basic premises, however, are the same. Although Silko offers a religious vision that postulates an inherently ordered universe, whereas Cruz Smith presents a rigorously secular view that emphasizes human limitations and imperfectability, both authors' critiques of the postnuclear world move beyond the immediate issues of weapons, war and power to question the sufficiency of rational thought itself.

Notes

[1]Poems by Wendy Rose and Linda Hogan are in Green 216-217 and 157-178, respectively; also see Hogan, *Seeing through the Sun.* For discussion of Rose's and Hogan's poems see Allen *The Sacred Hoop* 169-172. Paula Gunn Allen depicts a nuclear test explosion in a chapter from a novel-in-progress titled *Raven's Road* (Bartlett 51-63). Popkes' story, "Deathwitch," projects the traditional figure of Coyote into a post-nuclear future. An unreleased film produced by Leslie Silko also develops the theme of destruction of land through open-pit uranium mining.

[2]*Stallion Gate* and *Ceremony* will be cited in parentheses as *SG* and *C*, respectively, with page numbers in the text.

[3]As the sons of sisters, Tayo and Rocky are as closely related as brothers according to Pueblo family patterns; see Dozier 145-146.

[4]The dissection of frogs is apparently becoming a pervasive metaphor for the invasive, life-denying side of empirical science. In Gerald Vizenor's *Griever* the protagonist recalls liberating live but doomed frogs from a high school classroom. In Victorville, California, a high school student went to court in 1987 to establish her right to refrain from dissecting a live frog in her biology class; she won her case on appeal.

[5]See especially Garcia; Lincoln; Nelson. Silko has herself emphasized the theme in polemical writings (see, e.g., "An Old-Time Indian Attack").

[6]Navajo miners have spoken extensively of the hazardous working conditions, though much of their testimony has been buried in research documents. Oral historians have collected a great deal of testimony from men like John Billsie, hired during the 1940s at age 13, who recollected moving vanadium with shovel and wheelbarrow. Ventilation in the mines was poor, and though laws enforced by mine inspectors were supposed to protect the workers, "The mine inspector don't come around.... It's quite a while before

he gets there" (Oral History Collection. California State U Fullerton. OH 275). Ned Yazzie and Jimmie Singer were both disabled as a result of faulty equipment; Yazzie described how he was injured driving one of the mine's trucks: "It use to be bad before. The equipments were too old, out of order: [bad] brakes, no doors, no rear view mirrors" (Tr. Fern Charlie. OH 296). The full extent of the destruction to American Indian people and land through resource extraction has yet to be told. I am grateful to the Oral History program at California State University Fullerton for use of their collection on the development of the uranium industry in the Four Corners area.

Works Cited

Allen, Paula Gunn. *The Sacred Hoop: Recovering the Feminine in American Indian Traditions*. Boston: Beacon Press, 1986.

Bartlett, Mary Dougherty, ed. *New Native American Novels: Works in Progress*. Albuquerque: U New Mexico Press, 1986.

Boas, Franz. *Keresan Texts*. Publications of the American Ethnological Society Vol. 8, Part 1. New York: The American Ethnological Society, 1928.

Dozier, Edward P. *The Pueblo Indians of North America*. New York: Holt, Rinehart and Winston, 1970.

Fitzgerald, F. Scott. *The Great Gatsby*. 1925. New York: Charles Scribner's Sons, 1953.

Garcia, Reyes. "Senses of Place in *Ceremony*." *MELUS* 10.4 (1983): 37-48.

Green, Rayna, ed. *That's What She Said: Contemporary Poetry and Fiction by Native American Women*. Bloomington: Indiana U Press, 1984.

Hieb, Louis A. "The Ritual Clown: Humor and Ethics." *Forms of Play of Native North Americans*. Ed. Edward Norbeck and Claire R. Farrer. Proceedings of the American Ethnological Society, 1977. St. Paul, MN: West Publishing Company, 1979. 171-188.

Hinchman, Steve. "Rebottling the Nuclear Genie." *Native Self-Sufficiency* 8.4 (Spring 1987): 1, 9-11.

Hogan, Linda. *Seeing Through the Sun*. Amherst: U Massachusetts Press, 1985.

Horsman, Reginald. *Race and Manifest Destiny: The Origins of American Racial Anglo-Saxonism*. Cambridge, MA: Harvard U Press, 1981.

LaDuke, Winona and Ward Churchill. "Native America: The Political Economy of Radioactive Colonialism." *The Journal of Ethnic Studies* 13.3 (Fall 1985): 107-132.

Lewis, R.W.B. *The American Adam*. Chicago: U Chicago Press, 1955.

Lincoln, Kenneth. *Native American Renaissance*. Berkeley: U California Press, 1983.

Nelson, Robert M. "Place and Vision: The Function of Landscape in *Ceremony*." *Journal of the Southwest* 30.3 (Autumn 1988): 281-316.

Oral History Collection. California State University Fullerton.

Ortiz, Alfonso. *The Tewa World: Space, Time, Being and Becoming in a Pueblo Society*. Chicago: U Chicago Press, 1969.

Ortiz, Roxanne Dunbar. *Roots of Resistance: Land Tenure in New Mexico, 1680-1980*. Los Angeles: UCLA American Indian Studies Center, 1980.

Popkes, Stephen. "Deathwitch." *Isaac Asimov's Science Fiction Magazine* Feb. 1985, 76-88.

Seyersted, Per. "Two Interviews with Leslie Marmon Silko." *American Studies in Scandinavia* 13 (1981): 17-33.

Silko, Leslie Marmon. *Ceremony*. New York: Viking, 1977.

———— "An Old-Time Indian Attack Conducted in Two Parts: Part One: Imitation 'Indian' Poems [;] Part Two: Gary Snyder's Turtle Island." *The Remembered Earth: An Anthology of Contemporary Native American Literature*. Ed. Geary Hobson. Albuquerque: U New Mexico Press, 1979.

Smith, Martin Cruz. *Stallion Gate*. New York: Random House, 1986.

Vizenor, Gerald. *Griever: An American Monkey King in China*. New York; Boulder; Normal, IL: Illinois State U/Fiction Collective, 1987.

Ecofeminism, Nuclearism, and O'Brien's *The Nuclear Age*

Lee Schweninger

In the context of nuclear power production, Mary Daly, in *Gyn/Ecology* (1978), writes that "there are no adequate safeguards to prevent plutonium from being hijacked by terrorists. Moreover, the latter could use it to make atomic bombs." She goes so far as to suggest that the "civilized governments of patriarchy, however, are run by terrorists. The plutonium, therefore, has already been hijacked" (104).

In *The Nuclear Age* (1985), Tim O'Brien describes the stealing of "an armed nuclear warhead" by an underground, anti-superpower, terrorist group. Some members of the group want to detonate the bomb as a means of calling attention to the danger of nuclear buildup. As Sarah, one of the hijackers opposed to detonation, describes it, their purpose is "Blackmail. A demonstration project or some such shit. Set it off in the desert, wake up the rattlesnakes. I don't know. Headlines" (290). These nuclear terrorists seem unaware of the irony of using a bomb as a protest against the use of bombs, and in this sense they mirror the patriarchy in its attempt to protect one nation by threatening the nuclear destruction of another.

The similarity between Daly's contention and O'Brien's fiction suggests that an ecofeminist approach to nuclearism might provide a heuristics by which readers can enter both the actual nuclear texts such as plutonium waste and arms buildup and the fictional texts such as the one presented in O'Brien's novel. As the subtitle of Daly's book, *Gyn/Ecology: The Metaethics of Radical Feminism* indicates, her approach is radically feminist; there is little place for the phallocentric, the phallocratic, or what she calls the "male-authored and male-identified" metaethical, "masturbatory meditations by ethicists upon their own emissions" (13). Nonetheless, consideration of Daly's approach in the context of nuclearism defines one set of theoretical parameters by which nuclear texts—both fictional and actual—can be investigated and better understood.

The purpose of this essay, then, is to define a ecofeminist ethics as it relates to nuclearism in general and literature about nuclearism in particular. The essay illustrates a practical application of these speculations by applying this heuristics to O'Brien's novel, *The Nuclear Age*, a novel which ironically is as much about a "nuclear" family and the disintegration of that family in a nuclear age as about nuclearism per se.

177

Ynestra King defines ecofeminism as "a critical social movement, representing the convergence of two of the most important contemporary movements, feminism and ecology." King writes that "for ecofeminists, left projects of human liberation and the liberation of nature are inextricably connected, as are the ecological and social crises" (702). Because the movement concerns itself with "human liberation and the liberation of nonhuman nature," undeniable is its applicability to the patriarchy's nuclear buildup, to the phallocentric concept that power, success, peace, and safety depend on the literal total domination of all life as we know it.

Carolyn Merchant writes that "Juxtaposing the goals of the two movements [feminism and ecology] can suggest new values and social structures, based not on the domination of women and nature as resources but on the full expression of both male and female talent and on the maintenance of environmental integrity" (xv). If, as ecofeminists maintain, "the domination of nature and the domination of persons are inextricably connected" (702), then a nuclear arsenal epitomizes what is wrong with male oriented hegemonies. A nuclear warhead mounted on the top of a minuteman missile is the culmination of the phallotechnocracy and is certainly the ultimate symbol of the phallocentric attempt at total domination over all forms of life on the planet.

In an effort to protect his family (wife and child), William—the "hero" in O'Brien's novel—has begun digging the hole for a bomb shelter. As William digs, the hole takes on more and more personality until it finally commands William to take particular actions. Nonetheless, the narrator's subconscious, personified by "the hole," appears to be aware of the interconnectedness of all things. The hole says, "I am all there is...I am what happened to the dinosaurs. I am the ovens at Auschwitz, the Bermuda Triangle, the Lost Tribes, the Flying Dutchman, the Missing Link. I am Lee Harvey Oswald's secret contact in Moscow....I am the uncaused cause, the unnamed source,...I am you, of course. I am your inside-out" (298).

In *Le Feminsime oú la Mort* (Feminism or Death) (1974), Françoise d'Eaubonne in coining the term *ecofeminism*, suggests, as subsequent ecofeminists have argued, that without coming to terms with the interrelatedness of Homo sapiens and their environment, the race will not survive. Survival depends on a radical change of approach to the biosphere, and ecofeminism offers one radical possibility, an approach based on a new epistemology. In *Green Paradise Lost* (1979) Elizabeth Dodson Gray argues that a radical reorientation is necessary to bring about an understanding that difference is not necessarily superiority (10-11).

In an ecofeminist society there would be no nuclear arsenals because the patriarchal power structures would have no place in that new society. As Merchant and others have pointed out, the world is an organism; recognition that all parts are inextricably interrelated is necessary: "All parts are dependent on one another and mutually affect each other and the whole.... Ecology, as a philosophy of nature, has roots in organicism— the idea that the cosmos is an organic entity, growing and developing from within, in an integrated unity of structure and function" (Merchant 99-100). In *Gyn/Ecology*, Daly too affirms that everything is connected (11). The implication, of course, is that a system of total domination (as nuclear power totally dominates) should not exist because it denies the integration and interdependence of all parts. Nuclear power stands apart from and is antithetical to life on earth; therefore, it has no place.

In *Woman and Nature*, Susan Griffin writes satirically that "It is decided that...the particular (like the parts of a machine) may be understood without reference to the whole" (18). A good satirist, Griffin implies that preferable is just the opposite of what she writes; that is, nothing may be understood without reference to the whole. She infers that this refusal or inability on the part of the patriarchy to take into account the whole, the interrelatedness of everything, results in the separation of matter from spirit. It might be thus argued that such a misconception is part and parcel of the mentality that can allow nuclear arms and nuclear power production to proliferate. The ecofeminist argues that the separation of the particular from its context results in chauvinism, sexism, racism, nationalism, and other forms of bigotry. These forms of bigotry ultimately result in and are symbolized by the nuclear warhead. An ecofeminist approach quickly and incontrovertibly identifies the irony inherent in the nuclear industry's total disregard for human and nonhuman life under its pretense of safeguarding the very life it at the same time threatens to annihilate.

Overcoming the bias evident in a phallocentric approach to science, to the environment, and to the place of minorities and women in society will not be easy. The authors of *Green Politics* argue that "The majority of scientists and scientific institutions, [for example, still] cling to the mechanistic and reductionist concepts of Cartesian science and do not realize that such a framework is no longer adequate to solve social, economic, and technological problems in a fundamentally interconnected world" (Capra and Spretnak 118). The need for a post-Cartesian, or post-modern science is clear. As Merchant argues, "we must reexamine the function of our world view" (xvii).

In a recent unpublished paper, philosopher Frederick Ferré argues for the possibility of a post-modern "revolution in our thinking—and eventually in our living—comparable in importance to the one that turned us from pre-modern to modern epistemic norms" (15). That revolution, Ferré conjectures, would be based on ecology, which he calls the subversive science in reference to Paul Shepard's book by that title. Like feminism, ecology must consider whole systems rather than parts, must keep subordinate excessive abstraction and purely analytic methods. This post-modern, somewhat ecofeminist, holistic approach to biology, synecology, or geophysiology has recently been popularized by James Lovelock in *The Ages of Gaia* (1988) in which he argues that the entire planet is a living organism. Such notions as Lovelock's and Ferré's are ecofeminist and argue for a radical epistemological shift. According to Ferré, "We shall need new ways of coping...with the economic and military threats posed by suicidal parochialism joined to outmoded sovereignties, and with environmental retribution by depletion and pollution for modern, narrow-visioned practices and technologies" (19).

Although male, and although once an active participating part of the war machine in Vietnam, Tim O'Brien as a novelist seems to support the contention that the alienation of matter and spirit, the imposing of paternalistic forms of authority, and the resultant nuclear buildup create problems whose solutions demand radical shifts in the dominant epistemic norms. In *The Nuclear Age* he depicts just how interrelated the technological and the nontechnological are and asks for a radical reorientation. Indeed, the complexities and ambiguities of O'Brien's fiction suggest a fictional counterpart to an ecofeminist reading of the nuclear age, a reading which offers an essentially new world view.

An immediate indication of O'Brien's holistic approach to the problem of nuclearism is his use of chapter and section titles to suggest the interrelatedness of two apparently separate worlds (worlds certainly considered separate in the modern mentality): the world of science and technology which gave us the neutron bomb and the world of nature which gives us the "nuclear family," an expression coined in 1947, two years after the Advent of nuclear war. The three books of the novel are "Fission," "Fusion," and "Critical Mass." The titles echo the obvious correlation between what happens in the novel and the jargon of the nuclear industry. In the "Fission" section O'Brien breaks the account of his narrator's growing up into discrete parts, childhood, high school, and college. He also introduces the different parts of William's personality and describes his supposed insanity. The key motif in this description is the notion of parts; fission is the reproduction by spontaneous division, the breaking into parts. In the "Fusion" section he describes a literal political partnership, a group made up of several diverse college students forming an underground organization whose purpose is to assist the anti-war movement. Here the diverse elements are melded into a unified whole, analogous to the melding characteristics of a hydrogen bomb. In the final section, "Critical Mass," O'Brien describes the discovery of a mountain of uranium which the group buys and sells for enough profit to make each a multimillionaire. In this section William nearly reaches the breaking point, his madness nearly causes not only his own death but the deaths of his wife and daughter; nuclear family reaches critical mass, a point at which a chain reaction is sustainable.

Individual chapters within these sections also have titles which relate to nuclear or scientific terminology: "Civil Defense" contains an account of a child's attempt to build a bomb shelter under his Ping-Pong table; "Chain Reactions" describes the results of that troubled childhood; "Underground Tests" is a chapter describing basic training in the underground alliance; the "Fallout" chapter describes the fallout, outcome, or effect of the underground movement.

In the series of chapters entitled "Quantum Jumps" (abrupt changes in discrete energy states), O'Brien leaps from one past time to another as he narrates the story of William's digging a hole for a bomb shelter. In these interspersed chapters the narrator asks himself over and over whether he is sane. The figural quantum jumps are from sanity to insanity, but William finds it impossible to distinguish between the two states. He digs the hole because he is sane enough to see the danger; but his digging the hole is insanity. The quantum leaps O'Brien describes here are analogous to the leaps through mind, time, and space Barbara Starrett considers as a necessary facet of developing a radically new mental outlook.

In a chapter entitled "The Nuclear Age," O'Brien further indicates his awareness of the interrelatedness of apparently disparate parts by describing William's relationship with his wife, Bobbi, in patriarchal, political jargon: Bobbi suggests a "trial separation"; William responds with "I was comforted by the final passage of a poem in progress: The balance of power, our own, the world's, grows ever fragile" (295). Bobbi, too, uses the scientific and jargon from the nuclear industry in a poem "Relativity," describing her relationship with her husband: "Relations are strained / in the nuclear family. / It is upon us, the hour / of evacuation, / the splitting of blood / infinitives. / The clock says fission / fusion / critical mass" (122).

Besides O'Brien's use of language to suggest his holistic approach, the novel also presents an end-of-the-world metaphor which transcends the literal description of nuclear holocaust. Available to O'Brien as a metaphor for the end of the world is an actual nuclear warhead, but rather than on the bomb, the focus of the narrative is on the narrator's old girlfriend, underground compatriot, and war protester. She arrives at his door in a jeep carrying an armed nuclear warhead. "Sarah coughed and rubbed her eyes. She'd lost some weight—too much, I thought—and... she seemed skinny and poor-looking. Unhealthy, too. The blister at her lip was hard to ignore" (289). Thus the figural biblical image of the world's end finds its literal counterpart in Sarah's disfigured lip.

In *Gyn/Ecology* Daly compares the biblical end of the world as suggested in the book of Revelation with the potential for nuclear holocaust. Daly points out some of the salient features according to Revelation: "Among these phenomena are earthquakes, drought, horrors in the heavens (stars falling, sun going black, blinding flashes of light), and plagues causing disgusting and virulent sores" (Daly 102). One of Daly's points is that the prediction in the biblical Revelation could find its consummation in a nuclear age. According to Daly, we need not even fear the exploding of nuclear bombs; the millions of gallons of lethal nuclear waste will be potent enough to bring about the apocalypse. Daly maintains that "Through the 'peaceful use of nuclear energy' and other forms of pure pollution they have paved the way for planetary plagues causing disgusting and virulent sores— radiation sickness and various forms of cancer" (104). According to Revelation "ugly and painful sores broke out on the people" (16.2). Paralleling this symbolism in Revelation, in *The Nuclear Age*, the blister on Sarah's lip becomes all consuming: "A dark, thimble-sized scab formed at the corner of her mouth. Tiny black veins snaked across the surface of the blister. Her speech faltered. She had trouble coordinating past with present.... One evening she used a needle to drain the lip. There was infection and severe swelling. In the morning, when I brought breakfast to her room, she pulled a pillowcase over her head" (292). Sarah dies shortly after an operation she undergoes to treat her encephalitis, of which the blister was a single manifestation. Meanwhile the warhead she and her compatriots stole lies hidden in an outbuilding near the house, out of sight and essentially out of mind.

With Sarah's death as synecdoche, O'Brien, like an ecofeminist, calls into question traditional beliefs as he subverts the conventional patriarchal myth of the end of the world. According to Daly, "the technological true believers of the Book of Revelation live their faith, the faith of the Fathers" (104). For O'Brien that belief must be subverted in order for his characters to survive not only a nuclear holocaust which seems imminent, but also simply to survive the thought of or the possibility of such a holocaust.

O'Brien is not unaware of the irony implicit in his character's situation. The selling of a mountain to a uranium mining enterprise is blatant and perhaps hyperbolic but certainly emblematic and suggestive of our own complicity—if not duplicity—in the consumption of electricity generated by nuclear power or the paying of taxes to a government which spends billions supporting the nuclear industry.

In digging the hole for a bomb shelter, William asserts that his prime motivation is love for the nuclear family, his wife and daughter. As a child he had tried to convince his unheeding parents of the reality of the threat of nuclear war; in college he had attempted to convince his unmotivated, unconcerned, and basically ignorant classmates of the danger. As an adult, husband, and father, he begins to dig for a bomb shelter in an effort to protect his family. (In Revelation, we remember, the people hide from the storms to come in caves [6:15].) Ironically, the very digging—motivated by a desire to preserve the family—ultimately alienates the husband from his wife and the father from his daughter. But because he is obsessed with the fear of nuclear holocaust, the alienation from family does not stop him; he continues working nights with strings of Christmas bulbs for light. The lights themselves suggest an inversion of the Christmas myth in which the boy-child is born to die for humanity. Here the strings of lights (emblems of that lonely Star of Bethlehem) guide a lone digger as he works for the salvation of his family.

Unmistakable are the similarities between William, the Father in his efforts to preserve the family, and the Patriarchy in its efforts to "preserve" its family through balance of power. William formulates it thus: "We will kill for our children. Our children will kill for us. We will kill for families. And above all we will kill for love, as men have always killed. Crimes of passion. As terrorists kill. As soldiers kill for love of honor and love of country. Just love" (308). The passage is indicative of the patriarchal mentality, the mental trap William is in.

William has become so obsessed with his desire to keep his wife from leaving him—to keep the family intact, to keep all safe—that he drugs his wife and daughter, puts them sleeping into the hole he has dug, and wires the cave for dynamite. Analogously, our federal father, Uncle Sam, in his paternal care, protects us with silos in Kansas. As William sits through the night (a long night at another Gethsemane) with detonator in hand, visions of Revelation go through his head. There is noise like thunder, the light and dark of a lightning storm, and the imminent threat of detonation.

Once his daughter wakes, however, she is able to convince him of the importance of alternatives. She momentarily represents the interrelatedness of all; she reminds him of life outside the hole, literally the hole he has dug in order to protect them, symbolically the hole or trap humanity is in. She wants out, and her Father thinks "And if I could, I would do it. I would take her in my arms and be calm and gentle and find safety by saving." He would perform what the pre-moderns might have called a miracle; what the post-moderns might call a radical epistemological shift. "I'd do magic," he says. "I'd lead them into the house and brew up some hot chocolate and talk about the different kinds of spin you can put on a Ping-Pong ball. And the world would be stable. The balance of power would hold. A believer, a man of whole cloth [as opposed to the partial or incomplete], I would believe what cannot be believed. The power of love, the continuing creation—it cannot be believed—and I would therefore believe" (310). Here he asks for a shift (critical mass) in epistemic norms. As the Copernican revolution discarded the pre-modern, geocentric notion, so William moves into a post-modern world in which the phallocentric is discarded. The modern (post-Copernican) dependence on abstraction and mathematical formula to describe truth is found insufficient. William's willingness to believe the unbelievable epitomizes the ecofeminist notion of the need for a radical shift in world view.

Ultimately William does what he cannot do except in a post-modern context; he accepts the unacceptable. He believes in the unbelievable. Like an ecofeminist, he radically undermines the prevalent notions of modern patriarchal faith; through the paradox of his effort to save self, family, and planet, he finally realizes the solutions are extreme, but they are not to be achieved by maintaining the power of one person over another or of human over nature; he realizes solutions that are not even part of the traditional pattern of belief. The ecofeminist contention that women, men, and nature are inextricably related overcomes him. In a gesture symbolic of turning from the patriarchal's *ignis fatuus*, the "Light to lighten Gentiles" (Luke 3:2), he turns off the Christmas lights: "The sky at this hour is purple going to blue. The mountains [which in Revelation disappear or tumble into the sea] are firm and silent. There are morning birds in the trees, and the grass [which in Revelation is seared] is a pale dusty green" (311).

With his depiction of an obsessed character, O'Brien suggests that because the threat of nuclear war is real, the family faces both intellectual and emotional crises. The novel shows how that family—itself representative of the interrelatedness of life on earth—is in danger, and through the narrator O'Brien asks compelling questions of his readers. Given the possibility of an all-out, totally destructive war, how do we live? How can we love and laugh when all of Kansas is burning? Given the interrelatedness and interdependence in the ecosystem, how can we any longer enforce arbitrary separations or maintain false hierarchies?

Like his ecofeminist contemporaries, O'Brien turns from the Patriarchal answers; he retreats from the terrorism of established government and of underground movements. In re-mything, he will have to believe "what cannot be believed, that all things are renewable, that the human spirit is undefeated and infinite, always." He will know that humans and their environment are mutually interdependent. O'Brien's narrator maintains finally a faith that is hope. In an ecofeminist world, he will discard the modern acceptance of mathematical equations as the only truth. He will believe that "E will somehow not quite equal mc^2, that it's a cunning metaphor, that the terminal equation will somehow not quite balance" (312). His is a post-modern, ecofeminist vision, a vision of justice among groups, races, sexes, species. It is a vision of harmony, of wholeness in which, for example, coordination is seen as more fundamental than conflict (Gray 73); in which dangerous and insupportable patriarchal forms of oppression are replaced "with new attitudes without hierarchy, domination, exploitation and oppression" (Sale 302); and in which holistic notions of nature are "revived in ecology's premise that everything is connected to everything else" (Merchant 99). O'Brien suggests the validity of attempting to re-mythologize or re-theorize the world. The old theories and power structures are repressive and destructive; the new are critical but interdependent, constructive, and hopeful.

Works Cited

Daly, Mary. *Gyn/Ecology: The Metaethics of Radical Feminism*. Boston: Beacon Press, 1978.

d'Eaubonne, Françoise. *Le Feminsime oú la Mort*. Paris: Pierre Horay, 1974.

Capra, Fritjof and Charlene Spretnak. *Green Politics*. New York: E.P. Dutton, Inc., 1984.

Ferré, Frederick. "Cosmos, Science, and Environment from a Humanities Perspective." (Unpublished lecture, delivered at the University of North Carolina-Wilmington as part of the "Science, the Humanities, and Society" Lecture Series, funded by a grant from the National Endowment for the Humanities and University match.) 22 March 1990.

Grey, Elizabeth Dodson. *Green Paradise Lost*. Wellesley, Massachusetts: Rountable Press, 1979.

Griffin, Susan. *Woman and Nature*. New York: Harper and Row, 1978.

King, Ynestra. "What is Ecofeminism?" *The Nation* 245.20 (12 December 1987): 702, 730-31.

Lovelock, James. *The Ages of Gaia: A Biography of Our Living Earth.* New York: W.W. Norton, 1988.

Merchant, Carolyn. *The Death of Nature: Women, Ecology and the Scientific Revolution.* New York: Harper and Row, 1982.

O'Brien, Tim. *The Nuclear Age.* New York: Alfred A. Knopf, 1985.

Sale, Kirkpatrick. "Ecofeminism—A New Perspective." *The Nation.* 245.9 (26 September 1987): 302-305.

Shepard, Paul and Daniel McKinley. *The Subversive Science: Essays Toward an Ecology of Man.* Boston: Houghton Mifflin, 1969.

Starrett, Barbara. "I Dream in Female." *Amazon Quarterly.* 3i (November 1974): 13-27.

The Theme of Guilt in
Vonnegut's Cataclysmic Novels

Tom Hearron

Although with one exception—*Deadeye Dick*—the novels of Kurt Vonnegut do not deal explicitly with the idea of nuclear weapons, a recurrent image in his work is that of the massive cataclysm which annihilates human life. In four of his novels (*Cat's Cradle, Slaughterhouse-Five, Deadeye Dick* and *Galapagos*) some sort of tremendous disaster takes place. In *Cat's Cradle* it is the destruction of the world by ice-nine. In *Galapagos* the near extinction of humanity occurs as a result of a stock market crash leading to starvation and war. In *Deadeye Dick* it is the neutron bombing of Midland City, Ohio, while in *Slaughterhouse-Five* it is the firebombing of Dresden. In Vonnegut's works, though, the central issue is not so much the horrible event itself, but the effects of it—and, even more important, the degree to which one can assign blame to the humans who are the agents for its coming about: in other words, the theme of guilt.

Saint Paul expressed the concept of guilt like this: "For I know that in me (that is, in my flesh) dwelleth no good thing: for to will is present with me; but *how* to perform that which is good I find not. For the good that I would, I do not; but the evil which I would not, that I do. Now if I do that I would not, it is no more I that do it, but sin that dwelleth in me" (*Romans* 7: 18-20).

Throughout much of the work of Kurt Vonnegut, this same feeling of guilt manifests itself. In Vonnegut's case, though—unlike that of Saint Paul—the origin seems to have been a historical event, the fire bombing of Dresden.

The city of Dresden, Germany, attacked by saturation bombing, burned to the ground with a total loss of life greater than the more famous atomic bombing of Hiroshima in 1945. Among those who did not lose their lives in the attack was a young American soldier, a prisoner of war who survived because his unit was housed in a slaughterhouse deep beneath the city. The soldier's name, of course, was Kurt Vonnegut, and the experience shattered his life. Shattered it to such an extent that in most of Vonnegut's works there is an echo, at least, of that distant holocaust. Of this fire bombing Vonnegut has written that he was the only one to benefit from the slaughter:

Only one person on the entire planet benefited from the raid, which must have cost tens of thousands of dollars. The raid didn't shorten the war by half a second, didn't weaken a German defense or attack anywhere, didn't free a single person from a death camp. Only one person benefited—not two or five or ten. Just one.... Me. I got three dollars for each person killed. Imagine that. (*Palm Sunday* 94)

The feelings described here in Vonnegut's usual ironic way are quite common to survivors of some great disaster—feelings which are complex and difficult to describe but which certainly involve an element of guilt: his profiting, if only to the extent of three dollars per corpse, from the event. Indeed, although Vonnegut tells us that he planned to write his Dresden book from the moment that he returned from the war, the fact that its completion required over twenty years suggests the conflicting attitudes involved in its production.

Vonnegut's view of human depravity, as it develops throughout his novels, moves to the notion that although humans are capable of doing great harm to others, they are ultimately too much victims themselves to be held accountable for the disasters which they inflict on others. This concept first appears, though in immature form, in *Cat's Cradle*.

Published in 1963, *Cat's Cradle* is an account of the end of the world, brought about through the agency of a new substance called ice-nine. Ice-nine, the product of the scientist Felix Hoenikker, who was also the head of the atom bomb project, is a form of water whose freezing point is over one hundred degrees Fahrenheit. It has the property of freezing any water with which it comes in contact, even if that water is contained within living matter. Before he can fully explore his discovery, though, Dr. Hoenikker suddenly dies, leaving crystals of his invention behind to his three children, who exploit it for their own personal gain: a clear allegory of the folly of placing powerful forces in the hands of the military.

Paradoxically, the man whose discovery results in the end of the world is himself as innocent as a child. His daughter, talking to the freelance writer who narrates the book, insists that Hoenikker be viewed as the saint that he actually was. This saint, though, is quite morally innocent, as is illustrated in an incident when the atomic bomb is tested. According to one of Hoenikker's sons:

...do you know the story about Father on the day they first tested a bomb out at Alamogordo? After the thing went off, after it was a sure thing that America could wipe out a city with just one bomb, a scientist turned to Father and said, 'Science has now known sin.' And do you know what Father said. He said, 'What is sin?' (*Cat's Cradle* 21)

But naive, innocent people can perform acts which have terrible consequences, whether atomic bomb or ice-nine. As another character in the book remarks of Hoenikker, " 'how the hell innocent is a man who helps make a thing like an atomic bomb?' " (*Cat's Cradle* 53).

The key issue, then, is this: to what extent can the innocence of an individual be compromised by the person's role in a system which does loathsome deeds? Vonnegut himself appears to have grappled with this, not so much in the firebombing of Dresden, as in his reaction to the threat of nuclear annihilation in the post-war period, a reaction which he terms losing faith in his religion. The religion of which he speaks, though, was a faith in technology:

An enthusiasm for technological cures for almost all forms of human discontent was the only religion of my family during the Great Depression when I first got to know that family well. It was religion enough for me.... (*Palm Sunday* 69)

The effects of this change were devastating to Vonnegut's view of the world:

But the bombing of Hiroshima compelled me to see that a trust in technology, like all the other great religions of the world, had to do with the human soul. I will bet you...that every one of the tales of lost innocence you receive will embody not only the startling discovery of the human soul, but of how diseased it can be.

How sick was the soul revealed by the flash at Hiroshima? And I deny that it was a specifically American soul. It was the soul of every highly industrialized nation, whether at war or at peace. How sick was it? It was so sick that it did not want to live anymore. What other sort of soul would create a new physics based on nightmares...? (*Palm Sunday* 70)

In *Cat's Cradle* Dr. Hoenikker's "new physics" is left in the hands of his children—a clear metaphor for the scientists who put their work into the hands of government officials and generals—into the hands of those whose moral attitude is as clear, uncomplicated and egocentric as that of young children. Consider, for example, the research scientist who first describes ice-nine to the narrator. The goal, he says, is to find a substance that will prevent the U.S. Marines from becoming bogged down in the mud. If the Marines threw a crystal of ice-nine in a puddle:

'The puddle would freeze?' I guessed.
'And all the muck around the puddle?'
'It would freeze?'
'And all the puddles in the frozen muck?'
'They would freeze?'
'And the pools and the streams in the frozen muck?'
'They would freeze?'
'You bet they would!' he cried. 'And the United States Marines would rise from the swamp and march on!' (*Cat's Cradle* 40)

But not really. In fact, the Marines would be frozen, immobilized in the frozen muck. And if any of them touched the ice-nine and then touched their mouths, they too would freeze. The narrator suggests that things may not be as simple, as consequence-free as the scientist makes out. Exploring the idea further, he learns that all the streams in the swamp would freeze, and all the lakes and ponds that the streams feed, and the ocean, and even the rain when it fell. It would be, in short, the end of the world—exactly as happens later in the novel. The motives of the scientist might be purely practical: the desire to extricate Marines from the mud. What he does not see, though, is the long-range consequences stemming from the interconnectedness of all things. In such a case, then, as the earlier quotation from Saint Paul suggests, the concept of guilt is not applicable because guilt requires both knowledge of the consequences of the act and the ability to choose. And in Vonnegut's view humans are severely limited both in what they can know and in what degree of freedom of choice they have.

Both *Slaughterhouse-Five* and *Deadeye Dick* are concerned with the destruction of cities by bombing. And although the results are horrible, in both cases Vonnegut finds that the issue of blame is meaningless. Or as he himself puts it when discussing his work in the University of Chicago's Department of Anthropology:

> Another thing they taught was that nobody was ridiculous or bad or disgusting. Shortly before my father died, he said to me, 'You know—you never wrote a story with a villain in it.'
>
> I told him that was one of the things I learned in college after the war. (*Slaughterhouse* 8)

Why is the concept of guilt inapplicable? Because, as is suggested in the concept of time held by the Tralfamadorians who kidnap Billy Pilgrim, the concept of guilt involves choice. But both *Slaughterhouse-Five* and *Deadeye Dick* argue that humans are so much at the mercy of more powerful forces that the concept of choice—of free will—does not enter in. As the Tralfamadorians put it, all existence is like being a bug trapped in amber:

> 'Earthlings are the great explainers, explaining why this event is structured as it is, telling how other events may be achieved or avoided. I am a Tralfamadorian, seeing all time as you might see a stretch of the Rocky Mountains. All time is all time. It does not change. It does not lend itself to warnings or explanations. It simply is.' (*Slaughterhouse* 86)

When Billy objects that such a view contradicts the idea of free will, he is told, " 'I've visited thirty-one inhabited planets in the universe, and I have studied reports on one hundred more. Only on Earth is there any talk of free will' " (*Slaughterhouse* 86).

The Tralfamadorians even know how the universe will end—it is destroyed by a Tralfamadorian test pilot (the military again!) experimenting with new fuels. And this conversation ensues:

> 'If you know this,' said Billy, 'isn't there some way you can prevent it? Can't you keep the pilot from pressing the button?'
>
> 'He has *always* pressed it, and he always *will*. We *always* let him, and we always *will* let him. The moment is *structured* that way.' (*Slaughterhouse* 117)

In such a world, there is little wonder that in the face of the immense destruction of an entire city, only one man is singled out for punishment: Edgar Derby, a gentle schoolteacher, the oldest man in his unit—shot by a firing squad. His crime? He is guilty of stealing a teapot from the ruins of Dresden. Admittedly, he is guilty of the act, Vonnegut never denies the fact. However, Derby's crime is so minuscule in comparison with the larger crime of destroying an undefended city that if death is the proper punishment for his actions, what punishment should be given to those responsible for burning Dresden?

Like *Slaughterhouse-Five*, Vonnegut's *Deadeye Dick* counterpoints a massive catastrophe, the destruction of Midland City, for which no one is punished, with a smaller event which is punished severely: Rudy Waltz's accidental shooting of Eloise Metzger. Far from intending to harm anyone, Rudy shoots her through pure accident: given for the first time the keys to his father's gun room, Rudy decides to celebrate what he sees as initiation into manhood by firing one ritual shot at random. The random shot kills the pregnant woman in the midst of her vacuuming—on Mother's Day, no less. In such a world, life is dangerous, or as Rudy points out, "That is my principal objection to life, I think: It is too easy, when alive, to make perfectly horrible mistakes" (6). Indeed, the opening line of the narrative proper is "To the as-yet-unborn, to all innocent wisps of undifferentiated nothingness: Watch out for life" (1).

Rudy is taken to the jail's basement, where he is put on display to the local citizens—a tormenting ordeal. And although he is not tried for the crime (he is too young), his father, who assumes the blame, does spend time in prison for his role in giving Rudy the keys. The father, although he had no way of knowing his son's intent, takes all the guilt for his seemingly innocuous action. Ironically, though, the police chief, Francis Morrissey, who must confront the Waltzes, has himself killed a man in a hunting accident years before, a death for which no one is held accountable:

Morissey was one of the bunch who had been goose-hunting with Father and John Fortune back in 1916, when old August Gunther disappeared. Only recently have I learned that it was Morissey who killed old Gunther. He accidentally discharged a ten-gauge shotgun about a foot from Gunther's head. (*Deadeye Dick* 52)

Morissey, however, perhaps aware that Rudy's act was accidental (i.e., done with no intent of doing harm, but only with ignorance of the consequences of his firing the gun), is willing to let Rudy off, but Rudy's father insists on taking the blame—in a most public way, by destroying his precious gun collection, in a vain attempt to make atonement. For the rest of his life Rudy is known as the murderer Deadeye Dick, the family loses all it owns as a result of a suit by Eloise Metzger's husband, and life effectively ends for the entire Waltz family—all the result of an accident.

And when Midland City is destroyed by an accident involving a neutron bomb—which the newspapers ironically call "a friendly bomb"—no one is held to blame, even though the novel suggests that the "accident" might have been more sinister:

My own guess is that the American Government had to find out for certain whether the neutron bomb was as harmless as it was supposed to be. So it set one off in a small city which nobody cared about, where people weren't doing all that much with their lives anyway, where businesses were going under or moving away. The Government couldn't test a bomb on a foreign city, after all, without running the risk of starting World War Three. (*Deadeye Dick* 234)

"Accident." "Mistake." Words like these appear frequently in Vonnegut's later work. In a sense, he seems to say, we are all as much victims as villains. As Vonnegut once said to me in conversation, "You want to know why there aren't any villains in my work? It's because the villain is society" (Vonnegut interview).

In *Galapagos*, though, Vonnegut finds another villain: the human brain, which he suggests has become too large:

That, in my opinion, was the most diabolical aspect of those old-time big brains: They would tell their owners, in effect, 'Here is a crazy thing we could actually do, probably, but we would never do it, of course. It's just fun to think about.'

And then, as though in trances, the people would really do it—have slaves fight each other to the death in the Colosseum, or burn people alive in the public square for holding opinions that were locally unpopular, or build factories whose only purpose was to kill people in industrial quantities, or to blow up whole cities, and on and on. (*Galapagos* 226)

The human brain, then, is in Vonnegut's view too overly developed to be an efficient instrument of survival:

...Can it be doubted that three-kilogram brains were once nearly fatal defects in the evolution of the human race?

A second query: What source was there back then, save for our overelaborate nervous circuitry, for the evils we were seeing or hearing about simply everywhere?

My answer: There was no other source. This was a very innocent planet, except for those great big brains. (*Galapagos* 8-9)

It is appropriate that Vonnegut, the master of bitter irony, sees as the essential paradox of our time that people are equipped with such large brains that they have become extremely stupid when it comes to foreseeing the consequences of their action. Vonnegut's remarks on the world view of the radio comedians Bob and Ray are enlightening in this context. In an introduction to their collected works, Vonnegut wrote: "Man is not evil, they seem to say. He is simply too hilariously stupid to survive" (*Palm Sunday* 142).

Kurt Vonnegut's work expresses the same view of humanity: we are too hilariously stupid to survive.

Works Cited

Vonnegut, Kurt. *Cat's Cradle*. N.Y.: Dell, 1963.
——— *Deadeye Dick*. N.Y.: Ramjac, 1982.
——— *Galapagos*. N.Y.: Dell, 1986.
——— *Palm Sunday*. N.Y.: Ramjac, 1981.
——— Personal interview. 17 June 1988.
——— *Slaughterhouse-Five*. N.Y.: Dell, 1968.

Kurt Vonnegut's Ultimate

Jerome Klinkowitz

Every one of Kurt Vonnegut's novels encompasses destruction of one sort or another. In *Player Piano* (1952) it is a workers' revolt that smashes the machines of automation that have become a self-generating world in themselves. *The Sirens of Titan* (1959) climaxes with a Martian invasion that threatens the Earth. *Mother Night* (1962) is more personal: from the apocalyptic rubble of Nazi Berlin the protagonist emerges to live a secret non-life which in the end, under a wrongful sentence of death, he closes with his suicide. Then come the big ones: the actual end of the world, by freezing, in *Cat's Cradle* (1963); the vision of a firestorm destroying Indianapolis in *God Bless You, Mr. Rosewater* (1965); and finally the resolution to this first, proto-destructive phase of Vonnegut's career, the destruction of Dresden in *Slaughterhouse-Five* (1969). From there the author moves into a more intimately personal set of catastrophes, yet each of which includes a broader and more contemporary range of destructive technologies, from the Chinese experiments with gravity that run out of control in *Slapstick* (1976) to the neutron bomb that destroys the protagonist's home town in *Deadeye Dick* (1982).

Through all of this, nuclear holocaust itself is held off, perhaps for reason of irony. As the most expectable form of total destruction, it never comes, instead giving mankind the rude surprise of seeing the world otherwise frozen or conventionally incinerated. This reminder that the traditional elements are threat enough corresponds to a contrasting optimism in these same works: that however destructive the action has been, there is always hope of rebuilding. That's what the workers do, to their discredit, at the end of *Player Piano*, when unable to resist the urge to tinker with the broken machines they devise still more gadgets that will eventually put them back out of work. So too does the alien invasion in *The Sirens of Titan* unify the world in a new religion that makes survival more likely than under previous faiths that egotistically and selfishly assumed that God could be anything other than utterly indifferent to the fate of man. Even *Mother Night* and *Cat's Cradle*, with their supposedly ultimate conclusions, play little tricks with open endings, as Howard Campbell's last words are not "good-bye" but rather the German for "until we meet again," while the black ants surviving the general freeze are foreseen as wrapping themselves around droplets of ice-nine's frozen water and thawing them out with body heat, from which life may re-evolve. Eliot Rosewater's firestorm, one remembers, is only a vision, one that purges his madness so that he can finally dissolve his vexing fortune and bring good to the world. And even though Dresden is destroyed, both the author and his protagonist are able to confront its memory, making *Slaughterhouse-Five* itself possible.

To this point, of course, Vonnegut has yet to face actual nuclear annihilation. That comes in the form of a localized nuclear accident (or perhaps fiendishly amoral test) in *Deadeye Dick,* and then as the total catastrophe everyone fears in *Galápagos* (1985). It is with *Galápagos,* however, and in *Bluebeard* (1987), which returns to the memory of Dresden in order to contemplate something even worse, that we see Kurt Vonnegut transcending even the ultimate and most technologically feasible holocaust in order to go on living—specifically, to go on writing, which throughout his career he has always used as the index of both personal and universal survival.

The events Vonnegut has witnessed and struggled with as a fiction writer and public spokesman have certainly been inhibiting of promise. What he certainly must have thought was the worst, as close to the end as one can come, turned out to be just the beginning of a long train of catastrophes and atrocities, one example after another of humankind and nature conspiring to end the world. That Vonnegut didn't die in Dresden is a darkly comic accident; one of a hundred or so in the city center to escape the firestorm that incinerated or asphyxiated a quarter of a million, he survived to witness the uniquely scientific destruction of Dresden and its people, and then return home to learn about even more technically effective means of mass murder. At the height of his first great wave of popular fame, a time coinciding with America's great social turmoil of the Vietnam years, he addressed the graduating class at Bennington College, recalling his own transformation a quarter century before, when he was their age and his world was as volatile as their own:

I used to be an optimist. This was during my boyhood in Indianapolis. Those of you who have seen Indianapolis will understand that it was no easy thing to be an optimist there. It was the 500-mile Speedway Race, and then 364 days of miniature golf, and then the 500-mile Speedway Race again.

My brother Bernard, who was nine years older, was on his way to becoming an important scientist. He would later discover that silver iodide particles could precipitate certain kinds of clouds as snow or rain. He made me very enthusiastic about science for a while. I thought scientists were going to find out exactly how everything worked, and then make it work better. I fully expected that by the time I was twenty-one, some scientist, maybe my brother, would have taken a color photograph of God Almighty—and sold it to *Popular Mechanics* magazine.

Scientific truth was going to make us *so* happy and comfortable.

What actually happened when I was twenty-one was that we dropped scientific truth on Hiroshima. We killed everybody there. And I had just come home from being a prisoner of war in Dresden, which I'd seen burned to the ground. And the world was just then learning how ghastly the German extermination camps had been. So I had a heart-to-heart talk with myself.

"Hey, Corporal Vonnegut," I said to myself, "maybe you were wrong to be an optimist. Maybe pessimism is the thing." (Wampeters 161-62)

And so he has been a pessimist ever since, the few exceptions being when he had to persuade others or himself to continue on in the face of so little hope. Yet the formulations given to the graduates at Bennington indicate that within the elements of Vonnegut's pessimism are the very factors that allow him to turn his mood back around.

Consider his reading of Indianapolis. Here he degrades life in that city as a sentence to perpetual boredom, but elsewhere Vonnegut has praised his home town as an ideal place to live, rich in culture and industry and providing exceptionally fine conditions for the prospering of those extended families his anthropological perspective deems so necessary to human happiness. How then can the old days back in Indy be judged severely? Because the judgment is an adolescent one, finding the worst fate possible as being bored and measuring existence by the sole high and low of an auto race and miniature golf. The example is a deliberately circular one—from the race to golf to the race again—just as the examples themselves function as an endless circuit, as mindlessly repetitive as any game of idiot's delight. It is the fate suffered by the workers in his first novel, *Player Piano*, where boredom with a life of automation incites the destruction of machines, which in turn yields just another form of tedium that leads the people back to tinkering with the same machines.

Consider too what, in Vonnegut's example, serves to break the routine: science. Here again, both syntactically and materially, the route is circular, for what the author hopes to see by age 21 turns out to be destructive (rather than simply reductive). Yet just as the optimistic example is undercut by having it published not in a learned journal but in the lowbrow *Popular Mechanics*, so too do the weighty moral lessons of Hiroshima, Dresden, and Dachau yield not the lofty posturings of a Nobel laureate's speech but rather the shrug-of-the-shoulders/scratch-of-the-head decision made by a lowly and somewhat befuddled corporal in dialogue with himself, the only one around to provide a good listener.

At the start of his career, with his dedication to writing about the matter of Dresden, Kurt Vonnegut draws few distinctions among the styles of destruction his age has offered. Atom bombs, incendiary firestorms, and concentration camps figure in generally the same way: as eminently scientific solutions to situations perceived as problems. Such is the human manner, to find stability boring and to tinker around trying to fix something that isn't broken, until the project gets so overdeveloped that it blows up in one's face, making the "solution" a greater problem than the one began with. And from there follows an endless cycle of retinkering, with the catastrophes increasing in the proportionate black comedy of a Laurel & Hardy slapstick film.

For most readers, universal nuclear holocaust would seem the ultimate threat. But does Vonnegut see it that way? To do so would contradict the nature of his finest talent, which is to sustain the energy of creation just when conventional wisdom says the end is at hand. Such is the structural nature of jokes, to which Vonnegut has time and again used as the definition of his fictive technique. Jokes relieve the pressure of ultimacy, taking a situation which threatens to face a closed door and suddenly (and surprisingly) opening it again. To audiences he has explained how punch lines function: they relieve the pressure of a situation the listener feels confined in by magically revealing a way out, an excuse from responsibility. He will ask his listeners a serious question, such as what is the capital of an unfamiliar state. They won't know and in shame will have to accept his answer. Then he'll ask why the cost of cream is so high. Conditioned to search their memories and tax their intelligence, his audience will struggle for the correct answer, and of course come up with none. At this point Vonnegut supplies it: because the cows hate squatting over those little cartons. The result is guaranteed laughter, because it is a wonderful feeling of release. Excused from the responsibility of having to think—which is, after all, hard work—his listeners take pleasure in viewing the matter in an entirely different dimension, one that strips away the previous limits and clears the way toward something entirely new.

Then too there is the comforting nature of jokes. By using the form's open-ended structure, comedians relieve another type of pressure, that resulting from taking one's troubles too seriously. As a youth during the Great Depression, Kurt Vonnegut surely saw enough to worry about, but he also appreciated how the era's radio jokesters made life a little more endurable by using the pressure-and-release structure of their gags. His favorite from those years is recounted as a 1936 gem from radio's Henry Morgan: "You know that cat that inherited five million dollars last year? Well, he died. Left his money to another cat" (Klinkowitz and Somer 109).

One more feature of a joke's structure serves Vonnegut's art, and that is how the lead-up to a punch line (such as the first two sentences of Henry Morgan's joke) devises a tension much like the pressure resulting from setting a mouse trap. Punch lines then spring this tension, releasing enough energy to carry the listener or reader forward to the next set-up. Virtually every piece of fiction Vonnegut writes is designed this way, as a series of one joke leading to another and from there to another. Accommodating this technique are the more apparent features of his work, including short sentences as brief as a word and paragraphs often no longer than a sentence. Again, the Henry Morgan joke is a masterpiece of timing, and so are the pages of *Cat's Cradle* and Vonnegut's other works.

Nuclear holocaust, then, would serve Vonnegut as no more of an ultimate than any other pressure situation. It is one more tension to be relieved—perhaps as the biggest one, the tension most useful for springing open the author's most broadly reaching new perception.

That is the precise circumstance of *Galápagos*, where—like so many postmodern works—the narrative begins just where conventional novels would end, in this case with the virtually total destruction of the world's civilization in a nuclear war. The novel's strategy is that of the joke, replicated again and again. Having nuclear annihilation be the beginning rather than the end accomplishes the same release of pressure as a joke's punch line, and opens the same door of new possibilities. In this case the broad new horizon is that of re-evolution, in which humankind embarks on a one million year course of biological refitting so that all the design errors that produced nuclear war can be corrected. Brain size is the first factor. "Just about every adult human being back then had a brain weighing about three kilograms," we are told. "There was no end to the evil schemes that a thought machine that oversized couldn't imagine and execute" (*Galápagos* 8). Remembering the innocent foolishness of the workers in *Player Piano* and the dark comedy of those fighting over ice-nine in *Cat's Cradle*, one would agree that excess brain power has not served the race well. Now, from the perspective of one million years further on, Vonnegut's narrator can look back and decide that there were no other sources for all the evil, mischief, and simple pratfalls suffered by mankind. "There was no other source," he concludes. "This was a very innocent planet, except for those great big brains" (*Galápagos* 9). Nor is there any trick to straightening things out, for the simple operation of the law of natural selection sees that the type of human best suited to survive will do so, passing on his or her characteristics to the next.

A common criticism of Vonnegut's art is that its jokes are inappropriate, that the author's lack of seriousness prompts him to shrug off with a giggle what should properly be faced with more serious intent. If this were true, then the punch line set-up of *Galápagos* would be his most monstrous act. Yet a subtle irony underlies Vonnegut's use of nuclear holocaust, not the least of which is found in the volume's epigraph, the line from Anne Frank's diary attesting that in spite of everything, she still believes people are really good at heart. By the end of *Galápagos*, Vonnegut's readers would agree that they are—but only after the massive, million-year evolution that severely reduces their brain capacity and manual dexterity to do evil. In terms of such redirection, we see that Anne Frank's holocaust simply hasn't been enough, and that sentimental attempts to accept her wishes as having come true in our own times are premature.

As for the appropriateness of nuclear war being a joke, the broader sweep of Vonnegut's fiction clarifies his practice. From the start, his protagonists have been sufferers, and what they suffer from is life—a life that seems to them an unending series of practical jokes, of which they are the butt. By the time of *Slapstick*, Vonnegut can suggest that the best way to handle life is with the gracefulness some people can take practical jokes. Better not to complain and certainly better not to feel sorry for oneself. Rather try to do one's best with every one of these infuriating tests. Not that one stands a chance of winning this or that specific wager, but that in trying to do so people can, as did Laurel & Hardy in their film comedies, make themselves adorably funny and loveable. By bargaining in good faith with destiny, one at least purchases a superiority over it, just as one who can take a joke gracefully looks a great deal more dignified than one who can't. *Galápagos* takes this perspective and pushes it to include the most feasible ultimate our own times face.

Vonnegut's ultimate ultimate, however, is always something at once greater and more intimate than thematic issues of destruction and survival. And that is the book itself, what the author is writing and the reader is reading. Bringing the two together in this shared act is always the final purpose of each novel. The record of this practice is a long and consistent one. *Mother Night* is framed as the narrator's confessions, a set of memoirs enfolded in several elaborate textual devices which emphasize not just the protagonist's telling of the story but of Kurt Vonnegut's "editorial" handling as well. *Cat's Cradle* adds a further dose of irony and makes a reader as much of an involved partner as the author, for in setting out to write a book about the atomic bombing of Japan titled *The Day the World Ended* he in fact precipitates the actual ending of the world, yet survives long enough to write the history of human stupidity the readers now hold. *Slaughterhouse-Five*, which never actually describes the fire bombing of Dresden, does come into being as the author's attempt to write about it, matched by the reader's attempt to read sequentially a spatialized, non-sequential book. From here on Vonnegut adopts the practice of integrating autobiographical statement with his fiction, yet writer-characters remain crucial to the design, even to having the son of Kilgore Trout undertake the telling of *Galápagos*—with the success of his telling being as important as the physical survival and re-evolution he describes.

A nuclear-apocalyptic disaster for Kurt Vonnegut, then, functions much like the other disasters recounted in his works: as designs made by humans in their botched attempts to improve a style of life that is in truth no more malign than a practical joke. It is an ultimate only because our present society conceives it to be, yet in the long run of human events, it is no more ultimate than any previous apocalyptic visions. That life goes on is neither a blessing or a curse, but rather the necessary condition of things; without that perception, living (as does writing and reading) becomes impossible. If there is an ultimate in Vonnegut's work, it would be that.

Works Cited

Klinkowitz, Jerome, and Somer, John. eds. *The Vonnegut Statement*. NY: Delacorte Press/Seymour Lawrence, 1973.

Vonnegut, Kurt. *Galápagos*. NY: Delacorte/Seymour Lawrence, 1985.

———. *Wampeters, Foma & Granfalloons*. NY: Delacorte/Seymour Lawrence, 1974.

Contributors

Nancy Anisfield is an English lecturer at Saint Michael's College. She also teaches war literature courses at the University of Vermont and edited *Vietnam Anthology: American War Literature.*

Jan Barry is a poet and journalist based in New Jersey. He is an editor of three poetry anthologies on war and peace, and author most recently of *Morning in Moscow*, a collection of poems. His poetry on the Vietnam War appeared in the *New York Times, Chicago Tribune* and numerous other publications, including *Carrying the Darkness: The Poetry of the Vietnam War, The Lessons of the Vietnam War, A People and a Nation: A History of the United States, Unaccustomed Mercy: Soldier-Poets of the Vietnam War,* and *Vietnam Anthology.*

Jack Branscomb received his Ph.D. from the University of North Carolina, Chapel Hill (1972), and is a professor of English at East Tennessee State University. His major interests are in twentieth-century literature, and he has published articles on Robert Lowell, John Updike and Russell Hoban.

Paul Brians is author of *Nuclear Holocausts: Atomic War in Fiction 1895-1984* (Kent State University Press) and editor of *Nuclear Texts & Contexts*, newsletter of the International Society for the Study of Nuclear Texts and Contexts.

Jane Caputi is an Associate Professor of American Studies at the University of New Mexico, Albuquerque. She is the author of *The Age of Sex Crime*, a feminist analysis of serial sex murder, and collaborated with Mary Daly on *Websters' First New Intergalactic Wickedary of the English Language.* She is currently writing a book, *Gossips, Gorgons and Crones: Female Power and the Nuclear Age.*

Merritt Clifton, editor of *Samisdat*, is also the news editor of *The Animals' Agenda.* He is the author of *North American Fur Sources and Trade in the 1980s*, a former farmhand and firefighter, an active trapbuster, and an environmental journalist/activist since 1969.

Michael Dorris's novel, *A Yellow Raft in Blue Water*, appeared in 1987; his most recent non-fiction book is *The Broken Cord* (1989).

Louise Erdrich is the author of two books of poetry and three novels, *Love Medicine, The Beet Queen*, and *Tracks.*

H. Bruce Franklin is the author or editor of fifteen books and over a hundred articles on literature and society. The present essay is adapted from his widely-acclaimed *War Stars: The Superweapon and the American Imagination.* In the late 1950s, Franklin flew as a navigator and intelligence officer in the

Strategic Air Command. He is now the John Cotton Dana Professor of English and American Studies at Rutgers University in Newark.

Tom Hearron is a novelist and Professor of English at Saginaw Valley State University in Michigan.

Helen Jaskoski is editor of *SAIL—Studies in American Indian Literatures* and Professor of English and Comparative Literature at California State University Fullerton. She has published poetry and fiction in addition to articles on ethnic American literature, modernist poetry and poetry therapy. She is presently writing a book on Native American literature.

Jerome Klinkowitz is Professor of English at the University of Northern Iowa. His recent books include *Their Finest Hours: Narratives of the RAF and Luftwaffe in World War II, Slaughterhouse-Five: Reinventing the Novel and the World, Short Season and Other Stories,* and *Listen: Gerry Mulligan.*

Millicent Lenz is a specialist in literature for youth and conducts classes in children's and young adult materials at the University of Albany, School of Information Science and Policy. She co-edited with Ramona M. Mahood *Young Adult Literature: Background and Criticism* (1980), has contributed essays to the *ChLA Quarterly* and a variety of journals, and her monograph, *Nuclear-Age Literature for Youth: The Quest for a Life-Affirming Ethic* was published in 1990 by ALA Books.

Richard H. Minear is a Professor of History at the University of Massachusetts in Amherst. His most recent book, *Hiroshima: Three Witnesses,* includes translations of the three premier accounts by writer-survivors of the atomic bombing including Hara Tamiki *Summer Flowers.* He also wrote *Japanese Tradition and Western Law* and *Victors' Justice,* and translated Yoshida Mitsuru's *Requiem for Battleship Yamato.*

William J. Scheick is J.R. Millikan Centennial Professor of English and American Literature at the University of Texas at Austin, where he also serves as editor of *Texas Studies in Literature and Language.* His work has appeared in numerous journals and his best-known books include: *The Will and the Word: The Poetry of Edward Taylor; The Slender Human Word: Emerson's Artistry in Prose;* and *Fictional Structure and Ethics.*

Jim Schley is a former editor of *New England Review* (*NER/BLQ*), and editor of the anthology *Writing in a Nuclear Age* (University Press of New England, 1984). Since 1987 he has been a member of three experimental theater collectives: Bread and Puppet Theater, the Expanding Secret Company, and most recently Les Montreurs d'Images, a troupe based in Geneva but now active in Eastern Europe. "News" is the first section of a longer essay dealing with nuclear age poetry.

H. Wayne Schuth is a Professor in the Department of Drama and Communications at the University of New Orleans. He is the author of *Mike Nichols* (Boston: Twayne Publishers, 1978), has several essays in the *International Dictionary of Films and Filmmakers* and has a chapter on *Hiroshima, Mon Amour* in the book *Nuclear War Films,* edited by Jack G. Shaheen.

Lee Schweninger received his Ph.D. from the University of North Carolina, Chapel Hill, and is currently associate professor of English at the University of North Carolina, Wilmington. He edited *Departing Glory: Eight Jeremiads by Increase Mather*, contributed several entries for the *Encyclopedia of American Literature*, and wrote a critical biography of John Winthrop. He is currently working on a book-length study of Celia Parker Woolley.

Jacqueline Smetak is an assistant professor of English at Iowa State University, Ames, Iowa, where she teaches courses on American literature and culture. She has published extensively, including articles on Thomas Pynchon, Maya Deren, Vietnam War fiction, and nuclear holocaust stories.

Daniel L. Zins teaches a number of courses on war and peace issues in the liberal arts department of The Atlanta College of Art. His essays on nuclear weapons issues have appeared in *College English, Papers on Language and Literature, Science Fiction Studies,* and elsewhere. He is working on a book, *Exploding the Canon: Rethinking the English Department in an Age of Mass Death.*